*The Mitchell Beazley pocket guide to*

# STATELY HOMES AND CASTLES

IN GREAT BRITAIN AND IRELAND

---

John FitzMaurice Mills

Mitchell Beazley

**How to use this book**

The book is organized on a county (region in Scotland) basis, the properties in each area being listed alphabetically within that section. If you do not know which county or region a particular property is in, you can look it up in the Index. The map on pp 6–7 shows county divisions.

To assist in your selection, there are 26 easily recognized symbols providing essential information at a glance (see pp 8–10). If you are especially interested in the work of one particular craftsman or architect, there is also an index of architects, designers and craftsmen on pp 180–1. This can be used in conjunction with the date list on pp 167–175 to locate all the properties described with which that person was associated.

Edited and designed by
Mitchell Beazley Publishers
87–89 Shaftesbury Avenue, London W1V 7AD

ISBN 0 85533 269 7

Typeset by Servis Filmsetting Ltd, Manchester
Printed and bound in Yugoslavia by Mladinska Knjiga

**Chief Compiler** Alan Folly
**Editor** Michele Staple
**Designer** Sarah Jackson
**Illustrator** Gary Marsh
**Editor in Chief** Susannah Read
**Art Editor** Douglas Wilson
**Production** Sarah Goodden

# CONTENTS

# INTRODUCTION

*It is a reverend thing to see an ancient castle or building not in decay.*

Francis Bacon, Essays

From Fort Charlotte in the Shetland Isles to King Charles's Castle in the Scillies, from Blarney Castle in the west to Blickling Hall in the east, the stately homes and castles that stud Britain and Ireland provide, in their wealth and variety, a heritage unequalled anywhere else in the world. Each has a unique contribution to make, whether it be through the intimate domesticity of a lone writer's cottage, the magnificent Baroque showpiece of Vanbrugh's Blenheim Palace, or the bluff squat towers of Bodiam Castle. All reflect a way of life that is peculiar to their peoples, and afford the visitor an unrivalled opportunity to step back in time and glimpse at history.

The buildings described here have, in many cases, retained the contents which were chosen or carefully made for them at their genesis. Successive owners over the centuries, using their selective genius, may have added their own particular items of furniture, paintings or tapestries. The art treasures contained within some stately homes are often of astonishing quality and include works such as: paintings from the great masters; cabinets of exquisite porcelain and glass; furniture of supreme excellence; tapestries; rugs; silver from the hands of the great smiths; clocks; and priceless trinkets. Other buildings may house more modest furnishings, but be filled with charm and atmosphere. Their contents may be valued because of their associations with a particular person or period. The carefully preserved garden of the Kiplings at Bateman's, the reading desk used by Charles Dickens, a collection of manuscripts or the delightful sketches of Beatrix Potter at Hill Top may inspire even the casual observer, while thoughtfully displayed collections of bygones can provide hours of fascination and enjoyment. For example, the domestic details of a 100 years ago set out in a great kitchen, relics of medieval sporting events, items of folk history, collections of arms and armour, coaches and venerable cars, costumes, dolls, toys – the list is almost endless and rarely fails to include something of interest to everyone.

To visit and browse through these lived-in, loved-in, cared-for places is to share the tastes of a great variety of people, many of whom have enriched our heritage by their enlightened search for perfection. Their foresight, backed up by the necessary finance, provided the stimulus that released the creative energies of artists, architects and craftsmen. Many architects concerned themselves not only with the fabric of the building, but also with the design of the interior, down to the minutest details such as door-handles. Such uniformity of design can be witnessed in the Palladian perfection of William Kent's Holkham Hall or in the many undertakings of Robert Adam (Osterley Park House and Syon House are two fine examples).

Complementing these magnificent buildings are their settings, which are often breathtakingly beautiful. Perhaps the best-known landscape gardener was 'Capability' Brown, a man capable of moving hills, diverting streams and damming rivers to form lakes. Examples of his work may be found throughout Britain, his sweeping landscapes being in strong contrast to the formal gardens based on the ideas of Le Nôtre. The style of Gertrude Jekyll is different again: her gardens tend to be secluded places enclosed by hedges and linked by winding paths. Where the grounds are extensive it is not unusual to find wooded areas inhabited by herds of rare deer.

Today many owners are creating new attractions to enhance the pleasure of a visit. Wildlife parks in the mould of Longleat are being established, trips on disused waterways are being organized, and miniature railways to carry passengers around the grounds are becoming more commonplace. Many facilities are also provided to cater for the 'family day out', with picnic areas in wooded glades, amusement parks and nature and adventure trails.

The information presented in this pocket guide should enable you to make your choice of outing with comparative ease. Whether your day is spent at the ruins of some prehistoric fortification, at an almost-forgotten castle hidden away at the end of an unclassified road, or at a great and dignified stately home, each will evoke memories of the past and provide you with not just an entertaining day out, but a satisfying and rewarding educational experience.

# LOCATION MAP SHOWING COUNTY DIVISIONS/REGIONS

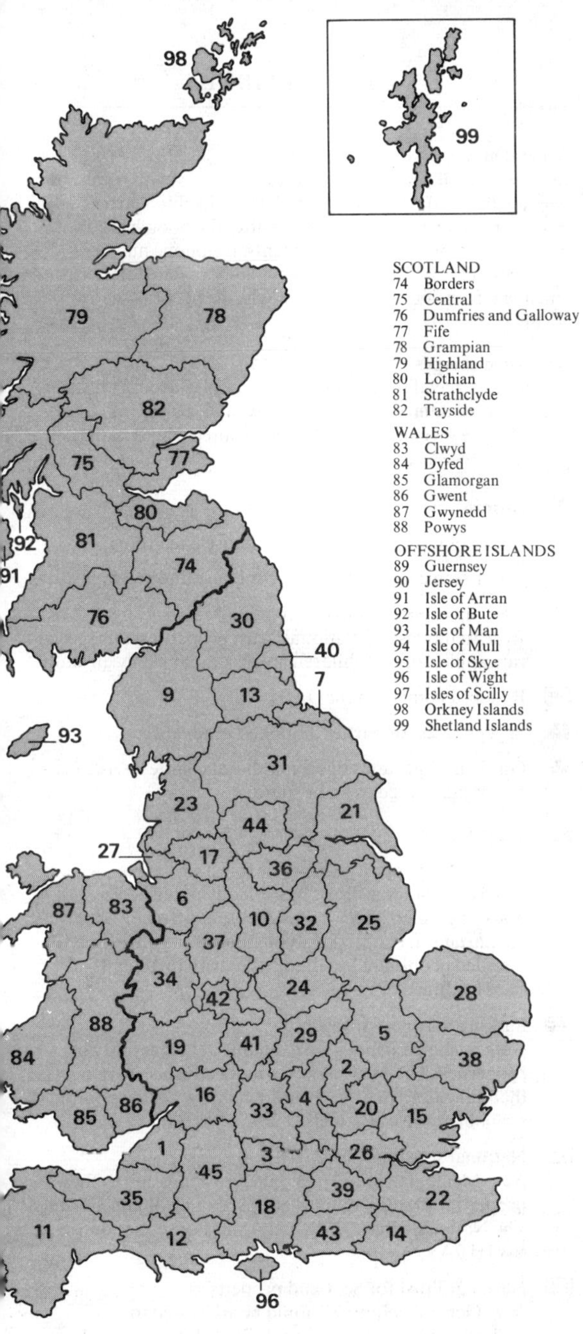
SCOTLAND
74 Borders
75 Central
76 Dumfries and Galloway
77 Fife
78 Grampian
79 Highland
80 Lothian
81 Strathclyde
82 Tayside
WALES
83 Clwyd
84 Dyfed
85 Glamorgan
86 Gwent
87 Gwynedd
88 Powys
OFFSHORE ISLANDS
89 Guernsey
90 Jersey
91 Isle of Arran
92 Isle of Bute
93 Isle of Man
94 Isle of Mull
95 Isle of Skye
96 Isle of Wight
97 Isles of Scilly
98 Orkney Islands
99 Shetland Islands

# KEY TO SYMBOLS

**General note**
Every effort has been made to ensure accuracy with regard to opening hours, dates, admission charges, facilities etc. However, changes inevitably occur after the book has gone to press: owners may alter arrangements, telephone numbers may be re-allocated, bus services cut and rail schedules amended. If in doubt it is always advisable to check in advance.

**Admission charges**
Since charges tend to rise season by season, only an indication of the level of admission charges is given: *Under £1* and *£1 or over*. If more specific information is required, check with the property concerned.

- Admission free
- Admission charge under £1 for house and grounds
- Admission charge £1 or over for house and grounds
- Free or reduced admission for children
  *Note* In the case of National Trust properties, this special rate applies only if children are accompanied by an adult
- OAP Reduced admission for OAPs
- Special rates for parties if booked in advance
- Gardens or grounds open at reduced charge to visitors not wishing to go over the house

**Special categories**

- Majority of property accessible to wheelchairs
  *Note* The National Trust has recently published a booklet entitled *Facilities for the Disabled and Visually Handicapped*. Properties giving special consideration to disabled people are listed, together with full details of their facilities
- Parking may be a problem
  *Note* Parking facilities are available at the majority of properties. This symbol serves as an advance warning that difficulties may be encountered, e.g. parking only available in nearby streets
- NT National Trust property
  *Note* Members of the Trust gain free admission to these properties. Details about the Trust can be obtained from: The National Trust, 42 Queen Anne's Gate, London SW1H 9AS
- NTS National Trust for Scotland property
  *Note* General enquiries should be addressed to: 5 Charlotte Square, Edinburgh EH2 4DU

Property in the care of the Department of the Environment, the Scottish Development Department, or the Welsh Office

Designated as an Ancient Monument

**General information**

Telephone number
*Note* The number and exchange are given wherever possible. The correct STD code for calls from the enquirer's area may be obtained from the local dialling code booklet, or from directory enquiries by dialling 192 (142 for local numbers in London)

Access
*Note* A large town or city is given as the reference point, with instructions for reaching the property via the nearest 'A' or 'B' road for most entries. Where directions are not specified, this is because the address (usually in a town) is sufficient

Opening times
*Note* Exact dates are not given, because they are liable to change from year to year. Where (DES) or (AMS) appears in the text, this refers to standard opening times, details of which are given on p. 10

Other nearby places of interest
*Note* These are properties near enough to visit on the same day if desired. An asterisk (*) indicates that the building does not have a main entry in the text

Nearest British Rail station within reasonable cycling distance of property
*Caution* There may well not be any other available form of transport from the station

Bus stop within walking distance of gates
*Note* Routes and timetables are subject to constant change. Always check availability before setting out

Nearest London Underground station

**Amenities available**

Gardens open (see note on dogs on p. 10)

Shop

Light refreshments available

Restaurant
*Note* Parties should always book in advance

Picnic area provided
*Note* Picnicking is often permitted in the grounds where there is no specific picnic area, but check beforehand

Children's play area or amusement park

*Note 1. Dogs*
Most properties have restrictions on when and how dogs may be brought into the grounds. Some will not admit them at all. Others insist 'only on lead'. Since these restrictions vary so widely, it is recommended that dog-owners who wish to take their pets with them check before setting out.

*Note 2. Standard opening times*
(For historic monuments in the care of the Secretaries of State for the Environment and for Wales and Scotland)
**England and Wales**
Where (DES) appears, the following opening times apply:
Mid-Oct to mid-Mar, weekdays 9.30–4, Sun 2–4
Mid-Mar to mid-Oct, weekdays 9.30–6.30, Sun 2–6.30
**Scotland**
Where (AMS) appears, the following opening times apply:
Apr to Sept, weekdays 9.30–7, Sun 2–7
Oct to Mar, weekdays 9.30–4, Sun 2–4

In England and Wales all monuments close on Jan 1, May Day and Dec 24 and 25. Those in Scotland close on Dec 25 and 26, also Jan 1 and 2. There may be other closures on Good Friday and during the Easter holidays, and for special events connected with some monuments. Parties of more than 11 people may obtain a 10% discount on admission and children under 5 are admitted free. Season tickets, valid for one year, admit holders free to all ancient monuments and historic buildings in State care in England, Wales and Scotland. Applications should be made to:
**The Secretary (AMHB/P)**, Department of the Environment, Room G1, 25 Savile Row, London W1X 2BT
**The Under-Secretary**, Department of the Environment, Scottish Headquarters, Argyle House, Lady Lawson Street, Edinburgh EH3 9SD
**The Director**, Ancient Monuments Branch, Department of the Environment, Ty-Glas, Llanishen, Cardiff CF4 5UP

Alternatively season tickets may be purchased from HMSO Bookshops in Belfast, Birmingham, Bristol, Cardiff, Edinburgh, London and Manchester.

## ABBREVIATIONS

AMS see *Note 2* above
C century
DES see *Note 2* above
DoE Department of Environment
Hol. holiday (plural hols)
HQ headquarters
incl including
kg kilogramme
m metre
NT National Trust

Standard abbreviations for days of the week and months of the year are also used.

# ENGLAND

## AVON

### Badminton House

*Badminton, near Chipping Sodbury*

Palladian mansion, home of Dukes of Beaufort since 17th C. English, Dutch and Italian paintings. Grounds by William Kent and 'Capability' Brown. Stables and hunt kennels open to visitors. Horse trials.

Badminton 202

Off B4040 5 miles E of Chipping Sodbury

Early June to early Sept, Wed only, 2.30–5

Dodington House, Dyrham Park, Horton Court, Little Sodbury Manor

BADMINTON HOUSE

### Claverton Manor

*Near Bath*

Built 1820 in Greek Revival style. Houses American Museum with 17th- to 19th-C room furnishings brought over from America. Exhibits include whaling, immigration, battles and trading with China. Outside reproduction of George Washington's flower garden, also herb garden.

Bath 60503

2½ miles from Bath via Bathwick Hill

End Mar to early Nov daily (except Mon) 2–5. Bank Hol. Mon and preceding Sun 11–5

Great Chalfield Manor, Westwood Manor

Bath (2½ miles)

### Clevedon Court

*Near Clevedon*

14th-C manor house incorporating 12th-C tower and 13th-C hall. Literary associations with Thackeray, who wrote much of *Vanity Fair* there, and Tennyson. Collections of Nailsea glass and Elton ware. Fine window tracery in 14th-C chapel. Garden with rare plants and shrubs.

Off Bristol road B3130 1½ miles E of Clevedon

Apr to end Sept, Wed, Thur, Sun and Bank Hol. Mon 2.30–5.30

Congresbury Vicarage (by appointment)*

### Dodington House

*Dodington, near Chipping Sodbury*

Probably the last great 18th-C house to be built in the Classic manner, created by James Wyatt for Christopher Codrington. The huge portico with Corinthian columns allows vehicles to approach the front door under cover. The Codrington family have lived in house since 1578. Has 700 acres of parkland laid out by 'Capability' Brown. Carriage Museum. Narrow-gauge railway. Model aviation collection. Children's adventureland with farm exhibits, nature trails and play area.

Chipping Sodbury 318899

From A46 Bath–Stroud road. Near exit 18 on M4

Easter to Sept daily, 11–5.30

Badminton House, Dyrham Park, Horton Court, Little Sodbury Manor

## Dyrham Park

*Near Chippenham*

£

Country mansion built *c.* 1698 by William Talman for William III's Secretary of State, William Blathwayt. Contents include book presses used by the diarist Pepys, also tapestries and portraits, good panelling. Part of front garden by Hauduroy. Deer park.

A46 Bath–Stroud road 2 miles S of Tormarton M4 interchange

Apr, May and Oct daily 2–6 except Thur and Fri; June to end Sept daily 2–6 except Fri

Bath Assembly Rooms*, Claverton Manor, Dodington House

## Georgian House

*7 Great George St, Bristol*

£

Small town house fully furnished in the manner of the period, useful for comprehensive study on a small but detailed scale.

Bristol 299771

Weekdays all year 10–5 except Christmas Holiday and New Year's Day

Clevedon Court, Dyrham Park, St Vincent's Priory

Templemeads

## Horton Court

*Near Chipping Sodbury*

£

Restored Cotswold manor house. 12th-C Norman great hall. Perpendicular ambulatory in garden.

3 miles NE of Chipping Sodbury, ¾ mile N of Horton, off A46

Apr to Oct, Wed and Sat 2–6

Badminton House, Dodington House, Dyrham Park, Little Sodbury Manor

(¾ mile)

## Little Sodbury Manor

*Near Chipping Sodbury*

£

15th-C mansion built for Sir John Welsh. Outstanding great hall and Queen Anne wing. Associated with William Tyndale, translator of the New Testament.

Chipping Sodbury 312232

From A46 2½ miles from Chipping Sodbury

Apr to Sept by appointment only

Badminton House, Dodington House, Dyrham Park, Horton Court

## Oakhill Manor

*Oakhill, near Shepton Mallet*

£

Excellent example of English small country house set in attractive gardens of some 8 acres. Remarkable collection of models connected with transport. Novel feature is miniature railway that carries visitors from car park along a scenic route.

Oakhill 840210

4 miles N of Shepton Mallet on A37. Car park beside the Mendip Inn

Easter to early Nov, daily 12–6

Nunney Castle

## Red Lodge

*Park Row, Bristol*

£

Late 16th-C house altered in 18th C with good collection of furniture from both periods, also carving and panelling.

Bristol 299771

Weekdays all year 2–5 except Dec 25–26 and Jan 1

Clevedon Court, Dyrham Park, Georgian House (Bristol)

Templemeads

## No. 1 Royal Crescent

*In Bath*

£

Georgian house restored as nearly as possible to original built by

NO. 1 ROYAL CRESCENT, BATH

John Wood the Younger in 1767. The whole crescent consists of a dignified sweep of 30 houses with 114 Ionic columns supporting a Palladian cornice. The transformation of Bath started with the work of John's father on Queen Square and was continued by such as Thomas Baldwin (the Pump Room and Guildhall) and Robert Adam (the delightful Pulteney Bridge over the Avon). Not far away is the mock Gothic façade of Sham Castle erected by Ralph Allen, the postal employee who accelerated the passage of letters to London.

- Bath 28126
- Early Mar to end Oct, weekdays (not Mon) 11–5, Sun 2–5
- Claverton Manor, St Catherine's Court, Westwood Manor
- Bath

## St Catherine's Court

*Near Bath*

A small Tudor house redolent of Henry VIII and Elizabeth I. Foundations laid on earlier buildings once in ownership of the Monks of Bath. Examples of early needlework and old furniture.

- 6 miles S from junction 18 on M4; 2 miles N of A4 at Batheaston
- Apr to end Sept, Sat, Sun and public hols, also by prior arrangement. Conducted tours 2.30–5.30 only
- Claverton Manor, Royal Crescent (Bath), Westwood Manor

## St Vincent's Priory

*Clifton, near Bristol*

A unique small Gothic Revival house erected over caves reputedly used as Christian sanctuary. Front elevation carries strange caryatid figures. First floor has relief modelled from murals at Pompeii.

- Bristol 39621
- Clifton, 100 m from the Suspension Bridge, Bristol
- July and Aug, Sat and Sun afternoons 2.15–6, other times by appointment
- Clevedon Court, Dyrham Park, Red Lodge
- Templemeads

# BEDFORDSHIRE

## Luton Hoo

*In Luton*

Robert Adam designed exterior in 1767. Interior converted to French style in early part of this century. One of finest house collections of the rare, beautiful and valuable, including: Beauvais tapestries; rare collections of Bristol, Chelsea, Derby, Liverpool, Rockingham, Staffordshire and Swansea ceramics; works by Fabergé; imperial Russian robes; and major works by Bermejo,

WOBURN ABBEY

Rembrandt and Titian. Surrounding park by 'Capability' Brown.

☎ Luton 22955

➜ By Park Street Gates, Luton

⏲ Early Apr to end Sept, Mon, Wed, Thur, Sat and Good Fri 11–6; Sun 2–6

▦ Hatfield House, Knebworth House

⇌ Luton (3 miles)

## Woburn Abbey

*Woburn, near Dunstable*

Family seat of Dukes of Bedford. Present building is mid-18th-C reconstruction by Henry Flitcroft and Inigo Jones although land was originally granted by Henry VIII to John Russell in 1539. The Orangery and house contain superb examples of paintings by Canaletto, Cuyp, Gainsborough, Holbein, Rembrandt, Reynolds, Teniers, Van Dyck and Velazquez. Other treasures include 18th-C silver, and the Sèvres dinner service presented by Louis XV to the 4th Duke. 3,000-acre deer park includes the renowned Père David herd. The 'Wild Animal Kingdom' has lions, tigers, giraffes, elephants, monkeys, a pets' corner and a dolphinarium. Safari boat trips on lake. Amusement park, 40 antique shops and banqueting and conference facilities.

☎ Woburn 666

➜ 5 miles from exits 12 or 13 on M1

⏲ Nov to Easter (except Dec 21–25) daily, Park 12–3.45, Abbey 1–4.45; Good Fri to end Oct, daily, Park 10–4.45 (Sun 10–5.45), Abbey 11–5.45 (Sun 11–6.15). Last entries to Abbey are 45 mins before closing time

▦ Wrest Park*

# BERKSHIRE

## Basildon Park

*Lower Basildon, near Reading*

Country house in Classical style by John Carr of York, dating from 1776. Interesting features are the Octagon Room and some excellent plasterwork. Contents include notable furniture and paintings. Beautiful setting overlooking Thames Valley.

☎ Pangbourne 3040

➜ Between Pangbourne and Streatley on A329

⏲ Apr to end Oct, Wed to Sun 2–6 (Oct 2–5); Bank Hol. Mon 11–6. Closed Good Fri

▦ Mapledurham House

⇌ Pangbourne (2½ miles)

## Donnington Castle

*In Donnington*

Surviving parts from the Civil War sieges of 1644–46 include 14th-C gatehouse and earthworks.

➜ 1 mile N of Newbury off B4494

⏲ Any reasonable time

▦ Ashdown House, Littlecote

## Dorney Court

*Dorney, near Windsor*

Tudor manor house, warm brick and timber. Quality paintings and furniture. Open for the first time in 1981.

- Burnham 4638
- 2 miles out from Windsor on B3026
- End Apr to end Sept, Tues, Wed, Sun and Bank Hol. Mon 2–5.30. Parties at other times by appointment
- Windsor Castle
- Windsor (2 miles)

## Swallowfield Park

*Near Reading*

18th-C reconstruction of earlier house built in 1689 to design of William Talman. Notable stucco decoration, also Baroque treatment of entrance. Gardens a good example of walled 4-acre plot with interesting trees, flowering shrubs and roses.

- Reading 883815
- From village of Swallowfield 6 miles SE of Reading off A33
- May to Sept on Wed and Thur 2–5
- Mapledurham House

## Windsor Castle

*Windsor*

Originally established by William the Conqueror, this is the largest inhabited castle. Many monarchs contributed to its impressive grandeur, but it was in Queen Victoria's reign that the castle finally assumed the form with which we are familiar today. A full day is necessary to appreciate the treasures that stock the State Apartments: paintings and drawings by masters; furniture, ceramics and armour; and that most spectacular of miniature creations, Queen Mary's Dolls' House (made one-twelfth natural size, this was designed by Sir Edwin Lutyens and has everything complete: books, ornaments, lighting fittings, carpets). Not to be missed is the magnificent St George's Chapel, high peak of rich Gothic in England. In its choir are the fine carved stalls of the Knights of the Garter.

- Windsor 68286. Enquiries re St George's Chapel: Windsor 65538
- From town of Windsor
- Precincts open daily, mid-Mar to end Apr, Sept to Oct 10–5.15; May to Aug 10–7.15; Oct to mid-Mar 10–4.15. State Apartments, Queen Mary's Dolls' House and Exhibition of Drawings open most days, but best to consult authorities, as also St George's Chapel. Schedules cannot be guaranteed because Castle can be subject to closure, often with little notice
  Entrance to Precincts
  State Apartments, Queen Mary's Dolls' House, Drawings £, , OAP
- Windsor Safari Park and Seaworld*, The Household Cavalry Museum in Combermere Barracks*, Cliveden, Eton College*, Mapledurham House, Osterley Park House
- Windsor

WINDSOR CASTLE

# BUCKINGHAMSHIRE

## Ascott

*Wing, near Leighton Buzzard*

Half-timbered hunting lodge built in 1870 housing a striking collection of beautiful objects brought together by Anthony de Rothschild: Ming and Sung porcelain; Chippendale and French furniture; also good paintings. Garden has unusual trees, water lilies, displays of naturalized bulbs and a topiary sundial.

Wing 242

2 miles SW of Leighton Buzzard, S side of A418

Early Apr to end Sept, Wed and Thur 2–6; also Sat in Aug and Sept and Bank Hol. Mon 2–6. Entry to house may be by timed ticket

Claydon House, Little Gaddesden, Woburn Abbey

Leighton Buzzard (2 miles)

## Chenies Manor House

*Chenies, near Rickmansworth*

Delightful small Tudor house set in the village of Chenies. Antique Fair and Flower Festival held end of June.

Little Chalfont 2888

Close to junction of A404 and B485 about 4 miles W of Rickmansworth

Early Apr to end Oct, Wed and Thur 2–5; Bank Hol. Mon 2–6

Moor Park Mansion

## Chicheley Hall

*Chicheley, near Newport Pagnell*

Baroque house built for Sir John Chester between 1719 and 1723. One of the best and least altered examples of the work of Georgian craftsmen, including brickwork, stone and wood carving and handling of plaster. Contents include the Chester 'hidden' library, mementoes and naval pictures collected by Admiral Lord Beatty.

North Crawley 252

2 miles E of Newport Pagnell on A422

Easter to late Sept, Sun and Bank Hol, also Wed in July and Wed and Sat in Aug 2.30–6 (Bank Hol. 11.30–6)

Stoke Park Pavilions

## Claydon House

*Middle Claydon, near Winslow*

Mid-18th-C extension to an earlier house on land that came to the Verney family in 1471. West front contains series of magnificent Rococo rooms with Chinese-inspired plasterwork. Paintings include fine Van Dyck portrait of Charles I, and a Mytens of Sir Francis Verney. Small museum of Florence Nightingale memorabilia and her bedroom.

Steeple Claydon 349

Close to Middle Claydon, 3½ miles SW of Winslow on Aylesbury–Buckingham road A413

Apr to end Oct, daily except Thur and Fri (incl Good Fri) 2–6; Bank Hol. Mon 2.30–6

Ascott, Waddesdon Manor, Wotton House

(not Sun)

## Cliveden

*Taplow, near Maidenhead*

The existing house, the 3rd to be constructed on the site overlooking the Thames, is currently let to Stanford University, California. Designed by Sir James Barry, architect of the House of Commons. Earlier buildings by William Winde, Thomas Archer and Giacomo Leoni. The grounds laid out by 'Capability' Brown contain a water garden, a series of Roman sarcophagi and a rustic theatre.

CLIVEDEN

☎ Burnham 5069

➔ 2 miles N of Taplow on B476

⏱ Apr to end Oct, Sat and Sun 2.30–5.30. Gardens daily all year, 11–6.30

Eton College*, Hughenden Manor

Taplow (3 miles)

## Dorton House

*Brill, near Thame*

£

Jacobean house erected in 1626 for Sir John Dormer. Worth a visit as a study piece for domestic architecture of the period. Fine Jacobean ceilings.

☎ Brill 238237

➔ 6 miles N of Thame off B4011

⏱ May to July and Sept, Sat and Sun 2–5

Hughenden Manor, Nether Winchendon House, Waddesdon Manor

(during school terms)

## Hartwell House

*Hartwell, near Aylesbury*

£

Jacobean mansion with E wing *c.* 1760 and 17th-C staircase. Louis XVIII stayed there for part of his exile (1807–14).

☎ Aylesbury 748355

➔ 2 miles SW of Aylesbury off A418

⏱ Mid-May to mid-July, Wed only, 2–5

Nether Winchendon House, Waddesdon Manor

## Hughenden Manor

*Near High Wycombe*

£ NT

Bought by Benjamin Disraeli in 1847, and reconstructed for him by Edward Buckton Lamb in 1862 in style of romanticized Tudor building. Contents include mementoes of the great statesman.

➔ A4128 1½ miles N of High Wycombe

⏱ Mar and Nov, Sat and Sun 2–5, Apr to end Oct, Wed to Sat 2–6, Sun and Bank Hol. 12.30–6 (closed Good Fri)

Cliveden, Stonor Park

High Wycombe (2 miles)

## Mentmore Towers

*Mentmore, near Wing*

£

Last surviving work by 19th-C architect Sir Joseph Paxton. This huge Victorian mansion was the home of Mayer Amschel de Rothschild and then the Earls of Rosebery. Acquired in 1978 by World Government of the Age of Enlightenment. Fine interiors include the great banqueting hall with impressive giltwork.

☎ Cheddington 668008

➔ 12 miles NE of Aylesbury; 2¼ miles SE of A418 at Wing

⏱ Mid-Mar to mid-Oct, Wed, Sun and Bank Hol. 1–5; mid-Oct to mid-Mar, Sun and Bank Hol. 1–4

Ascott, Little Gaddesden, Woburn Abbey

Cheddington (2 miles)

## Milton Cottage

*In Chalfont St Giles*

This small cottage has been preserved as it was in 1665. Here John Milton completed *Paradise Lost* and started *Paradise Regained*. Small library and number of souvenirs of the writer.

- Chalfont St Giles 2313
- Close to A413
- Early Feb to end Oct daily except Mon (but open Bank Hol. Mon) 10–1, 2–6; Sun 2–6. Nov, Sat 10–1, 2–5; Sun 2–5
- Cliveden, Moor Park Mansion House
- Gerrards Cross (4 miles)

## Nether Winchendon House

*Lower Winchendon, near Aylesbury*

Tudor house incorporating medieval core, altered in 17th C and again in 18th C when exterior was given Gothic look with windows and battlements. Was home of Sir Francis Bernard, Governor of New Jersey and Massachusetts in 1760. His conduct of British policy helped to precipitate the American War of Independence.

- Haddenham 290101
- 1 mile N of A418 Aylesbury to Thame road, close to Lower Winchendon
- Apr to Sept, Thur, also Bank Hol. Mon 2–5.30
- Claydon House, Waddesdon Manor, Wotton House
- Aylesbury (6½ miles)

## Princes Risborough Manor

*In Princes Risborough*

17th-C red-brick house restored by Lord Rothschild in 1880s. Noteworthy Jacobean oak staircase and later wainscoting.

- Just off Princes Risborough market square opposite the church
- May to end Sept, Wed 2.30–4.30
- Hughenden Manor, Stonor Park
- Princes Risborough

## Waddesdon Manor

*Waddesdon, near Aylesbury*

Built in the 1880s for Baron Ferdinand de Rothschild in style of a French Renaissance château. Outstanding collection of 17th- and 18th-C French antiques, ceramics, Savonnerie carpets, textiles, small arms and 7 exquisite terracottas by Claude Michel, known as 'Clodion'. Paintings include work by Gainsborough, Reynolds, Romney and Dutch, Flemish and Italian schools. In the grounds are a herd of Sika deer and a free-flight aviary.

- Waddesdon 211
- A41 Aylesbury–Bicester road, about 6 miles NW of Aylesbury
- End Mar to end Oct, Wed to Sun 2–6; Good Fri and Bank Hol. Mon 11–6. Closed on Wed following Bank Hol.
- No children under 12 in house
- Claydon House, Nether Winchendon House, Wotton House
- Aylesbury (6 miles)

WADDESDON MANOR

## West Wycombe Park

*Near High Wycombe*

Palladian style house built mainly by Sir Francis Dashwood, possibly using designs by Robert Adam. Unusual 2-storeyed colonnade on south front. Fine classical interiors, some with painted ceilings by Italian artist Borgnini, subjects being after works by Raphael, the Caracci and Guido Reni. Worth noting are Brussels tapestries and staircase made of red polished mahogany with inlaid risers of box and yew wood. Grounds landscaped by Thomas Cook, a pupil of 'Capability' Brown, and later by Humphry Repton who retained the general scheme of Cook's layout, including a number of temples and ornaments. Swan-shaped lake.

High Wycombe 24411

In village of West Wycombe to s of A40

Grounds only: Easter and Spring Bank Hol. Sun and Mon 2.15–6; closed Good Fri. House and grounds: June, Mon to Fri 2.15–6, July and Aug daily (except Sat) 2.15–6

Cliveden, Hughenden Manor, Stonor Park

High Wycombe (2½ miles)

## Winslow Hall

*Winslow, near Buckingham*

One of the very few domestic buildings that can almost certainly be attributed to Sir Christopher Wren. Tall building of red brick built for William Lowndes, Secretary to the Treasury, completed *c.* 1702. Most of interior fixtures and features such as the staircase have been retained in their original manner. Contents include good examples of Chinese art and 18th-C furniture.

Winslow 2323

From A513 between Buckingham and Aylesbury

July to Sept daily (except Mon) 2.30–5.30 (other times by appointment)

Claydon House, Waddesdon Manor, Wotton House

Aylesbury (10 miles)

Not Sun

## Wotton House

*Wotton Underwood, near Aylesbury*

Built in 1704 to a plan almost identical to that for Buckingham House (later Buckingham Palace). Sir John Soane reconstructed the interior in 1820. Of interest is fine ironwork by Tijou and Thomas Robinson. The grounds were given 'Capability' Brown treatment between 1757 and 1760.

Brill 363

2 miles to s of A41 between Aylesbury and Bicester

July to Sept, Wed 2–6. Children under 12 not admitted

Claydon House, Nether Winchendon House, Waddesdon Manor

Bicester (9½ miles)

# CAMBRIDGESHIRE

## Anglesey Abbey

*Lode, near Cambridge*

Founded in 1135 for Canons of Augustinian Order, and converted into a private house after 1591. Contains Fairhaven collection of paintings, tapestries, ceramics, furniture and clocks. The gardens of some 100 acres were developed in 1926. An encouraging example of 20th-C landscaping.

Cambridge 811200

6 miles NE of Cambridge on B1102

Apr to mid-Oct, Tues, Wed, Thur, Sat, Sun and Bank Hol. Mon 2–6. Closed Good Fri

Ickworth, Sawston Hall*

Cambridge ($6\frac{1}{2}$ miles)

## Hinchingbrooke House

*Near Huntingdon*

Early 13th-C nunnery, converted to private use about middle of 16th C. Additions made in 17th and 19th C. Today a sixth-form centre for Hinchingbrooke School, but Sandwich family paintings are still housed there.

Huntingdon 51121

$\frac{1}{2}$ mile to W of Huntingdon

Mar to end July, Sun, Easter and Spring Bank Hol. Mon 2–5

Kimbolton Castle, Rippington Hall*

Huntingdon ($\frac{1}{2}$ mile)

## Kimbolton Castle

*Kimbolton, near St Neots*

OAP

The early building which had associations with Katherine of Aragon partially collapsed at beginning of 18th C. The then owner, 1st Duke of Manchester, commissioned Vanbrugh to completely remodel the castle, work being completed *c.* 1720. Gatehouse reputedly by Robert Adam. There are a number of quality murals by Pellegrini.

8 miles NW of St Neots off A45

Easter and Spring Bank Hol. Sun and Mon; mid-July to end Aug, Sun and Bank Hol. Mon 2–6

Hinchingbrooke House, Hinwick House

St Neots ($8\frac{1}{2}$ miles)

## King's School

*Ely, near Cambridge*

Dates mainly from 12th and 14th Cs. Of architectural and historical interest as there are considerable remains of original stonework and vaulting.

Ely 2837

In Ely, 16 miles NE of Cambridge, on A10

Late July and most Aug, Mon to Fri 10–4. For permission to view interior apply to the Seneschal

Anglesey Abbey

Ely ($\frac{1}{4}$ mile)

## Leverington Hall

*Near Wisbech*

Quality house, part Elizabethan and part late 17th C. Further alterations in 18th C. Notable staircase, chimney-breasts.

Wisbech 2055

From village of Leverington 2 miles NW of Wisbech off B1169

By written appointment (donation to charity)

Peckover House

March (13 miles)

## Peckover House

*In Wisbech*

NT

Built *c.*1722, was first owned by Southwell family and passed from them to Jonathan Peckover at end of 18th C. He was member of the Society of Friends and founded local bank of Gurney, Birkbeck and Peckover, which merged with Barclays at end of 19th C. Interior is principally noted for fine plasterwork. Well-kept Victorian garden contains rare trees and there are orange trees under glass.

Wisbech 3463

On N bank of River Nene

Early Apr to mid-Oct, Tues, Wed, Thur, Sat, Sun and Bank Hol. Mon 2–6

Leverington Hall, Raynham Hall*

March (11 miles)

## Wimpole Hall

*Arrington, near Royston*

NT

Quality red-brick and stone 18th-C country house. Originally built for Sir Thomas Chicheley and later bought by 1st Earl Hardwicke who extended it to present elegant symmetry. Long gallery and library particularly worth noting, also chapel (decorated by Thornhill) and Sir John Soane's Yellow Drawing Room. Large park landscaped by Bridgeman, Brown and Repton who included a castle as a folly.

☎ Arrington 257

→ Off A603 8 miles SW of Cambridge, or A14 6 miles N of Royston

Apr to mid-Oct, Tues, Wed, Thur, Sat, Sun and Bank Hol. Mon 2–6

Anglesey Abbey, Hinchingbrooke House

Royston (6 miles)

Not Sun ($1\frac{1}{2}$ miles)

# CHESHIRE

## Adlington Hall

*Adlington, near Macclesfield*

Black-and-white Tudor house built round courtyard, with additions. Great hall constructed between 1450 and 1505, Elizabethan black-and-white *c.* 1581 and Georgian south front in mid-18th C. House of Legh family since 14th C. The organ by Bernard Smith was installed *c.* 1670 and Handel is reputed to have played it. Garden contains a 'shell cottage' and fine yews and limes.

☎ Prestbury 829206

→ 5 miles N of Macclesfield on A523

Good Fri to early Oct, Sun and Bank Hol.; July and Aug, Wed and Sat, 2.30–6

Gawsworth Hall, Little Moreton Hall

Adlington ($\frac{3}{4}$ mile)

## Beeston Castle

*Beeston, near Nantwich*

DoE

Impregnably sited on very steep hill, castle was built by Earl of Chester in 13th C. Example of skilled masonry carried out under extreme difficulties, with much man-haulage as opposed to wagons.

→ About 15 miles N of Whitchurch, off A49

Mon to Fri 9.30–4.30

Dorfold Hall, Hodnet Hall*

Nantwich (10 miles)

## Bramall Hall

*Bramhall, near Stockport*

Half-timbered and good example of 'magpie'-style, built between the 14th and 16th Cs and contains interesting plasterwork. Worth visit just to appreciate this type of architecture in beautiful parkland setting. Home of Davenport family for many years, it contains portraits dating from 1575.

→ 4 miles S of Stockport off A5102

All year (except Dec) daily except Mon (but open Bank Hol. Mon), Apr to Sept 12–5, Oct to Mar 12–4

Adlington Hall, Lyme Park, Tatton Park

Bramhall ($1\frac{1}{2}$ miles)

BRAMALL HALL

## Capesthorne Hall

*Capesthorne, near Macclesfield*

Interesting Jacobean-style house dating from *c.* 1722, probably work of Francis and William Smith of Warwick. At beginning of 19th C it was considerably altered by Blore and Salvin. Contents include antique vases, silver, furniture, paintings, family documents and Americana. Small adjoining chapel could be one of earliest surviving works by John Wood of Bath. Close to Jodrell Bank.

Chelford 861221

7 miles s of Wilmslow on A34. 5½ miles w of Macclesfield A537–A34

End Mar to end Sept, Sun, Good Fri and Bank Hol., also Wed and Sat from May, and Tues and Thur from July, 2–5

Adlington Hall, Gawsworth Hall, Little Moreton Hall, Lyme Park

Macclesfield (6 miles)

(1½ miles)

## Churche's Mansion

*Hospital Street, Nantwich*

Late 16th-C black-and-white H-plan building. Restoration began in 1930 and continues with aim of restoring quality of work by original craftsmen. Fine interior oak panelling. Walled garden.

Nantwich 65933

Apr to Oct daily 10–5.30

Dorfold Hall, Hodnet Hall*, Little Moreton Hall

Nantwich

## Dorfold Hall

*Near Nantwich*

Built *c.* 1616 by Ralph Wilbraham, with wing added to E side in 18th C. Outstanding Jacobean panelling and decorative plasterwork.

Nantwich 65245

From A51 1 mile outside Nantwich heading w

Apr to Oct, Tues and Bank Hol. Mon 2–5

Churche's Mansion, Little Moreton Hall

Nantwich (1 mile)

## Dunham Massey

*Dunham, near Altrincham*

NT

Main house reconstructed in early 18th C. Restoration in progress, also with stables. Historical portraits include Lady Jane Grey; noteworthy collection of Huguenot silver.

Manchester 945 1025

3 miles sw of Altrincham off A56

Apr to end Oct daily except Mon and Good Fri (but open Bank Hol. Mon) 12–5.30

Churche's Mansion, Dorfold Hall, Tatton Park

Altrincham (3½ miles)

## Gawsworth Hall

*Near Macclesfield*

Tudor black-and-white manor house set in park with medieval jousting ground. Associated with Mary Fitton, Maid of Honour at Court of Elizabeth I, possibly the 'dark lady' of Shakespeare's sonnets. Note armour, sculpture, paintings and furniture. Carriage museum.

North Rode 456

3 miles s of Macclesfield on A536

Late Mar to late Oct daily 2–6

Adlington Hall, Capesthorne Hall, Little Moreton Hall

Macclesfield (4 miles)

## Little Moreton Hall

*Scholar Green, near Congleton*

NT

Fine example of black-and-white architecture with good carving on gables which tower up romantically; house surrounded by own moat. Inside much evidence of skill of original craftsmen joiners in handling massive timbers and fine panelling. 16th-C wall paintings have been recently discovered and restored.

Congleton 2018

4 miles SW of Congleton off A34. 1 mile N of Scholar Green

Mar, Sat and Sun 2–6; Apr to end Oct daily (except Tues and Good Fri) 2–6

Capesthorne Hall, Dorfold Hall, Gawsworth Hall

Kidsgrove (2½ miles)

Scholar Green (1 mile)

LITTLE MORETON HALL

## Lyme Park

*Disley, near Stockport*

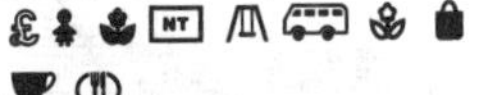

Main building dates from Elizabeth I and has been home of Legh family for some 600 years. Present Palladian exterior and other alterations were carried out *c.* 1720 by the Venetian Giacomo Leoni. Grinling Gibbons' carvings should be sought out. Large gardens and park of more than 1,300 acres with herd of red deer, also nature trails.

Disley 2023

½ mile W of Disley on A6

House: Apr to end Oct daily (except Mon), Tues to Sat 2–4.30 (2–4 in Oct), Sun and Bank Hol. Mon 1–5.30 (Sun 1–4.30 in Oct). Park and garden all year 8–sunset

Adlington Hall, Capesthorne Hall, Tatton Park

Disley (½ mile)

## Tatton Park

*Near Knutsford*

The earlier house here dates from time of Charles II; that built round it was started late in 18th C and designed by Samuel Wyatt. Four-column portico was constructed of local Cheshire stone, each column being cut from a single block of stone. Excellent assembly of furniture, silver, ceramics, glass and paintings for the connoisseur. Tenant's Hall museum contains veteran cars, state coach. Grounds include 50-acre garden with broad walk of fine trees leading to Greek monument, Japanese water garden, terraced Italian garden, orangery, show house and fernery, as well as 1,000-acre deer park. The Golden Brook is home of ornamental waterfowl, and wildfowl flourish on nearby Melchett Mere. Tatton Mere, a mile long stretch of water, offers sailing, swimming and fishing. Other pursuits include a medieval village trail, a nature trail and riding.

Knutsford 3155

3½ miles N of Knutsford off A50

Mid-Apr to mid-Oct daily except Mon (but open Bank Hol. Mon and Mon in Aug); mid-Oct to mid-Apr, Sun and Bank Hol. Mon only but closed completely from mid-Nov to early Mar. Open afternoons, but times vary. Check in advance.

Adlington Hall, Capesthorne Hall, Lyme Park

Knutsford (3½ miles)

# CLEVELAND

## Ormesby Hall

*Ormesby, near Middlesbrough*

Mid-18th C house containing quality plasterwork. The stable block is thought to be by Carr of York. Courtyard and stables are leased to the Mounted Police.

3 miles SE of Middlesbrough near junction of A171 and A174

Apr to end Oct, Wed, Sun and Bank Hol. Mon 2–6

Gisborough Priory*

Ormesby (1½ miles)

# CORNWALL

## Antony House

*Torpoint, near Plymouth*

Built by Sir William Carew between 1711 and 1721, it is one of finest Queen Anne houses in country to have survived unspoilt and unaltered. Sole addition is 19th-C entrance porch for carriages on S side. Contents include notable portrait of Charles I by Edward Bower, possibly worked from sketches made during the King's trial at Westminster Hall—Carew of Antony was one of the judges. Other paintings of note are Kneller's portrait of Admiral Van Tromp, said to have come from the Captain's cabin of a Dutch man-of-war captured by a Carew; three by Reynolds, a Benjamin Wilson and two hunting scenes by John Wyck and John Wootton. Early embroidery and furniture.

Plymouth 812191

2 miles NW of Torpoint (take car ferry from Plymouth)

Apr to end Oct, Tues, Wed, Thur and Bank Hol. Mon 2–6

Cotehele, Lanhydrock, Buckland Abbey, Saltram House

Plymouth (6 miles)

## Cotehele

*St Dominick, near Tavistock*

Medieval manor house of true grey Cornish granite that has weathered the years well. For centuries seat of Edgcumbe family and still contains fine collection of tapestries, needlework, armour and furniture. Chapel clock was installed by Sir Richard Edgcumbe *c.* 1489; it claims to be the earliest clock in England still unaltered and in its original position. Made entirely of hand-wrought iron, its driving power is supplied by 2 40-kg hollow iron weights. In a field immediately to N of house is the strange 3-sided Prospect Tower. 18 m high it may have been intended for signalling or erected just as a folly. Also worth visiting is nearby Cotehele Watermill, restored to working order.

COTEHELE

☎ St Dominick 50434

➔ 8 miles SW of Tavistock, 2 miles E of St Dominick, on E side of A388

⏱ Apr to end Oct daily except Mon (but open Bank Hol. Mon) 11–6. Garden all year daily during daylight hours

Antony House, Buckland Abbey, Lanhydrock House, Launceston Castle

Calstock (1½ miles via steep footpath)

Calstock

## Ebbingford Manor

*In Bude*

Small, representative example of old Cornish manor house, dating from 12th C. Walled garden.

☎ Bude 2808

➔ Near town centre

⏱ June to mid-Sept, Tues, Wed, Thur, also Sun from July, 2–5.30

Tintagel Castle

## Godolphin House

*Godolphin Cross, near Helston*

For a long time this was country home of the Earls of Godolphin. Earliest parts date from Tudor period, Doric-colonnaded front being added in 1635. Contains notable painting of 'The Godolphin Arabian' by John Wootton.

➔ 5 miles NW of Helston, 1½ miles S of B3280 at Townshend

⏱ May to June, Thur 2–5; July to Sept, Tues and Thur 2–5

St Michael's Mount

## Lanhydrock

*Treffry Cross, near Bodmin*

Begun by the 2nd Lord Robartes in 1634, it was one of the few great houses to be finished in Cornwall during the Commonwealth. In 1780 George Hunt removed the E wing leaving 3 sides of the square, the plan being as it is today. In 1881 a serious fire destroyed a large part of house. The original long gallery survives and the rest has been sensitively restored. The gallery is some 35 m long and has notable plastered barrel ceiling modelled in high relief with scenes from the Old Testament. Kitchen and domestic quarters are as in Victorian times. The formal gardens beside and in front of the house date from 1857, and contain bronze urns modelled by Louis Ballin, goldsmith to Louis XIV and given to Marie Antoinette by Comte d'Artois.

☎ Bodmin 3320

➔ From Bodmin–Lostwithiel road B3268

⏱ Apr to end Oct daily 11–6. Gardens all year daily during daylight hours

Antony House, Cotehele, Trerice

Bodmin Road (3 miles)

## Launceston Castle

*In Launceston*

OAP DoE

Formerly known as Dunheved, the strong cylindrical Norman keep still stands imposingly on a conical earthwork. N and S gates are good examples of way in which early masons treated problems of arching.

⏱ Daily except public hols (DES)

Cotehele

## Mount Edgcumbe House

*Cremyll, near Plymouth*

Massive Tudor-style mansion destroyed in 1941 Blitz on Plymouth and now restored. Still home of 7th Earl Mount Edgcumbe and contains good examples of Hepplewhite furniture. Outstanding coastal views from gardens.

➔ Take pedestrian Cremyll ferry across the Tamar from Plymouth

⏱ House and higher gardens early May to end Sept, Mon

and Tues 2–6; lower gardens daily all year

Antony House, Buckland Abbey, Saltram House

Plymouth (via ferry)

## Pencarrow House

*Washaway, near Bodmin*

Noteworthy Georgian house with good collection of paintings, furniture, particularly Oriental examples, and ceramics. Gardens include lake, rockery and remains of ancient encampment. Specialized plantation of conifers.

St Mabyn 369

4 miles NW of Bodmin off A389

Easter Sat to end Sept daily except Mon 1.30–5.30; Bank Hol. Mon 11–5.30. Gardens daily during season

Lanhydrock, Launceston Castle

## Pendennis Castle

*Near Falmouth*

With St Mawes Castle across Carrick Roads from Falmouth, this was part of Henry VIII's coastal defence system against possible invasion by the French. There is a central circular keep with semicircular bastions, enclosed by a curtain wall with gun emplacements. Held out for 5 months when under siege from the Cromwellians, but was savaged after this.

On Pendennis Point close to town of Falmouth

Daily except public hols (DES)

Godolphin House, St Mawes Castle*

Falmouth

## Restormel Castle

*Near Lostwithiel*

Originally part of manor of Bodardle, Restormel was probably built by Baldwin Fitz Turstin *c.* 1100. Keep is 38 m in diameter, made from local slate with dressings of white Pentewan stone. Walls are 2½ m thick and there is a wall-walk 7½ m above the level of the courtyard protected by a battlemented parapet.

1 mile N of Lostwithiel off A390

Daily except public hols (DES)

Lanhydrock, St Mawes Castle*

Lostwithiel (1 mile)

## St Michael's Mount

*Marazion, near Penzance*

A place of legend, the Cornish name for the Mount being *Cara clowse in cowse* meaning 'the hoar rock in the wood'. Jack the Brave Cornishman is said to have slain the giant, Cormoran, here. The latter's clumsy wife dropped the chapel rock from her apron to where it now stands on the shore of Marazion. Some say the place is the Ictis of the Phoenicians. In the year A.D. 495 fishermen told how they saw a vision of St Michael standing suffused in light on a ledge of rock. A monastery built here *c.* 12th C was in later centuries converted to present imposing hybrid castle–mansion–church. Truly a unique place with collections of armour, furniture, paintings, moulded plasterwork and 14th-C chapel.

ST MICHAEL'S MOUNT

Marazion 710507

From Marazion on the A394. Approach across causeway if tide is out, otherwise make use of floating transport

Nov to end Mar, Mon, Wed and Fri (guided tours only—check availability and times); Apr to end May, Mon, Wed and Fri 10.30–4.45, June to end Oct, Mon, Tues, Wed, Fri, 10.30–4.45

Pendennis Castle, Trerice

Penzance (3½ miles)

## Tintagel Castle

*In Tintagel*

Said by some to be the romantic fortress of the great King Arthur, high on the cliffs overlooking the angry seas below. What can the imagination make of the rugged rambling remains of ancient masonry? Are the spirits of Merlin, King Mark, Tristan and Iseult wandering here? Historians date the castle remains as *c.* 13th C, and remains of the early Celtic monastry *c.* 6th C. If you have the head for heights, dwell here a moment with the piskies and the rest.

From village of Tintagel off A39

Daily except public hols (DES)

Lanhydrock, Old Post Office (Tintagel)*, Trerice

Not weekends

## Trerice

*Kestle Mill, near Newquay*

16th-C manor house rebuilt by John Arundell on site of earlier building. Has uncommon curling treatment given to gables and impressive great window in hall with 24 lights, mullioned and transomed with 576 panes, much of the early glass remaining. Interior plasterwork worth noting; similar motifs appear at Buckland Abbey.

Newquay 5404

3 miles SE of Newquay. Turn off A3058 at Kestle Mill

Apr to end Oct daily 11–6

Lanhydrock, Trewithen

Newquay (3½ miles)

## Trewithen

*Probus, near Truro*

Good early Georgian house standing in garden internationally famous for display of beautiful flowering shrubs, particularly camelias, magnolias and rhododendrons.

St Austell 882763/4

1½ miles E of Probus, S of A390

Garden: Mar to Sept, weekdays 2–4.30. House: Apr to July, Mon and Tues 2–4.30

Lanhydrock, Pendennis Castle, Trerice

# CUMBRIA

## Abbot Hall

*In Kendal*

18th-C house probably by Carr of York. Notable collections of paintings, glass, furniture and china. Garden landscaped in 1759.

Kendal 22464

All year daily, Mon to Fri 10.30–5.30, Sat and Sun 2–5 (closed 2 weeks Christmas and New Year, also Good Fri)

Belle Isle, Hill Top, Levens Hall, Sizergh Castle

Kendal

## Belle Isle

*Near Bowness-on-Windermere*

Late 18th-C house set on delightful island in middle of Lake

Windermere. Interior by the Adam brothers with Romney paintings and Gillow furniture.

Bowness 3353

By ferry from Bowness

Mid-May to mid-Sept, Sun, Mon, Tues and Thur 10.30–5

Browsholme Hall, Hill Top, Holker Hall

Windermere ($1\frac{1}{2}$ miles)

Bowness Pier

## Brantwood

*Near Coniston*

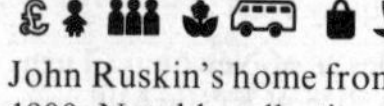

John Ruskin's home from 1872 to 1900. Notable collection of drawings and watercolours, also memorabilia. Woodland gardens and nature trails.

Follow signs from Coniston

Easter to end Oct daily except Sat 11–5.30

Belle Isle, Hill Top

## Brough Castle

*Brough, near Appleby*

£ OAP DoE

Remains of late 12th-C keep in commanding position on hill that was earlier site of Roman fort of Verterae. Burnt down by Scots in 1521 and restored by Lady Anne Clifford in late 16th C.

8 miles SE of Appleby off A66 to Barnard Castle

Daily except public hols (DES)

Brougham Castle

Appleby (8 miles)

## Brougham Castle

*Near Penrith*

£ OAP DoE

Built on site of Roman fort of Brocavum. Keep dates from *c.* 1170, with considerable remains, also of other buildings. Added to and restored by Lady Anne Clifford in late 16th C.

$1\frac{1}{2}$ miles E of Penrith off A66

Daily except public hols (DES)

Brough Castle, Carlisle Castle

Penrith ($1\frac{1}{2}$ miles)

## Carlisle Castle

*In Carlisle*

£ OAP DoE

One of the great border fortresses built *c.* 1092 by William Rufus and enlarged 100 or so years later. Mary Queen of Scots was welcomed as a visitor and stayed as a captive. Cromwell's men took it and in 1745 it fell to Bonnie Prince Charlie. Time has spared the impressive keep, the early gate and Queen Mary's Tower.

Daily except public hols (DES)

Brough Castle, Brougham Castle, Lanercost Priory

Carlisle (1 mile)

## Dalemain

*Dacre, near Penrith*

£

Imposing early Georgian mansion grown from medieval beginnings, through Tudor to present impressive façade. Collections of paintings, ceramics and furniture. Interesting museum of agricultural implements, also museum of Westmorland and Cumberland Yeomanry.

Pooley Bridge 450

A592 3 miles from Penrith

Easter Sat to end Sept daily (except Fri) 2–5.15

Carlisle Castle, Hill Top, Hutton-in-the-Forest, Sizergh Castle

Penrith ($3\frac{1}{2}$ miles)

## Dalton Castle

*Dalton-in-Furness, near Barrow-in-Furness*

£ NT

14th-C pele tower built originally by monks from Furness Abbey. On view is small but noteworthy collection of arms and armour and documents.

In centre of Dalton-in-Furness

Daily (key from Mr Whitehead, 18 Market Place) at any reasonable time

Belle Isle, Hill Top, Holker Hall

Dalton-in-Furness

## Hill Top

*Sawrey, near Bowness-on-Windermere*

17th-C farmhouse which became the beloved retreat of Beatrix Potter and the setting for several of her books including: *Tom Kitten*, *Jemima Puddle-Duck*, *Samuel Whiskers* and *Pigling Bland*. On view are some of her original drawings, also her china, furniture and pictures. As house is small, entry may have to be restricted at peak times.

- Hawkshead 334
- In village of Sawrey, 2 miles S of Hawkshead. Also by car ferry across Lake Windermere 2 miles S of Bowness
- Apr to end Oct, Mon to Sat (closed Fri) 10–5.30, Sun 2–5.30
- Belle Isle, Dalton Castle, Holker Hall
- Hawkshead (2½ miles)

## Holker Hall

*Cark in Cartmel, near Ulverston*

Originally built in 16th C, it suffered a fire in 19th C and has since been restored. Former home of Dukes of Devonshire, it is now owned by Mr Hugh Cavendish, a relative of the present Duke. Contains some of the finest wood carving in the North of England. Connected attractions include a motor museum, an art gallery and seasonal sporting activities of horse driving trials, sheep dog trials and hot-air ballooning. Large park with herds of fallow, red and sika deer. Adventure playground, children's farm and extensive gardens.

- Flookburgh 328
- 5 miles E of Ulverston (10 miles by road) off B5278
- Easter Sun to end Sept daily (except Sat), 11–6
- Belle Isle, Dalton Castle, Hill Top
- Cark in Cartmel (1 mile)

## Hutton in the Forest

*Unthank, near Penrith*

Another 14th-C pele tower, this time with interesting additions. Pele towers (or barmkins) were erected all over the northern counties in 14th and 15th Cs by the lesser gentry who felt the need to live in some kind of fortification. They could not afford a full-scale castle so made do with a rectangular tower house and a courtyard enclosed with a strong wall, thus hoping to protect their families and possessions from the swords and hands of raiding Scots. This one contains a fine collection of pictures, tapestries and furniture spanning more than 4 centuries. There is a charming woodland walk.

- Skelton 207
- 6 miles NW of Penrith on B5305
- Late May to mid-Oct, Thur and Bank Hol. Mon; also some Sun in Aug
- Carlisle Castle, Dalemain, Hill Top, Sizergh Castle
- Penrith (6½ miles)

## Lanercost Priory

*Brampton, near Carlisle*

Augustinian Canons' house founded *c.* 1166 by William de Vaux. Remains of choir, transepts, refectory, claustral buildings and gatehouse. In transepts are tombs of Dacre and Howard families. Nave of church still used for parish worship and not under DoE.

- 13 miles NE of Carlisle, 2 miles from A69 at Brampton
- Daily except public hols (DES)
- Carlisle Castle, Hadrian's Wall*
- Brampton (2 miles)

## Levens Hall

*Levens, near Kendal*

Architecturally interesting, it shows the evolution of an

Elizabethan house from a pele tower. Contents are rich in treasures: a Sèvres coffee service brought back by the Duke of Wellington after Waterloo (it was apparently lying ready packed to be sent to Napoleon's mother), good furniture, silver and richly decorated Cordova leather. In part of the buildings harpsichords are made; in another there is a collection of steam engines from 1820 to 1930. Half-scale traction engine gives rides for children. In garden is famous topiary laid out in 1692 and still maintained.

Sedgwick 60321

5 miles S of Kendal on A6

Easter Sun to end Sept. House: Tues, Wed, Thur, Sun and Bank Hol. Mon 2–5. Gardens: daily 10–5

Belle Isle, Hill Top, Leighton Hall, Sizergh Castle

Oxenholme (5 miles)

## Muncaster Castle

*Ravenglass, near Whitehaven*

At one time sheltered Henry VI and has been seat of Pennington family since 13th C. The pele tower incorporated with the rest of the building rests on Roman foundations. Contents include paintings by Gainsborough, Hoppner, Lely, Reynolds, Van Dyck and Velazquez; outstanding furniture; ceramics; and tapestries. Gardens have fine flowering shrubs, and feature a teenager's commando course, tree and nature trails, ornamental birds, flamingo pool and bear garden.

Ravenglass 614

On A595 1 mile SE of Ravenglass

Easter to early Oct, Tues, Wed, Thur and Sun 2–5

Belle Isle, Dalton Castle, Hill Top

Ravenglass (1 mile)

## Rydal Mount

*Ambleside, near Windermere*

Home of Wordsworth from 1813 to 1850. Lived in today by descendant. Memorabilia of the poet. Garden, originally laid out by Wordsworth, has superb view across Rydal Water and Windermere.

Ambleside 3002

$1\frac{1}{2}$ miles N of Ambleside off A591

Mar to end Oct daily 10–5.30; Nov to mid-Jan 10–12.30, 2–4

Belle Isle, Hill Top

Windermere (6 miles)

## Sizergh Castle

*Sedgwick, near Kendal*

Another building that has developed from a pele tower, this time one of some 18 m, with additions made in 15th, 16th and 18th Cs. Good examples of panelling and ceiling decoration, also Stuart and Jacobite memorabilia.

Sedgwick 60285

$3\frac{1}{2}$ miles S of Kendal near junction of A6 and A591

Apr to end Sept, Wed and Sun and Bank Hol. Mon; also Thur in July and Aug 2–5.45

Belle Isle, Hill Top, Leighton Hall, Levens Hall

Oxenholme (4 miles)

## Wordsworth House

*Cockermouth, near Workington*

Medium-sized merchant's town house built 1745. Wordsworth's birthplace (1770). Staircase, fireplaces and panelling are original, also garden mentioned in his 'Prelude'. Contains a static and audio-visual display.

Cockermouth 824805

In main street of Cockermouth

Apr to end Oct daily (except Thur and Good Fri) 11–5, Sun 2–5

Carlisle Castle, Hill Top, Muncaster Castle

Maryport (7 miles)

## Bolsover Castle

*Bolsover, near Chesterfield*

Although earliest parts of castle buildings date from Norman times, the keep was erected *c.* 1615, possibly by John Smythson, who may also have been responsible for reconstructions and enlargements. Unusual feature is riding school and gallery built *c.* 1660, probably by Samuel Marsh for 1st Duke of Newcastle.

- 6 miles E of Chesterfield on A632
- Daily except public hols (DES)
- Chatsworth, Haddon Hall, Hardwick Hall, Thoresby Hall
- Chesterfield (6 miles)

## Chatsworth

*Edensor, near Bakewell*

Fine Classical mansion designed by William Talman for 1st Duke of Devonshire in 1687; took 20 years to build. The 4th Duke had James Paine convert kitchen into entrance hall and also erect stables. At beginning of 19th C, 6th Duke employed Jeffry Wyatville to make further alterations, and Orangery was then built. Distinguished collection of books, drawings, furniture and paintings. For some, the water gardens will have most fascination. Here, starting in 1688, George London created an original layout of canals and fountains to which was later added a large cascade by Thomas Archer. Farming and forestry exhibitions in grounds.

- Baslow 2204
- 4 miles NE of Bakewell off B6012 at Edensor
- Apr to early Nov daily except Mon (but open Bank Hol. Mon) 11.30–4.30
- Bolsover Castle, Haddon Hall, Hardwick Hall
- Matlock (9 miles). Not Sun

## Haddon Hall

*Near Bakewell*

Earliest parts date from 13th C when Richard Vernon obtained a licence to erect a defensive wall round his manor house. Progressively enlarged and restored, it passed to Dukes of Rutland when Dorothy Vernon eloped with Sir John Manners. Gardens noted for their roses.

- Bakewell 2855
- 2 miles SE of Bakewell off A6
- Apr to end Sept daily (except Sun and Mon) 11–6; also Easter and Bank Hol. Sun (2–6) and Mon (11–6)
- Bolsover Castle, Chatsworth, Hardwick Hall
- Matlock ($6\frac{1}{2}$ miles). Not Sun

## Hardwick Hall

*Doe Lea, near Chesterfield*

Built between 1591 and 1597 by Elizabeth, Dowager Countess of Shrewsbury ('Bess of Hardwick') who lived to be 90, and after Queen Elizabeth was the most formidable and richest lady in England. Her 4 marriages added to treasures in the Hall. These include: the 'Revolution Chair' in which 4th Earl of Devonshire is said to have sat when plotting to make William of Orange king in 1688; exquisite panels of needlework in *petit-point*, some on 'cloth of golde velvett'; fine Mortlake tapestries; superb plasterwork in the High Great Chamber; rugs; furniture; silver. Herb and flower garden.

- Chesterfield 850430
- About 9 miles SE of Chesterfield, 4 miles from exit 29 on M1
- Apr to end Oct, Wed, Thur, Sat, Sun and Bank Hol. Mon 1–5.30
- Bolsover Castle, Chatsworth, Haddon Hall
- Chesterfield (7 miles)

HARDWICK HALL

## Kedleston Hall

*Kedleston, near Derby*

Built on foundations of 12th-C manor house, the hall must be finest existing example of work of Robert Adam. He was called in by the Curzons, who have lived at Kedleston for 800 years, to complete earlier work started by Matthew Brettingham and James Paine. Adam was also responsible for exquisite interiors, including Marble Hall and State rooms. Outstanding collection of paintings and beautiful gilt gesso-on-wood-framed mirrors and gilt furniture. Museum contains weapons and works of art collected by the Marquis Curzon when Viceroy of India at the turn of the century.

Derby 840396

4 miles NW of Derby, 2 miles N of A52

Easter Sun, Mon and Tues, then Sun from last in Apr to last in Sept, also Bank Hol. Mon and Tues 2–6

Melbourne Hall, Wollaton Hall

Derby (5 miles)

## Melbourne Hall

*Melbourne, near Derby*

Today the home of Marquess of Lothian, earlier the seat of Lord Melbourne. Contains important collection of antiques and paintings. Superb formal gardens containing shell grotto, yew tunnels, fountains, statuary and an unusual wrought iron birdcage pergola by the blacksmith Robert Bakewell. Much of garden layout was probably work of William Wise, inspired by gardens at Versailles.

Melbourne 2502

8 miles S of Derby on A514

Mid-Apr to end Sept, Wed, Thur and Sun, also Tues and Sat in July and Aug 2–6; Bank Hol. weekends Sat to Tues 2–6 (Mon 11–6)

Kedleston Hall, The Moat House*, Prestwold Hall, Thrumpton Hall

Derby (8 miles)

## Sudbury Hall

*Sudbury, near Uttoxeter*

Fine brick-built 17th-C house, with some of richest Charles II rooms in country. Wood carvings by Grinling Gibbons, murals by Laguerre and plasterwork by Bradbury and Pettifer. Enjoyable museum with exhibits of childhood. Gardens and a lake.

6 miles E of Uttoxeter off A50

Apr to end Oct, Wed to Sun and Bank Hol. Mon 1–5.30

Kedleston Hall, Melbourne Hall, Shugborough

Uttoxeter (6 miles)

## Winster Market House

*Winster, near Matlock*

Late 17th- or early 18th-C market house with five original arches filled in. NT Information Centre.

➔ 4 miles w of Matlock on s side of B5057

⏲ Apr to end Sept, Wed, Sat, Sun and Bank Hol. Mon 2–6

Chatsworth, Haddon Hall

Matlock (4 miles)

# DEVON

## A la Ronde

*Near Exmouth*

Strange and unique late 18th-C house with 16 sides. The house, with its fascinating shell gallery and staircase, was designed by Jane and Mary Parminter, ancestors of present owners.

☎ Exmouth 5514

➔ 2 miles N of Exmouth just off A377

⏲ Apr to Oct daily 10–6

Blackbury Castle, Cadhay, Powderham Castle

Lympstone (1 mile)

## Arlington Court

*Arlington, near Barnstaple*

Early 19th-C mansion set in wooded estate. Interesting collections of old pewter, costumes, shells and ship models. Good showing of horse-drawn vehicles in stables. Carriage rides available. Park holds Jacob sheep and Shetland ponies. Nature trail beside lake.

☎ Shirwell 296

➔ 7 miles NE of Barnstaple on A39

⏲ Apr to end Oct, Tues to Sun and Bank Hol. Mon 11–6. Gardens all year daily

Castle Hill (South Molton), Tapeley Park, Youlston Park*

Barnstaple (8 miles)

Tues, Fri, Sat only

## Bickleigh Castle

*Bickleigh, near Tiverton*

Some parts of castle date from medieval period. Great hall worthy of notice, also guard room and armoury. 11th-C chapel and moat.

☎ Bickleigh 363

➔ Off A396 3 miles s of Tiverton

⏲ Easter to end May, Wed, Sun and Bank Hol. Mon; June to mid-Oct daily except Sat, 2–5

Killerton House

## Blackbury Castle

*Southleigh, near Honiton*

DoE

Oval-shaped camp probably dating from Iron Age, with single ditch and bank with complex protective entrance on s side.

➔ 6 miles s of Honiton, off B3174

⏲ At any time

Cadhay, Powderham Castle, A la Ronde

Honiton (6 miles)

## Bradley Manor

*In Newton Abbot*

NT

Medieval period, interesting example of domestic Gothic. E wing with chapel is 15th C. Great hall dates from *c.* 1420.

➔ w side of Newton Abbot

⏲ Late Apr to end Sept, Wed 2–5

Compton Castle, Dartington Hall, Dartmouth Castle, Powderham Castle

Newton Abbot (1 mile)

## Buckland Abbey

*Yelverton, near Tavistock*

13th-C Cistercian monastery bought by Sir Richard Grenville

BUCKLAND ABBEY

in 1541. 40 years later it came into possession of Sir Francis Drake and remained with family until recent years. Now a Naval and Devon Folk Museum. Drake's celebrated drum may be seen, also plaster frieze in the great hall, internal dog gates, banners and portraits of the great sailor.

- ☎ Yelverton 3607
- ➔ 11 miles N of Plymouth via A386
- ⏱ Good Fri to end Sept daily 11–6, Sun 2–6. Oct to Easter, Wed, Sat and Sun 2–5
- 🏠 Antony House, Cotehele, Saltram House

## Cadhay

*Ottery St Mary, near Honiton*

Charming Tudor manor house *c.* 1550.

- ☎ Ottery St Mary 2432
- ➔ ½ mile from Fairmile on A30
- ⏱ Spring and Summer Bank Hol. Sun and Mon, also mid-July to end Aug, Wed and Thur 2–6
- 🏠 Blackbury Castle, Killerton House
- ⇌ Honiton (6 miles)

## Castle Drogo

*Drewsteignton, near Moretonhampstead*

NT

20th-C castle standing 275 m above sea level and looking out over wooded gorge of the Teign. One of Sir Edwin Lutyens most remarkable works. Terraced garden with splendid views of Dartmoor and miles of walks through unspoilt country.

- ☎ Chagford 3306
- ➔ 2 miles NE of Chagford off A382
- ⏱ Apr to end Oct daily 11–6
- 🏠 Powderham Castle

## Castle Hill

*Filleigh, near South Molton*

Palladian mansion erected between 1730 and 1740, seat of Fortescue family. Collection of paintings, tapestries, ceramics and furniture. Ornamental and other gardens.

- ☎ Filleigh 227
- ➔ 3½ miles W of South Molton on A361
- ⏱ Apr to Oct. By telephone appointment only
- 🏠 Arlington Court, Tapeley Park

## Compton Castle

*Marldon, near Paignton*

NT

Fortified manor house built by Gilbert family over 3 main periods: 1320, 1440 and 1520. Sir Humphrey Gilbert was colonizer of Newfoundland and half-brother of Sir Walter Raleigh. The castle was depicted on a 2-cent Newfoundland stamp issued in 1933.

- ☎ Kingskerswell 2112
- ➔ 1 mile N of Marldon off A381
- ⏱ Apr to end Oct, Mon, Wed

and Thur, 10–12, 2–5; other times by appointment only

Bradley Manor, Dartington Hall

Paignton ($3\frac{1}{2}$ miles)

## Dartington Hall

*Near Totnes*

Only banqueting hall of 14th-C origin open to public. Attractive gardens and interesting woodlands.

Totnes 862271

From village of Dartington, 2 miles NW of Totnes off A384

All year daily at any reasonable time (but may be closed for special functions)

Bradley Manor, Compton Castle, Totnes Castle*

Totnes (2 miles)

## Dartmouth Castle

*In Dartmouth*

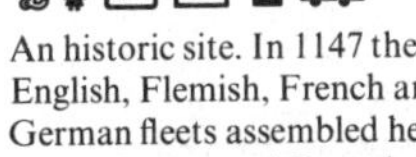

An historic site. In 1147 the English, Flemish, French and German fleets assembled here bound for Second Crusade. The Tudors later built castle to fend off possible raids from across the Channel. Close by in Royal Avenue Gardens is an original Newcomen steam engine.

1 mile SE of Dartmoor on W side of Dart estuary

Daily except public hols (DES)

Compton Castle, Dartington Hall, Saltram House

Paignton ($6\frac{1}{2}$ miles); Kingswear on Torbay and Dartmouth Railway ($\frac{1}{2}$ mile via ferry)*

## Killerton House

*Broadclyst, near Exeter*

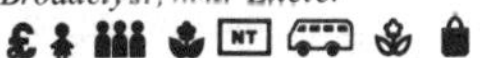

Late 18th-C house designed by John Johnson. Contains outstanding Paulise de Bush collection of costumes shown in rooms with different period furnishings. In grounds are fine flowering shrubs and conifers, also 19th-C chapel and Ice House.

Hele 345

7 miles NE of Exeter off B3181

Apr to end Oct daily 11–6

Bickleigh Castle, Powderham Castle

Exeter (7 miles)

## Knightshayes Court

*Bolham, near Tiverton*

Completed in 1874, it is a good example of work of William Burges. Decoration by J. D. Grace. Houses Sir John Amory's collection of paintings, also some early oak furniture. Recently established garden with formal terraces, rare shrubs and specimen trees.

Tiverton 4665

2 miles N of Tiverton off A396

Apr to end Oct daily 1.30–6

Killerton House

Tiverton Junction (8 miles)

## Lydford Castle

*Lydford, near Tavistock*

Remains of mid-12th C stone keep. Lower floor has been a prison, and upper floor was used as a Stannary Court concerned with local tin mines. Nearby is scenic Lydford Gorge with the 'White Lady' waterfall.

Midway between Okehampton and Tavistock off A386

At any reasonable time (DES)

Buckland Abbey, Cotehele, Lydford Gorge*, Okehampton Castle

Not weekends

## Okehampton Castle

*Castle Lane, Okehampton*

11th-C fortress built by Baldwin de Brionne to safeguard travellers

SALTRAM HOUSE

to West Country. There is a keep, chapel and hall, part dating from 14th C. Stands on edge of Dartmoor.

Daily except public hols (DES)

Killerton House, Powderham Castle

## Powderham Castle

*Kenton, near Exeter*

Family home of Courtenay family for nearly 600 years, it was built by Sir Philip *c*. 1390. Mauled during the Civil War, restoration took place in 18th and 19th Cs. The delightful music room with finely handled dome was work of Wyatt. Delicate plasterwork on walls surrounding great staircase. Banqueting hall has fine linenfold panelling and series of coats of arms tracing history of family. Contents include Brussels tapestries, portraits by Richard Cosway and ceramics.

Starcross 890243

8 miles sw of Exeter off A379 to Dawlish

Easter to mid-May, Sun (incl Easter Mon); mid-May to late Sept daily (except Fri and Sat) 2–6

Bradley Manor, Compton Castle, Killerton House

Starcross (1 mile)

## Saltram House

*Plympton, near Plymouth*

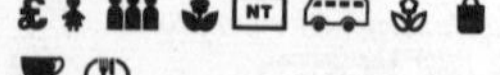

Possibly the jewel of houses in Devon. There appears to have been a manor or homestead on this site as early as 1249, then in late Tudor times came the buildings which comprise part of present mansion. Bought by Parker family in 1712, house was considerably remodelled in 18th C. Saloon and dining room are work of Robert Adam. Fine and well-cared-for furniture abounds; look for chandeliers and Zucchi decorations in saloon and Angelica Kauffman allegorical paintings on staircase walls. Above all Saltram is associated with Sir Joshua Reynolds; no less than 13 of his portraits hang here. Reynolds was a frequent visitor and his diary records hunting forays here with John Parker. Attractive gardens with Orangery. Great Kitchen on display.

Plymouth 336546

2 miles w of Plympton off A38

Apr to end Oct, Tues to Sun and Bank Hol. Mon 12.30–6. Garden all year daily

Antony House, Buckland Abbey, Cotehele

Plymouth (5 miles)

## Tapeley Park

*Instow, near Bideford*

William-and-Mary mansion on hill overlooking the Taw and Torridge estuary and across to Westward Ho! Quality plasterwork and carefully chosen selection of furniture and ceramics. Quiet and pleasant woodland walks. Devon cream teas in the Queen Anne Dairy.

Instow 860528

→ 1½ miles W of Instow on A39

Good Fri to late Oct daily (except Mon but open Bank Hol. Mon) 10–6

Arlington Court, Okehampton Castle

Barnstaple (6½ miles)

## Tiverton Castle

*In Tiverton*

£ OAP

Henry I fortress founded in 1106. See Joan of Arc gallery with portraits of her and her family, and Chapel of St Francis dedicated to animal welfare. Also note fine medieval gatehouse. Good collection of clocks.

Tiverton 3200

→ On outskirts of town

Easter, then mid-May to mid-Sept daily (except Fri and Sat) 2.30–5.30

Killerton House

Tiverton Junction (5½ miles)

## Ugbrooke

*Chudleigh, near Bovey Tracey*

£

18th-C house by Robert Adam set in 'Capability' Brown parkland with 2 lakes. Large silver ewer and dish made by Johann Jaeger of Augsburg and outstanding collection of quality embroidery.

Chudleigh 852179

→ 8 miles S of Exeter on A380

Spring Bank Hol. Sun and Mon, then June to Sept, Mon, Tues, Wed, Thur and Sun 2–6

Bradley Manor

Newton Abbot (6½ miles)

# DORSET

## Athelhampton

*Puddletown, near Dorchester*

£

Fine Tudor stone manor house, restored by various owners. It survives with its own sense of the past: secret staircases, old linenfold panelling, hall designed by Sir William Martyn with oriel window and heraldic glass. Outside 10 acres of well kept formal and landscaped gardens.

Puddletown 363

→ Off Dorchester – Bournemouth road A35, 5 miles NE of Dorchester

Apr to mid-Oct. Wed, Thur, Sun and Bank Hol.; also Tues and Fri in Aug 2–6

Cerne Abbas Giant*, Hardy's Cottage

Dorchester (5 miles)

## Christchurch Castle

*In Christchurch*

Rectangular tower mounted on Norman motte. Part of first floor of castle survives; building *c.* 1160, Norman chimney and few original windows.

Daily except public hols (DES)

Beaulieu, Corfe Castle

Christchurch

## Clouds Hill

*Bovington, near Wareham*

£ NT

For those interested in T. E. Lawrence (Lawrence of Arabia), here is the atmospheric little hideaway he bought when he rejoined the RAF in 1925; contains his sparse bare pieces of furniture, large horned gramophone and other relics.

→ 1 mile N of Bovington Camp, 1½ miles E of B3390

Apr to end Sept, Wed, Thur, Fri, Sun and Bank Hol. Mon 2–5; Oct to end Mar, Sun only 1–4

Cerne Abbas Giant*, Maiden Castle

Wool (4 miles)

## Compton House

*Over Compton, near Sherborne*

Manor house built in 16th C and substantially re-styled in 19th. Although people still live there, it is really a place of butterflies, a reserve where they are bred. Exhibits include a typical jungle setting and butterfly breeding hall. Visit the Lullingstone Silk Farm which has produced silk for many important Royal occasions.

Yeovil 4608

From A30 between Sherborne and Yeovil

Early Apr to end Oct daily 10–5

Lytes Cary, Montacute House, Wardour Castle

Yeovil ($2\frac{1}{2}$ miles)

## Corfe Castle

*Near Wareham*

12th- to 16th-C fortress with keep and inner bailey. Earliest parts once had fine set of domestic quarters erected in reign of John. Cromwell's troops treated it savagely but jagged and looming walls still carry feeling of great strength. Close by is small museum that has on show dinosaur footsteps from 130 million years ago.

SE of Wareham on A351

Mar to Oct daily 10 to dusk; Nov to Feb afternoons only

Athelhampton, Moignes Court*

Wareham (6 miles)

## Forde Abbey

*South Chard, near Chard*

OAP

Founded by Cistercian monks in 1138. Great hall built by Thomas Chard, the last Abbot. After the Dissolution became a private house, and was later occupied by Sir Edmund Prideaux, Cromwell's Attorney General. Fine Mortlake tapestries. 25 acres of beautiful gardens. Fruit in the orchards may be picked by visitors.

South Chard 20231

1 mile E of Chard Junction off B3162

Easter Sun and Mon, then May to Sept, Sun, Wed and Bank Hol. Mon 2–6

Montacute House, Shute Barton*

Axminster (7 miles)

## Hardy's Cottage

*Higher Bockhampton, near Dorchester*

NT

Thatched cottage which was birthplace of Thomas Hardy in 1840. Not changed since it was built by novelist's great-grandfather.

Dorchester 236

3 miles NE of Dorchester just S of A35. 10-min walk from car park through woods

Viewing only by prior appointment with tenant

Athelhampton, Corfe Castle, Maiden Castle

Dorchester (3 miles)

($\frac{1}{2}$ mile)

HARDY'S COTTAGE

## Maiden Castle

*Near Dorchester*

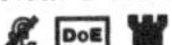

Most impressive example of prehistoric fortress in Britain. Immense earthworks with elaborate entrances. Dates from Iron Age and follows a neolithic siting. Remains of a Roman temple from 4th C have come to light within castle.

- 2½ miles SW from Dorchester on unclassified road off A354
- At any time
- Hardy's Cottage
- Dorchester (2½ miles)

## Milton Abbey

*Milton Abbas, near Blandford*

15th-C abbey dissolved by Henry VIII. In late 18th C Sir William Chambers erected a new Gothic house for Lord Milton. Contains James Wyatt ceilings.

- 9 miles SW of Blandford, N of A354
- For one week in early Apr, then late July to end Aug 10–7.30
- Athelhampton, Cerne Abbas Giant*, Forde Abbey
- (2¾ miles)

## Parnham House

*Beaminster, near Bridport*

Tudor mansion that has grown with the centuries and has additions by John Nash. Today houses John Makepeace Furniture Workshop and School for Craftsmen in Wood. Construction may be viewed as well as exhibitions in great hall and drawing room. Outside are formal terraces with cascades and water-channels and riverside walks.

- Beaminster 862204
- 1 mile S of Beaminster on A3066
- Early Apr to end Oct, Wed, Sun and Bank Hol. 10–5
- Cerne Abbas Giant*, Forde Abbey
- Crewkerne (6 miles)

## Portland Castle

*In Portland*

Originally built by Henry VIII but added to in 17th and 18th Cs.

- S from Weymouth on neck of Portland Bill
- Apr to Sept daily (DES)
- Maiden Castle, Moignes Court*
- Weymouth (3½ miles)

## Purse Caundle Manor

*Purse Caundle, near Sherborne*

Well-preserved medieval house with great hall and chamber. Pleasant garden.

- Milborne Port 400
- 4 miles E of Sherborne off A30
- Mar to Oct, Wed, Thur, Sun and Bank Hol. Mon 2–5
- Montacute House
- Sherborne (4 miles)

## Sandford Orcas Manor House

*Near Sherborne*

Good example of Tudor period house. Stained glass, quality paintings and furniture.

- Corton Denham 206
- 4 miles N of Sherborne
- Easter Mon 10–6, then May to Sept, Sun 2–6, Mon 10–6
- Purse Caundle Manor, Sherborne Castle

## Sherborne Castle

*In Sherborne*

Originally built by Sir Walter Raleigh and enlarged by Sir John Digby in 1625. Paintings by Gainsborough, Kneller, Lely, Reynolds and Van Dyck. 20 acres of 'Capability' Brown gardens and newly restored 50-acre lake.

- Sherborne 3182
- 5 miles E of Yeovil off A30
- Easter Sat to end May, Thur,

Sat, Sun and Bank Hol. Mon 2–6, June to Sept daily 2–6

Montacute House, Sherborne Old Castle*, Sandford Orcas Manor, Purse Caundle Manor

Sherborne

## Smedmore

*Kimmeridge, near Wareham*

17th- and 18th-C manor house still lived in by family who first built it. Contains collection of interesting old dolls and Dutch marquetry furniture. Walled gardens with flowering shrubs.

Corfe Castle 480717

7 miles s of Wareham on unclassified roads

Early June to early Sept, Wed 2.15–5.30

Athelhampton, Corfe Castle, Moignes Court*

Wareham ($7\frac{1}{2}$ miles)

## Wolfeton House

*Near Dorchester*

Fine medieval Elizabethan manor with exceptional wood and stone work; note fireplaces and ceilings. Good example of period furniture and some paintings. Chapel and cider house of interest.

Dorchester 3500

$1\frac{1}{2}$ miles from Dorchester on A37

Early May to end Sept, Tues, Wed, Sun and Bank Hol. Mon 2–6; daily in Aug 2–6 (except Sat). Other times by appointment

Athelhampton, Cerne Abbas Giant*, Moignes Court*

Dorchester ($1\frac{3}{4}$ miles)

# DURHAM

## Auckland Castle Deer House

*In Bishop Auckland*

Animal shelter erected in 1760 by Bishop Trevor in park of bishops of Durham. Provides interesting glimpse of Gothic style of period.

100 m to NE of Auckland Castle, in N outskirts of town

When park is open

Bowes Museum*, Raby Castle

Bishop Auckland ($\frac{3}{4}$ mile). Not Sun

## Durham Castle

*In Durham*

Norman building *c.* 1070, with additions by Bishop Hugh le Puiset; most striking remains from his time being main entrance to hall. Since 1832 castle has been used by Durham University.

Durham 65481

In centre of city

First 3 weeks in Apr, then July to Sept, weekdays 10–12, 2–4.30; other months, Mon, Wed and Sat 2–4

Auckland Castle Deer House, Bowes Museum*, Finchale Priory, Raby Castle

Durham ($\frac{1}{2}$ mile)

DURHAM CASTLE

## Finchale Priory

*Near Durham*

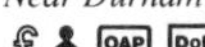

Impressive remains of Benedictine priory built on site of chapel of hermit St Godric (1115–70). Parts of church and claustral buildings date from mid-13th C.

➡ 5½ miles N of Durham on banks of River Wear, 2 miles E of A167 at Kimblesworth

Daily (DES), but Sun from Apr to Sept at 9.30

Auckland Castle Deer House, Bowes Museum*, Raby Castle

Durham (5½ miles)

## Raby Castle

*Staindrop, near Bishop Auckland*

14th-C fortified mass of masonry with great hall that could hold 700 knights. Alterations in 1765, also in 19th C by William Burn. Fire engines and horse-drawn coaches.

Staindrop 60202

➡ 1 mile N of Staindrop

Easter to end June, Wed and Sun; July to end Sept daily except Sat; also Bank Hol. weekends (Sat to Tues) 2–5

Bowes Museum*

Bishop Auckland (8 miles)

# EAST SUSSEX

## Alfriston Clergy House

*Alfriston, near Seaford*

14th-C half-thatched pre-Reformation priest's house. Bought in 1896 by the NT, the first building it acquired.

Alfriston 870001

➡ 4 miles NE of Seaford, off B2108

Apr to end Oct daily 11–6; Nov to Dec 23rd, Wed, Fri, Sat and Sun, 11-sunset

Bateman's, Firle Place

Seaford (4 miles)

## Bateman's

*Burwash, near Etchingham*

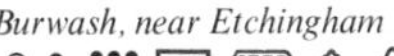

Built in 1634 for a local ironmaster, this was Rudyard Kipling's home from 1902 until 1936. Kipling, a keen early motorist, told how he and his wife found Bateman's hidden down an almost subterranean lane. His study is as it was when he was alive. The surrounding countryside was described in *Puck of Pook's Hill* and *Rewards and Fairies*. The NT has restored the mill which now grinds corn. Flour is sold in the shop.

Burwash 882302

➡ Just S of Burwash on A265

Mar to end May and Oct daily except Fri (but open Good Fri) 2–6; June to end Sept, Mon to Thur 11–6, Sat and Sun 2–6

Bodiam Castle, Charleston Manor*, Glynde Place

Etchingham (3 miles)

## Bodiam Castle

*Bodiam, near Robertsbridge*

Impressive expression of military strength in romantic setting.

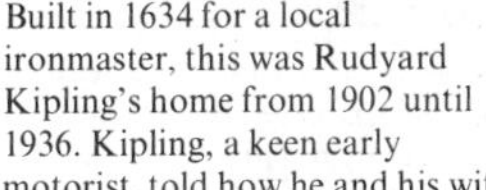

BODIAM CASTLE

Originally built as protection against French raids, it is one of the best-preserved examples of medieval fortification. Plan is a simple rectangle enclosed within massive curtain walls. Some floors have recently been replaced in the towers and it is possible to ascend by circular stairs to better judge the layout and area commanded by the castle. Small museum should not be overlooked as it contains interesting relics.

☎ Staplecross 436

→ 3 miles S of Hawkhurst, 1 mile E of A229

⏱ Apr to end Oct daily 10–7; Nov to Mar, Mon to Sat 10–sunset. Closed for Christmas

Bateman's, Sissinghurst Castle

Robertsbridge (5 miles)

Not Sun

## Brickwall House

*Northiam, near Rye*

£

Early 17th-C gabled house. Fine example of richly decorated plaster ceiling in drawing room.

☎ Northiam 2494

→ 7 miles NW of Rye off B2088

⏱ Late Apr to late May, early June to early July, Wed and Sat 2–4. Check dates in advance

Bateman's, Bodiam Castle, Smallhythe Place

Rye (7 miles)

## Firle Place

*West Firle, near Lewes*

£

Georgian house built round earlier Tudor building *c.* 1730. Has been home of Gage family since 15th C. General Sir Thomas Gage was Commander-in-Chief of British Army at start of American War of Independence. On view are items he brought home with him, also quality English, Dutch and Italian paintings; Sèvres ware; and French and English furniture.

☎ Hailsham 843902

→ 4 miles SE of Lewes off A27

⏱ June to Sept, Wed, Thur and Sun; also Easter, Spring and Summer Bank Hol. Sun and Mon 2.15–5.30

Bateman's, Glynde Place

Glynde (2 miles)

## Glynde Place

*Glynde, near Lewes*

£

Elizabethan house largely reconstructed in 18th C. Collections of bronzes and documents.

☎ Glynde 337

→ 4 miles E of Lewes, 1 mile N of A27

⏱ Late May to mid-Oct, Wed and Thur, also Bank Hol. Sun and Mon 2.15–5.30

Bateman's, Firle Place

Glynde (½ mile)

## Great Dixter

*Northiam, near Rye*

£

Charming half-timbered house with 15th-C great hall of unique construction. Restoration work and design of delightful gardens by Sir Edwin Lutyens.

☎ Northiam 3160

→ Just N of Northiam off A28

⏱ Apr to mid-Oct daily except Mon (but open Bank Hol. Mon) 2–5

Bateman's, Bodiam Castle, Smallhythe Place

Rye (7 miles)

## Haremere Hall

*Hurst Green, near Hawkhurst*

£

Early 17th-C manor house with minstrel staircase and fine panelled great hall with Flemish fireplace. Antiques include rugs and plate from Far East.

☎ Etchingham 245

→ Between Etchingham and Hurst Green near junction of A21 and A265

⏱ Bank Hol. weekends, 2.30–5.30

Bateman's, Bodiam Castle

Etchingham (1 mile)

## Lamb House

*West Street, Rye*

£ NT

Small Georgian house with walled garden, it was home of Henry James from 1898 to 1916. The study contains mementoes of author.

Apr to end Oct, Wed and Sat 2–6

Bateman's, Bodiam Castle, Smallhythe Place

Rye ($\frac{1}{2}$ mile)

## Michelham Priory

*Upper Dicker, near Hailsham*

Augustinian Priory, founded in 1229, with one of largest moats in Britain. A working watermill grinds wholemeal flour. Much to see with stained glass, musical instruments, dolls' house, forge, wheelwright's shop and wagons.

Hailsham 844224

7 miles N of Eastbourne, $1\frac{1}{2}$ miles W of A22

Early Apr to mid-Oct daily 11–1, 2–5

Charleston Manor*, Firle Place, Glynde Place, Pevensey Castle

Berwick (3 miles)

## Old Minthouse

*Pevensey, near Eastbourne*

£

Coins were struck on this site in 1076. Building dates from *c.* 1342 and was once occupied by Edward VI. Examples of fresco, carving and panelling; also priests' and smugglers' hideaways.

Eastbourne 762337

Opposite Pevensey Castle on A259

All year Mon to Sat 9–5; mid-July to mid-Sept Sun 1–5; also Bank Hols, except Christmas and New Year

Charleston Manor*, Firle Place, Glynde Place, Michelham Priory, Pevensey Castle

Pevensey and Westham

## Pevensey Castle

*Pevensey, near Eastbourne*

£ DoE

3rd-C Roman fort with Norman and 13th-C additions including keep, gatehouse and curtain wall. The wall served as a defence work during the Second World War when the Home Guard sited machine guns amongst the ruins.

3 miles NE of Eastbourne on A259

Daily except public hols (DES)

Charleston Manor*, Firle Place, Glynde Place, Michelham Priory, Old Minthouse

Pevensey and Westham

## Preston Manor

*Preston Park, Brighton*

£

Thomas-Stanford/Macquoid collections of antiques and paintings in quality Georgian house.

Brighton 552101

Off A23 Brighton to London road at Preston Park

All year Wed to Sat 10–5, Sun 2–5. Closed Christmas and Good Fri

Firle Place, Glynde Place, Royal Pavilion

Brighton (1 mile)

## Royal Pavilion

*In Brighton*

£

This impressive building started out as small house leased by Prince of Wales in 1786. Altered and reconstructed by Henry Holland and John Nash. Silhouette comprised of huge onion-shaped dome, minarets and tent-shaped roofs strikes unique note in its surroundings. Bought by town in 1850. Since Second World War has been well restored and holds interesting collections of pictures and furniture.

Brighton 603005

In centre of town

All year daily except public hols and possibly a few days

in first week of June. End June to early Oct 10–7.30; rest of year, 10–5

Firle Place, Glynde Place, Preston Manor

Brighton (¾ mile)

## Sheffield Park

*Near Uckfield*

Attractive Tudor house reconstructed by James Wyatt. Rare books, weapons and number of Charles Dickens' letters.

Dane Hill 790531

3 miles N of Chailey, off A275

Easter Sun and Mon, then May to end Oct, Wed, Thur, Sun and Bank Hol. Mon 2–5

Firle Place, Glynde Place, Michelham Priory

Uckfield (4 miles); Bluebell Railway: Sheffield Park from Horsted Keynes

(2½ miles)

# ESSEX

## Audley End House

*Audley End, near Saffron Walden*

Originally Benedictine Monastery of Walden stood here; at the Dissolution Henry VIII gave site to Lord Audley. A huge Jacobean building was erected and in 18th C Sir John Vanbrugh carried out considerable changes, including pulling down outer court. Exceptional collection of paintings and carved decoration.

1 mile W of Saffron Walden off A11

Apr to early Oct daily except Mon (but open Bank Hols) 10.30–6; not Good Fri or Maundy Thur

Gosfield Hall, Melford Hall

Audley End (1 mile)

## Belchamp Hall

*Belchamp Walter, near Sudbury*

Queen Anne House with period furniture and family portraits.

Sudbury 72744

5 miles SW of Sudbury

May to Sept, by prior appointment only

Castle House, Gosfield Hall

## Bradwell Lodge

*Bradwell-on-Sea, near Maldon*

Interesting small mansion, part Tudor, mainly Georgian with Adam wing. Belvedere tower and octagon room. Popular with 18th-C celebrities.

12 miles E of Maldon off B1021

By appointment only

Layer Marney Tower

Southminster (5 miles)

## Castle House

*Dedham, near Colchester*

Attractive home of late Sir Alfred Munnings PRA; his studio as well as the house display a number of his works.

Colchester 322127

7 miles NE of Colchester just off A11

Mid-May to mid-Oct, Wed, Sun and Bank Hol. Mon; also Thur and Sat in Aug 2–5

Layer Marney Tower, St Osyth's Priory

Manningtree (4 miles)

## Colchester Castle

*In Colchester*

Erected by Normans in late 11th C on and around remains of early Roman temple. Strong keep contains bricks from earlier structure; also incorporates original vaulting. Important collection of Roman and early antiquities.

Colchester 77475

- From town centre
- All year (except one day in early Apr and Dec 25–27) weekdays 10–1, 2–5 (2–4 Sat Oct to Mar); Sun (Apr to Sept only) 2.30–5
- Layer Marney Tower, St Osyth's Priory
- Colchester ($\frac{3}{4}$ mile)

## Gosfield Hall

*Gosfield, near Halstead*

Tudor courtyard house with 19th-C additions and restorations. Noteworthy panelled long gallery.

- $2\frac{1}{2}$ miles sw of Halstead off A1017
- May to Sept, Wed and Thur 2–5
- Audley End House, Melford Hall
- Braintree (5 miles)

## Ingatestone Hall

*Ingatestone, near Chelmsford*

Built *c.* 1540 for Henry VIII's Secretary of State, Sir William Petre. Long gallery with portraits, 16th-C virginal and armorial china. Archives hold huge collection of documents.

- 6 miles s of Chelmsford off B1002
- Early Apr to early Oct, Tues to Sat and Bank Hol. Mon 10–12.30, 2–4.30
- Bradwell Lodge, Layer Marney Tower
- Ingatestone ($\frac{1}{2}$ mile)

## Layer Marney Tower

*Layer Marney, near Colchester*

Striking 16th-C house with 8-storey gate-tower, highest Tudor gatehouse in country. Terracotta windows and low turrets treated in Italian style. Gardens with formal yew hedges and beautiful roses.

- Colchester 330202
- 3 miles NE from Tiptree, 1 mile s of B1022
- Apr to end Sept, Sun and Thur 2–6, Bank Hol. Mon 11–6; also Tues in July and Aug 2–6
- Castle House, St Osyth's Priory
- Colchester (9 miles)
- By arrangement

LAYER MARNEY TOWER

## Paycocke's

*Coggeshall, near Braintree*

NT

Merchant's house, *c.* 1500, with exceptionally rich wood carving and panelling.

- s side of West Street, in Coggeshall
- Apr to end Sept, Wed, Thur, Sun and Bank Hol. Mon 2–5.30
- Castle House, Layer Marney Tower, St Osyth's Priory
- Kelvedon ($2\frac{1}{2}$ miles)

## St Osyth's Priory

*St Osyth, near Clacton*

Among finest monastic remains in country. It was an Augustinian Abbey for 400 years until the Dissolution by Henry VIII.

- 4 miles from Clacton off A1027
- Gardens and ancient monuments only, May to Sept and Easter weekend 10–5
- Castle House, Layer Marney Tower
- Clacton ($4\frac{1}{2}$ miles)

## Spains Hall

*Finchingfield, near Braintree*

Remains of earlier building give added interest to this attractive Elizabethan manor. Noteworthy tapestries, paintings and antiques. Massive cedar of Lebanon in garden.

10 miles NW of Braintree off B1053

May to early Aug, Sun 2–5.30, also Bank Hol. Mon

Audley End, Gosfield Hall

Braintree (10 miles)

## Tilbury Fort

*Near Tilbury*

Dating from time of Henry VIII, it was here Queen Elizabeth I held her celebrated review of troops raised to resist the Spanish Armada. More recently the take-off point for forces during the final phases of the Second World War.

S of town off A13

Weekdays except public hols (DES)

Hadleigh Castle*

Tilbury Riverside

# GLOUCESTERSHIRE

## Arlington Mill

*Bibury, near Cirencester*

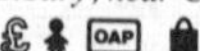

Late 17th-C mill with trout pool. Contents include machinery, Staffordshire china, furniture by Peter Waals and costumes.

Bibury 368

7 miles NE of Cirencester off A433

Mar to Oct daily, weekends in winter 10.30–7

Kelmscott Manor, Owlpen Manor*, Sudeley Castle

Kemble (11 miles)

## Berkeley Castle

*Berkeley, near Bristol*

Home of the Berkeleys, built in 1153, the oldest inhabited castle in England. Huge Norman keep, dungeon, kitchen and great hall are original. Here Edward II was murdered in 1327. State apartments have fine silver, paintings, tapestries and furniture. Ancient bowling alley, terraced gardens and park with fallow and red deer.

Berkeley 810332

Midway between Bristol and Gloucester off A38

Apr and Sept daily except Mon 2–5; May to Aug weekdays except Mon 11–5, Sun 2–5; Oct, Sun only 2–4.30, also Bank Hol. Mon 11–5

Badminton House, Horton Court, Little Sodbury Manor, Owlpen Manor*

Stonehouse ($11\frac{1}{2}$ miles)

## Buckland Rectory

*Buckland, near Evesham*

Dates from *c.* 1520. Great hall has timber-frame roof and stained glass windows of period. Oldest rectory in country. Connections with John Wesley.

Broadway 852479

6 miles SE of Evesham, off A46 $1\frac{1}{2}$ miles W of Broadway

May to July and Sept, Mon 11–4; Aug, Mon and Fri 11–4

Snowshill Manor, Sudeley Castle

Evesham (6 miles)

## Chavenage

*Tetbury, near Stroud*

Elizabethan Cotswold manor house with 2 tapestried rooms. Medieval barn.

Tetbury 52329

2 miles N of Tetbury off A433

May to Sept, Thur, Sun and Bank Hol. 2–5

Berkeley Castle, Kelmscott Manor, Owlpen Manor*

Kemble (7½ miles)

## Clearwell Castle

*Clearwell, near Coleford*

By repute oldest 'Mock Gothic' castle in country. Regency interior restored. 8 acres of formal gardens, bird sanctuary and lake.

Dean 32320

5 miles SE of Monmouth on B4231

Easter to early Oct daily 11–6

Goodrich Castle

Lydney (5½ miles)

## Kelmscott Manor

*Kelmscott, near Lechlade*

£

The house of William Morris, a 16th-C Cotswold building. Designs and possessions of Morris.

1 mile E of Lechlade

Apr to Sept, first Wed only in each month 11–1, 2–5

Snowshill Manor

## Painswick House

*Near Stroud*

Palladian Georgian house with fine reception rooms. Chinese wallpaper especially notable.

Painswick 813646

Just outside Painswick off A46, 3 miles N of Stroud

July to end Sept, Sat, Sun, and Bank Hol. Mon 2–6

Chastleton House, Snowshill Manor

Stroud (4 miles)

## Snowshill Manor

*Near Broadway*

Manor of Snowshill (Snawesille) dates back to pre-Conquest times and was in ecclesiastical ownership from Saxon period to the Dissolution. House was reconstructed in Tudor period, but has front elevation of later date. Fascinating collections: bicycles, clocks, armour, scientific instruments, spinning wheels, firefighting equipment, toys and dolls. Terraced garden.

Broadway 852410

3 miles S of Broadway and A44

Apr and Oct, Sat, Sun and Bank Hol. Mon 11–1, 2–6; May to end Sept, Wed to Sun and Bank Hol. Mon 11–1, 2–6

Buckland Rectory, Chastleton House

Evesham (10 miles)

(3 miles)

## Sudeley Castle

*Winchcombe, near Cheltenham*

Tudor home of royalty for many years. Katherine Parr lived here. Elizabeth I visited and Charles I used it as an HQ. Paintings by Constable, Rubens and Van Dyck. On show are Shakespeare costumes, Emma Dent collection of Victorian autographs, letters and photographs.

Winchcombe 602308

6 miles NE of Cheltenham off A46

Mar to Oct daily 12–5.30

Chastleton House, Snowshill Manor

Cheltenham (7½ miles)

## Upper Slaughter Manor

*Near Stow-on-the-Wold*

£

Fine Elizabethan house with extensive terraced gardens.

Bourton-on-the-Water 20927

2½ miles SW of Stow-on-the-Wold off A436

May to late Sept, Fri 2–6

Chastleton House, Ditchley Park, Snowshill Manor

Kingham (8 miles)

## GREATER MANCHESTER

### Heaton Hall
*Heaton Park, near Prestwich*

Impressive mansion built by James Wyatt in 1722, formerly home of Earls of Wilton. Amongst items of interest are: Etruscan rooms; organ built by Samuel Green; Assheton Bennett collection of English silver; and works of art from 17th to 19th Cs.

- Manchester 773 1231
- 6 miles N of Manchester city centre, ½ mile W of M66 exit 5
- Apr to Sept, weekdays 10–6, Sun 12–6 (2–6 Apr and Sept). Times subject to alteration
- Newton Hall, Platt Hall, Tatton Park
- Heaton Park

### Newton Hall
*Near Hyde*

Carefully restored Cruck-framed manor hall, built *c.* 1380. Original beams.

- Manchester 308 2721
- 1 mile N of Hyde near exit 3, M67
- All year Mon to Fri 10–4
- Heaton Hall, Platt Hall, Tatton Park, Wythenshawe Hall
- Hyde Central (1 mile). Not Sun

### Platt Hall
*Rusholme, near Manchester*

Designed by John Carr of York, *c.* 1760; houses distinguished collection of English costume covering fashions from 17th C to today.

- Manchester 224 5217
- 2 miles S of Manchester city centre off A6010
- Apr to Sept, weekdays 10–6, Sun 12–6 (2–6 Apr and Sept). Times subject to alteration
- Heaton Hall, Tatton Park, Wythenshawe Hall
- Manchester Piccadilly (2 miles)

### Wythenshawe Hall
*Northenden, near Altrincham*

Timber-framed Georgian brick manor house. Selective collections of 17th-C furniture, arms and armour, oriental ceramics, ivories, Japanese prints and paintings.

- Manchester 236 9422
- 7 miles S of Manchester city centre in Wythenshawe Park
- Apr to Sept, weekdays 10–6, Sun 12–6 (2–6 Apr and Sept). Times subject to alteration
- Heaton Hall, Newton Hall, Platt Hall, Tatton Park
- Gatley (2 miles). Not Sun

## HAMPSHIRE

### Avington Park
*Itchen Abbas, near Winchester*

Compact and old red-brick mansion, visited by Charles II and George IV. Fine portico surmounted by statues. Note ballroom ceiling and the Red Drawing Room.

- Itchen Abbas 202
- 4 miles NE of Winchester, just S of B3047
- May to Sept, Sat, Sun and Bank Hols 2.30–5.30
- Beaulieu, Broadlands, Mottisfont Abbey
- Winchester (4½ miles)
- Sun and Bank Hols only

BEAULIEU ABBEY

## Beaulieu Abbey and Palace House

*Near Lyndhurst*

£ OAP

Cistercians founded Abbey here early in 13th C. Great gatehouse of Abbey was converted to private home in 1538 and is known as Palace House. Contents include Montagu family portraits, Victorian stained glass and keyboard instruments. Outside are ruins of Beaulieu Abbey, a Winepress and the celebrated National Motor Museum with over 300 veteran and vintage cars, motor cycles and pedal cycles. Other attractions include monorail, veteran bus rides and model railway.

- Beaulieu 612345
- In Beaulieu, junction of B3054 and B3506
- Daily all year except Dec 25th. Apr to Oct 10–6, Nov to Mar 10–5
- Broadlands, Christchurch Castle, Mottisfont Abbey
- Beaulieu Road (3½ miles)
- From Hythe (Hants)

## Breamore House

*Breamore, near Fordingbridge*

£

Gabled manor house built in 1583, home of Hulse family; Sir Edward Hulse was physician to George II. Severely damaged by fire in 1856, now restored. Good collection of furniture, paintings and tapestries. Carriage museum and countryside collections.

- Breamore 233
- 3 miles N of Fordingbridge just W of A338
- Apr to end Sept daily except Mon and Fri (but open Bank Hol.) 2–5.30
- Beaulieu, Broadlands, Mottisfont Abbey
- Salisbury (7½ miles)

## Broadlands

*In Romsey*

£

Built in 1536, it belonged to the Abbey of Romsey until sold to Lord Palmerston in 1736. Landscaping and architecture by 'Capability' Brown. Special exhibition and audio-visual show illustrate the life and career of the late Lord Mountbatten whose wife Edwina inherited the estate in 1939.

- Romsey 516878
- Immediately S of Romsey off A31
- Apr to Sept daily except Mon (but open Bank Hol. and Mon in Aug and Sept) 10–6
- Beaulieu, Breamore House, Mottisfont Abbey
- Romsey

## Hurst Castle

*Near Lymington*

£ OAP DoE

Built in 1544 under direction of Henry VIII, and occupied by Cromwell's men in Civil War. Restored in 1873. Accessible by boat or on foot at low tide.

- On thin peninsula 4 miles SW of Lymington, 2 miles from B3058
- Daily except public hols (DES)
- Beaulieu, Broadlands, Christchurch Castle
- Lymington Town (4½ miles)

## Jane Austen's House

*Chawton, near Alton*

Houses many mementoes and souvenirs of the author and her family.

Alton 83262

1 mile sw of Alton off A32

All year, Apr to Oct daily, Nov to Mar, Wed to Sun 11–4.30. Closed Dec 25 and 26

Avington Park, Stratfield Saye House

Alton (1 mile)

## Mottisfont Abbey

*Near Romsey*

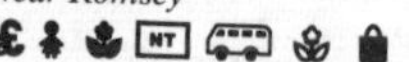

Augustinian Priory dating from 12th C and becoming a private dwelling at the Dissolution. Worth seeing is Gothic *trompe l'oeil* by Rex Whistler. Delightful walled garden with old roses and peaceful grounds bordering on river Test.

Lockerley 40278

4½ miles NW of Romsey, 1 mile E of B3084

Apr to end Sept, Wed and Sat 2.30–6. Grounds Tues to Sat (closed Good Fri) 2.30–6

Beaulieu, Breamore House, Broadlands

Dunbridge (¾ mile)

## Portchester Castle

*Portchester, near Portsmouth*

Originally a Saxon 4th-C shore fort, with 12th-C keep and Assheton's Tower (1367). Parish church (1133) in sw corner of outer curtain-walled enclosure.

Off A27, 3 miles w of Portsmouth

Daily except public hols (DES)

Beaulieu, Broadlands, Netley Abbey*

Portchester

## Stratfield Saye House

*Stratfield Saye, near Reading*

Early 17th-C mansion presented to Duke of Wellington in 1817. Comprehensive collection of paintings, furniture, prints, effects and relics of the great soldier. Wildfowl sanctuary. Wellington country park provides walks, fishing and boating.

Turgis Green 601

1 mile N of Stratfield Turgis on A33 between Basingstoke and Reading

House: mid-Apr to end Sept daily except Fri 11.30–5.30; Wellington Country Park and National Dairy Museum: Mar to end Oct daily 10–5.30, and winter weekends

Avington Park, The Vyne

Mortimer (3½ miles)

## The Vyne

*Sherborne St John, near Basingstoke*

Outstanding early 16th-C house, with diapered brickwork, built by

STRATFIELD SAYE HOUSE

William, 1st Lord Sandys, Lord Chamberlain to Henry VIII. Classical portico added in 17th C by Chaloner Chute, almost certainly from design by John Webb, the disciple of Inigo Jones. Noteworthy encaustic tiles in the chapel. Lawns, borders, trees and lake.

- Basingstoke 881 337
- 4 miles N of Basingstoke on unclassified road to Bramley
- Apr to end Oct, Tues, Wed, Thur, Sat and Sun 2–6 (Oct 2–5.30); Bank Hol. Mon 11–1, 2–6 (closed Tues following)
- Mapledurham House
- Bramley ($2\frac{1}{2}$ miles)

## West Green House

*Hartley Wintney, near Basingstoke*

£ NT

Small early 18th-C house in red brick with considerable charm and an enjoyable garden.

- 1 mile W of Hartley Wintney, 1 mile N of A30
- Apr to end Sept, Wed 2–6; garden only: Thur and Sun 2–6
- Loseley House, The Vyne
- Winchfield (2 miles)

# HEREFORD AND WORCESTER

## Berrington Hall

*Ashton, near Leominster*

£ NT

Built between 1778 and 1781 by Henry Holland, architect of Carlton House, London. Good plasterwork and painted ceilings. Extensive park laid out by 'Capability' Brown.

- 3 miles N of Leominster off A49
- Apr and Oct, Sat, Sun and Easter Mon; May to end Sept, Wed to Sun and Bank Hol. Mon 2–6. Joint tickets available with Croft Castle
- Croft Castle, Dinmore Manor, Eye Manor
- Leominster (3 miles). Not Sun
- Only at weekends

## Brilley: Cwmmau Farmhouse

*Whitney-on-Wye, near Kington*

£ NT

Early 17th-C timber-framed and stone-tiled farmhouse.

- 4 miles SW of Kington, 1 mile N of Whitney on A438
- Weekends (Sat, Sun and Mon) of Easter, Spring and Summer Bank Hols 2–6
- Dinmore Manor
- Only by prior arrangement

## Burton Court

*Eardisland, near Leominster*

£

14th- to 18th-C house with original 14th-C great hall. Fine collection of Chinese and European costumes. Model fairground.

- Pembridge 231
- $5\frac{1}{2}$ miles W of Leominster just S of A44
- Whitsun to mid-Sept, Wed, Thur, Sat, Sun and Bank Hol. Mon 2.30–6
- Croft Castle, Dinmore Manor, Eye Manor
- Leominster ($5\frac{1}{2}$ miles). Not Sun

## The Commandery

*Sidbury, Worcester*

£ OAP

Late 15th-C timber-framed building originally used as pre-Reformation hospital. Impressive great hall, late 15th-C wall paintings. In 1651 was Royalist headquarters during Battle of Worcester. Today houses important collection of Civil War items, also material illustrating history of Worcester since Roman times.

- Worcester 25371

In centre of Worcester

All year Tues to Sat 10.30–5, Sun (Apr to Sept) 2.30–5. Also Bank Hol. Mon

Hanbury Hall, Lower Brockhampton, Spetchley Park*

Worcester (1 mile)

## Croft Castle

*Near Leominster*

This well-weathered and impressive building has been in continuous possession of Croft family from Domesday, except for break of 170 years from 1750 to 1920. Acquired by NT in 1957.

5 miles NW of Leominster off B4362

Apr and Oct, Sat, Sun and Easter Mon; May to end Sept, Wed to Sun and Bank Hol. Mon 2–6. Joint tickets available with Berrington Hall

Berrington Hall, Dinmore Manor, Eye Manor

Leominster (7 miles). Not Sun

Not Sun

## Dinmore Manor

*Near Hereford*

16th-C house with medieval chapel that was once a Commandery of the Knights Hospitallers of St John of Jerusalem. Rock garden.

6 miles N of Hereford on A49

All year daily 2–6 (except Dec 25 and 26)

Croft Castle, Eye Manor, Lower Brockhampton

Hereford (6½ miles)

## Eastnor Castle

*Eastnor, near Ledbury*

Built in 1814 by John, 1st Earl Somers. Collections of paintings, tapestries, armour. Arboretum.

Ledbury 2304

2 miles E of Ledbury on A438

Mid-May to end Sept, Sun and Bank Hol. Mon, also Wed and Thur in July and Aug 2.15–6

Goodrich Castle, Hellen's

Ledbury (2 miles)

## Eye Manor

*Eye, near Leominster*

OAP

Erected 1680 for Ferdinando Gorges, a Barbados sugar-planter. Fine plasterwork, furniture and pictures. Collections of corn dollies, costumes, private press books and the Beck Costume Dolls.

Yarpole 244

4 miles N of Leominster, 1 mile E of B4361 on unclassified road to Eye

Apr to Sept daily 2.30–5.30

Berrington Hall, Croft Castle, Dinmore Manor

Leominster (4 miles)

## Goodrich Castle

*Near Ross-on-Wye*

OAP

First mentioned under name of 'Godric's' in a record of *c.* 1101. Massive Norman keep is late 12th C. When Edward I set out on conquest of Wales, William de Valence, half-brother to Henry III, made many alterations. Slighted during Civil War.

S of Ross-on-Wye off B4227

Daily except public hols (DES)

Eastnor Castle, Hellen's

GOODRICH CASTLE

## Hanbury Hall

*Near Droitwich*

£

Red-brick house in Wren style built *c.* 1700. Fine ceilings painted by Thornhill. Watney collection of porcelain.

- Hanbury 214
- $2\frac{1}{2}$ miles E of Droitwich just off B4091
- Apr and Oct, Sat, Sun, Easter Mon and following Tues; May to end Sept, Wed to Sun, Bank Hol. Mon and following Tues 2–6
- Coughton Court, Spetchley Park*
- Droitwich ($2\frac{1}{2}$ miles)

## Harvington Hall

*Near Kidderminster*

£

Elizabethan manor house with moat, priests' hiding places and some wall paintings.

- Chaddersley Corbett 267
- 4 miles SE of Kidderminster off A448
- Feb to end Nov daily except Mon and Fri following Bank Hol. (but open Bank Hol. Mon) 2–6. Also 11.30–1 from Easter to Sept. Closed Good Fri
- Hanbury Hall, The Commandery
- Kidderminster (4 miles)

## Hellen's

*Much Marcle, near Ledbury*

£

Stone manor house occupied since 1292. In the great hall stands stone table at which the Black Prince dined. Also on view is bedroom prepared for Mary I ('Bloody Mary'). 19th-C carriages.

- In Much Marcle on A449, 4 miles SW of Ledbury
- Easter to early Oct, Wed, Sat and Sun 2–6. Other times by written appointment only
- Eastnor Castle, Goodrich Castle
- Ledbury ($4\frac{1}{2}$ miles)
- By prior arrangement

## Kentchurch Court

*Kentchurch, near Hereford*

£

14th-C manor house with alterations by John Nash. Contains carving by Grinling Gibbons and paintings. Owen Glendower's tower.

- Golden Valley 240228
- 3 miles SE of Pontrilas just off B4347
- May to Sept for parties only. Prior appointment necessary
- Llanfihangel Court, Tretower Court and Castle
- Hereford (14 miles)

## Lower Brockhampton

*Bringsty, near Bromyard*

£

14th-C half-timbered moated manor house. Interesting gatehouse.

- 2 miles E of Bromyard off A44. Hall reached by rough narrow unclassified road through $1\frac{1}{2}$ miles of woods and farmland
- Medieval hall only, Feb to end Dec, Mon, Wed, Fri (not Good Fri), Sat 10–1, 2–6; Sun 10–1
- Spetchley Park*, Wichenford Dovecote
- Worcester ($12\frac{1}{2}$ miles)
- (1 mile)

## Moccas Court

*Moccas, near Hereford*

£

Mansion designed by Adam and built by Keck in 1775. Stands beside River Wye.

- Moccas 381
- 13 miles W of Hereford, 1 mile off B4352
- Apr to Sept, Thur 2–6
- Dinmore Manor, Goodrich Castle, Kentchurch Court
- Hereford ($13\frac{1}{2}$ miles)

## Pembridge Castle

*Welsh Newton, near Monmouth*

£

Romantic 13th-C border castle standing within a moat.

➔ 4 miles N of Monmouth just off A466
◷ May to Sept, Thur 10–7
▦ Tretower Court and Castle

### Wichenford Dovecote

*Near Worcester*

£ NT

Rare 17th-C black-and-white dovecote.

➔ 5½ miles NW of Worcester off B4204
◷ Daily 10–6
▦ Harvington Hall, Lower Brockhampton, Spetchley Park*
⇄ Worcester (6 miles)
🚌 (1 mile). Not Sun

## HERTFORDSHIRE

### Ashridge

*Little Gaddesden, near Berkhamsted*

£

Begun in 1808 by James Wyatt for 7th Earl of Bridgwater, house is example of early Gothic Revival. A previous building, a 13th-C monastery, had for a time after the Dissolution been home of Henry VIII's children. Park was landscaped by 'Capability' Brown and gardens laid out by Repton.

☎ Little Gaddesden 3491
➔ 3½ miles N of Berkhamsted, 1 mile W of A4146
◷ Ring to ascertain dates and times
▦ Gorhambury House, Little Gaddesden, Piccotts End
⇄ Berkhamsted (3½ miles)

### Berkhamsted Castle

*In Berkhamsted*

£ DoE

11th-C motte and bailey castle with a later circular keep. The Black Prince lived there, as did Chaucer, and it was the prison of King John of France.

◷ Daily except public hols and weekends (DES)
▦ Ashbridge, Little Gaddesden, Piccotts End
⇄ Berkhamsted

### Gorhambury House

*Near St Albans*

£ OAP

Late Georgian mansion in modified Classical style built between 1777 and 1784 by Sir Robert Taylor. Contents include noteworthy enamelled glass and some interesting historical portraits.

☎ St Albans 54051
➔ 2½ miles N of St Albans and 1 mile from M1 exit 7
◷ May to Sept, Thur 2–5 (guided tours only)
▦ Ashridge, Hatfield House, Piccotts End
⇄ St Albans (3 miles)

### Hatfield House

*In Hatfield*

£

This famous Jacobean house was built between 1607 and 1611 by Robert Cecil, 1st Earl of Salisbury and Prime Minister to James I. Exceptionally fine tapestries woven from engravings by Marten de Vos; 'Rainbow' portrait of Elizabeth I by Zucchero; collections of armour and fine furniture. National collection of model soldiers. Chapel has beautiful original stained glass. In the gardens stands the existing wing of the Royal Palace of Hatfield, built 1497, where Elizabeth spent part of her childhood and where in 1558 she held her first Council of State. Large park with lake.

☎ Hatfield 62823
➔ In centre of old Hatfield
◷ End Mar to Mid-Oct except

HATFIELD HOUSE

Mon (but open Bank Hol. Mon 11–5), weekdays 12–5, Sun 2–5.30. Closed Good Fri

Gorhambury House, Knebworth House, Luton Hoo, Piccotts End

Hatfield (opposite gates)

## Knebworth House

*Near Stevenage*

Built in 1492 as Tudor mansion, house was given an external Gothic style decoration by Edward Bulwer-Lytton in mid-19th C. Deer park, adventure playground with Astroglide, narrow gauge railway, skate park, roundabout and funbag.

Stevenage 812661

1 mile S of Stevenage from A1(M)

Apr to end Sept daily except Mon (but open Bank Hol. Mon) 11.30–5.30; Oct, Sun only

Hatfield House, Luton Hoo, Piccotts End

Stevenage (2 miles)

## Moor Park Mansion

*Near Rickmansworth*

£

Built in 1670 for James, Duke of Monmouth, who led revolt against James II. In 1727 Sir James Thornhill and Giacomo Leoni carried out reconstructions. Fine interior decorations by Thornhill and Verrio. Club House of Moor Park Golf Club.

1 mile SE of Rickmansworth near junction of A404 and A4145

All year on Mon except Bank Hols. Visitors should report to reception

Cliveden, Gorhambury House, Osterley Park House

Moor Park or Rickmansworth (1 mile)

## Piccotts End House

*Near Hemel Hempstead*

£

15th-C house with remarkable and strange medieval wall paintings. In 1826 Sir Astley Cooper Bart., Surgeon to King George IV, founded the first Cottage Hospital in England here.

Hemel Hempstead 56729

¾ mile N of Hemel Hempstead off A4146

Mar to Dec daily 10–6

Ashridge, Gorhambury House, Hatfield House, Luton Hoo

Hemel Hempstead (1 mile)

## Shaw's Corner

*Ayot St Lawrence, near Welwyn*

£ NT

Home of George Bernard Shaw from 1906 until his death in 1950. Many literary and personal relics.

Stevenage 820307

SW end of Ayot St Lawrence, 2 miles E of B651

Mar and Nov, Sat and Sun; Apr to end Oct daily except Mon, Tues and Good Fri (but open Bank Hol. Mon) 11–1, 2–6

Gorhambury House, Hatfield House, Knebworth House, Piccotts End

Welwyn North (3½ miles)

## Blaydes House

*6 High Street, Hull*

Mid-Georgian merchant's house restored by East Yorkshire Georgian Society 1974–75. Noteworthy panelling and staircase.

Hull 26406

All year Mon to Fri 10.30–1, 2–4 (except Bank Hol.) by telephone appointment only with Blackmore & Son & Co.

Burton Constable, Maister House, Thornton Abbey, Wilberforce House

Hull

## Burton Agnes Hall

*Near Bridlington*

Large Elizabethan mansion built between 1598 and 1610, it has bow windows which were an unusual feature for the period. Fine carved ceiling, also oriental china. Pictures include Impressionists, Post-Impressionists and some Moderns.

Burton Agnes 324

In village of Burton Agnes on A166, 5 miles SW of Bridlington

Apr to end Oct daily except Sat 1.45–5, Sun 1.45–6

Burton Constable House, Sledmere House

Bridlington (6½ miles). Not Sun in winter

## Burton Constable House

*Near Hull*

Built *c.* 1570 it has oriel windows and is castellated. Adam, Wyatt, Carr and Lightoler reconstructed interior some 200 years later. Delightful grounds with park and lakes by 'Capability' Brown.

Skirlaugh 62400

At Burton Constable on A166, 6 miles NE of Hull

Easter to Spring Bank Hol. Sat and Sun, then daily except Mon and Thur until end Sept, 12–5. Open Bank Hol. Mon

Blaydes House, Burton Agnes Hall, Sledmere House

Hull (9 miles)

## Epworth Old Rectory

*In Epworth*

Built early in 18th C after previous rectory had been destroyed by fire. John and Charles Wesley were born there. Restored in 1957 it is the oldest Methodist memorial building.

Epworth 872268

On A161 3 miles N of Haxey

Mar to Oct, weekdays 10–12, 2–4, Sun 2–4

Conisbrough Castle, Thoresby Hall

Crowle (5½ miles). Not Sun

By prior arrangement only

## Maister House

*160 High Street, Hull*

NT

Rebuilt in 1744 with very fine staircase and hall designed in Palladian manner; ironwork by Robert Bakewell.

Hall and staircase only all year Mon to Fri 10–4. Closed Bank Hol. Mon, Good Fri and Jan 1

Blaydes House, Burton Constable House, Thornton Abbey, Wilberforce House

Hull

## Normanby Hall

*Normanby, near Scunthorpe*

Regency house designed by Sir Robert Smirke, with furnishings and décor of the period. In the stable complex are craft works and a countryside centre. Display of costumes. Riding school.

Scunthorpe 720215

4½ miles N of Scunthorpe just off B1430

All year daily except Sat (and Tues, Apr to Oct) 10–12.30, 2–5.30 (10–12.30, 2–5 Nov to Mar)

Epworth Old Rectory, Thornton Abbey

Scunthorpe (4½ miles)

### Sledmere House

*Sledmere, near Driffield*

Fine Georgian house begun in 1751 and not completed until 1787. Some interior plasterwork in Adam manner by Joseph Rose. Unusual room decorated with Turkish tiles. Good collection of English and French furniture. Stands in a 'Capability' Brown park.

Driffield 86208

9 miles NW of Driffield on B1252

Good Fri to late Sept daily except Mon and Fri (but open Bank Hol. Mon) 1.30–5.30

Burton Agnes Hall, Castle Howard

Driffield (8½ miles)

### Thornton Abbey

*Thornton, near Brigg*

OAP DoE

Founded in 1139 for community of Augustinian canons. Fine example of 14th-C gateway approached across dry moat spanned by long bridge.

SE of Barton-upon-Humber, N of A160

Daily except for public hols (DES)

Blaydes House, Maister House

Habrough (4½ miles)

### Wilberforce House

*23–25 High Street, Hull*

The 17th-C house where the slave emancipator William Wilberforce was born.

Hull 223111 ext. 2737

Daily 10–5, Sun 2.30–4.30 (closed Good Fri, Dec 25–26 and Jan 1)

Blaydes House, Burton Constable House

Hull

## KENT

### Allington Castle

*Allington, near Maidstone*

13th C moated castle with later alterations by Wyatt. Castellated curtain wall, great hall and gatehouse were retained. Medieval market.

Maidstone 54080

1½ miles N of Maidstone, 1 mile from M20 exit 4

Daily 2–4 (except Dec 25)

Aylesford Priory, Boughton Monchelsea Place

Maidstone (2 miles)

Available May to Sept

### Aylesford Priory

*Aylesford, near Maidstone*

13th- and 14th-C Carmelite house with outstanding cloisters. Place of pilgrimage and retreat. Modern sculpture and ceramics. Rose garden.

Maidstone 77272

3½ miles N of Maidstone, ½ mile from M20 exit 4

Daily 10.30–12.45, 2–5

Allington Castle, Boughton Monchelsea Place, Eyhorne Manor

Aylesford

### Boughton Monchelsea Place

*Near Maidstone*

Battlemented Elizabethan house built of Kentish ragstone. Altered in Regency times but still retains Tudor kitchen and nearby tithe barn. Manor records from 1570, late 17th-C tapestries and displays of costume, ancient vehicles and farm implements. Walled gardens and deer park.

Maidstone 43120

In Boughton Monchelsea, 5 miles s of Maidstone just off B2163

Easter to early Oct, Sat, Sun, Bank Hol. and Wed during Aug 2.15–6

Allington Castle, Godinton Park, Old Soar Manor, Leeds Castle

Maidstone ($4\frac{1}{2}$ miles) or Marden (4 miles)

## Chartwell

*Near Westerham*

Former home of Sir Winston Churchill, his house, garden, studio and 79 acres of park being bought by a group of friends and given to the NT in 1946. Small museum with memorabilia of the great man.

Crockham Hill 368

2 miles s of Westerham, forking left off B2026

Mar to end Nov, Tues to Thur 2–6, Sat, Sun and Bank Hol. Mon 11–6 (closed Tues following Bank Hol.). Also Wed and Thur mornings in July and Aug. All Tues mornings reserved for prebooked visitors only

Hever Castle, Ightham Mote, Quebec House, Squerryes Court

Oxted (6 miles)

## Chiddingstone Castle

*Near Edenbridge*

18th-C Gothic Revival built round a much earlier manor house. Royal Stuart and Jacobite collection; ancient Egyptian items; Japanese lacquer; Buddhist images; paintings. Lake and caves. Fishing by arrangement.

Penshurst 870347

In Chiddingstone, 5 miles E of Edenbridge and 1 mile s of B2027

Late Mar to end Oct, Tues to Fri 2–5.30, Sat, Sun and Bank Hols 11.30–5.30

Chartwell, Hever Castle, Penshurst Place

Penshurst (3 miles)

## Cobham Hall

*Cobham, near Rochester*

Interesting combination of styles; latest additions and alterations being by James Wyatt, earlier work probably by Inigo Jones and John Webb. Gardens and landscaping by Humphry Repton and his son John. Now a girls' public school.

Shorne 3371

4 miles w of Rochester, $\frac{3}{4}$ mile from junction of A2 and B2009

Few days in early Apr, then end July to early Sept, Wed, Thur, Sun and Summer Bank Hol. Mon 2–6

Lullingstone Castle, Ightham Mote, Knole, Owletts

Sole Street (2 miles)

## Deal Castle

*In Deal*

Built *c.* 1540 by Henry VIII as part of defence system against invasion from France. Plan here is in form of a Tudor Rose with 6 semi-circular bastions and an outer curtain wall with 6 more semi-circular bastions; all were equipped with guns, there being 145 openings for artillery.

On sea front at Deal

All year except for public hols, Maundy Thur and Good Fri (DES)

Dover Castle, Lympne Castle, Walmer Castle

Deal

## Dover Castle

*In Dover*

Main fortifications date back to 12th and 13th C. Keep was built under Henry II, surrounding outer bailey completed under John and

Henry III. Contains underground passages, a 74-m deep well and a Roman 'Pharos' or lighthouse.

E side of Dover

All year except for public hols, Maundy Thur and Good Fri (DES)

Deal Castle, Lympne Castle, Smallhythe Place, Walmer Castle

Dover Priory ($1\frac{1}{2}$ miles)

In summer months

DOVER CASTLE

## Down House

*Downe, near Orpington*

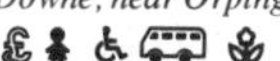

Built in 18th C, the home of Charles Darwin for 40 years. On view are mementoes of Darwin and other important scientists.

Farnborough 59119

In Downe, 5 miles S of Bromley, $1\frac{1}{2}$ miles E of A233

Early Mar to end Jan daily (except Mon and Fri, but open Bank Hol. Mon) 1–6. Closed Dec 24–26

Lullingstone Castle, Old Soar Manor, Quebec House

Orpington ($2\frac{1}{2}$ miles)

## Eyhorne Manor

*Hollingbourne, near Maidstone*

Early 15th-C timber-framed manor with additions from 17th C. Unusual features include smoking bay and laundry museum. In garden are old-fashioned roses and herbs.

5 miles E of Maidstone off B2163

Good Fri to end Sept, Sat and Sun, also Bank Hols and Tues, Wed, Thur, Sat and Sun in Aug 2–6

Allington Castle, Boughton Monchelsea Place, Old Soar Manor

Hollingbourne

## Eynsford Castle

*Eynsford, near Swanley*

OAP DoE

Dating from 12th C, here are remains of hall, walls and defensive ditch.

$7\frac{1}{2}$ miles N of Sevenoaks on A225

Daily except for public hols (DES)

Ightham Mote, Knole, Lullingstone Castle

Eynsford

## Finchcocks

*Near Goudhurst*

Built 1725, good example of Georgian baroque. Outstanding collection of harpsichords, chamber organs and early pianos. An opportunity not only to see these instruments but also to enjoy their being played. Exhibitions of harpsichord building, arts and crafts.

Goudhurst 211702

$1\frac{1}{2}$ miles W of Goudhurst off A262

Mid-Apr to late Sept, Sun and Bank Hol. Mon, also Wed to Sat in Aug 2–6

Boughton Monchelsea Place, Old Soar Manor, Penshurst Place

Marden (7 miles)

## Godinton Park

*Near Ashford*

Dating from 15th C, it is now outwardly mid-17th C.

Exceptional carving and panelling in the hall and staircase. Formal garden designed by Sir Reginald Blomfield.

Ashford 20773

$1\frac{1}{2}$ miles W of Ashford off A20

Easter weekend, then June to Sept, Sun and Bank Hol. 2–5

Allington Castle, Leeds Castle, Lympne Castle, Old Soar Manor

Ashford (2 miles)

## Great Maytham Hall

*Rolvenden, near Tenterden*

Built in 1910, noteworthy example of domestic architecture by Sir Edwin Lutyens.

W side of Rolvenden off A28

May to Sept, Wed and Thur 2–5

Bodiam Castle, Great Dixter, Smallhythe Place

Appledore (10 miles)

## Hever Castle

*Hever, near Edenbridge*

Mostly dates from 13th and 15th Cs and was home of Henry VIII's second wife Anne Boleyn, mother of Queen Elizabeth I. Paintings include Jean Clouet, Mabuse, Holbein, Geerarts, Coello, Moro, Titian and Cranach. There are also personal treasures: toilet articles reputed to have belonged to Elizabeth I; casket given by city of Venice to Marie de Medici; baby's head-dress worked by Anne Boleyn; and Martin Luther's Bible. In the keep is a torture chamber with medieval instruments. Italian garden has collection of statues, sculpture, bronze vases and huge pottery jars. The river Eden flows through the 35-acre lake.

Edenbridge 862205

3 miles SE of Edenbridge, 2 miles S of B2027

Late Mar to end Sept, Tues and Fri (not Good Fri) 1.30–6; Wed, Sun and Bank Hol. 1.30–7

Chartwell, Chiddingstone Castle, Penshurst Place

Hever (1 mile)

HEVER CASTLE

## Ightham Mote

*Ivy Hatch, near Sevenoaks*

One of the most complete remaining examples of a moated manor house, mainly dates from *c.* 1340. Great hall still retains its original oak ceiling.

Sevenoaks 62235

6 miles E of Sevenoaks just off A227

Mar to Oct, Fri 2–5; Nov to Feb, Fri 2–4; Apr to Sept, Sun 2–5

Chartwell, Hever Castle, Knole, Old Soar Manor, Penshurst Place

Sevenoaks (6 miles)

## Knole

*Near Sevenoaks*

NT

One of the most famous and largest private houses in country. First known reference to Knole is in the Lambeth papers. Sold in 1456 to Thomas Bourchier, Archbishop of Canterbury, who built much of present house. Later it was greatly enlarged by Thomas Sackville, 1st Earl of Dorset. State rooms contain works by Van Dyck, John Wootton,

Wouverman, Berchem, Lely, Kneller, Rosa, Reynolds, Romney and Gainsborough; rugs; tapestries and furniture. 26-acre garden is enclosed by wall of Kentish ragstone, and there is a delightful rustic area, the Wilderness.

- Sevenoaks 53006
- Just S of Sevenoaks off A225
- Apr to end Sept, Wed to Sat and Bank Hol. Mon 11–5, Sun 2–5; Oct and Nov, Wed to Sat 11–4, Sun 2–4
- Chartwell, Hever Castle, Igtham Mote, Old Soar Manor, Penshurst Place
- Sevenoaks ($1\frac{1}{2}$ miles)

## Leeds Castle

*Leeds, near Maidstone*

£ OAP

Home of the medieval Queens of England, takes its name from Led, Chief Minister to Ethelbert, 3rd son of Ethelwulf, King of Kent in 857. Built on 2 islands in a lake in a beautiful landscaped parkland. Museum of medieval dog collars. Woodland gardens and aviary.

- Maidstone 65400
- 6 miles SE of Maidstone just off A20 and B2163
- Apr to end Oct, Tues, Wed, Thur, Sun and Bank Hol. Mon 12–5.30 (daily from July to Sept, 12–5.30)
- Allington Castle, Boughton Monchelsea Place
- Hollingbourne (2 miles)

## Long Barn

*Weald, near Sevenoaks*

£

14th-C house, probably birthplace of William Caxton. Restored by Sir Edwin Lutyens, and enlarged by incorporating 16th-C barn. Associations with the Bloomsbury Set.

- Sevenoaks 282
- 2 miles S of Sevenoaks, 1 mile W of A21
- Apr to Sept, Wed 2–6
- Chartwell, Ightham Mote, Knole, Quebec House
- Sevenoaks (3 miles)

## Lullingstone Castle

*Near Eynsford*

£

First house stood here at time of Domesday Book. Mostly rebuilt in 18th C but Henry VII gateway remains. Portraits and armour.

- Farningham 862114
- About $\frac{1}{2}$ mile from Eynsford station, off A225
- Apr to Sept, Sat, Sun and Bank Hol. 2–6
- Ightham Mote, Knole
- Eynsford ($\frac{1}{2}$ mile)

## Lympne Castle

*Lympne, near Hythe*

£

Restored medieval building with earlier Roman, Saxon and Norman connections. Has outstanding views across Channel, and stands some 90 m above early Roman fort of Stutfall Castle, now in ruins.

- Hythe (Kent) 67571
- $2\frac{1}{2}$ miles W of Hythe off B2067
- June to Sept and Bank Hol. weekends daily 10.30–6
- Godinton Park, Smallhythe Place, Walmer Castle
- Sandling ($3\frac{1}{2}$ miles)

## Old Soar Manor

*Plaxtol, near Borough Green*

£ OAP NT DoE

The solar wing of an early medieval knight's house. Of specialist architectural interest.

- 2 miles S of Borough Green, E of A227
- Apr to end Sept, Mon to Sat 9.30–6.30, Sun 2–6.30
- Allington Castle, Ightham Mote, Knole, Leeds Castle
- Borough Green and Wrotham ($2\frac{1}{2}$ miles)
- Plaxtol (1 mile)

## Owletts

*Cobham, near Rochester*

£ NT

Red-brick house *c.* 1685, with contemporary plasterwork and staircase. Pleasant gardens.

1 mile s of A2 at w end of Cobham

Apr to end Sept, Wed and Thur 2–5

Allington Castle, Knole, Lullingstone Castle

Sole Street ($1\frac{1}{2}$ miles)

## Pattyndenne Manor

*Goudhurst*

Outstanding example of 15th-C timber house on site of earlier building thought to have been a prison. Personal standard bearer of Henry VIII and Elizabeth I lived there. Fine dragon beams and king post. House is furnished to demonstrate skills of craftsmen through the centuries.

Goudhurst 211361

1 mile s of Goudhurst off B2079

July to Sept, Sun, also Spring and Summer Bank Hol. Mon 2–5.15. Open all year for parties by arrangement

Bodiam Castle, Boughton Monchelsea Place

Marden (5 miles)

## Penshurst Place

*Near Tunbridge Wells*

Outstanding medieval, Tudor and Jacobean house, birthplace of Sir Philip Sydney. Contents include portraits, china, silver, furniture, arms and armour and historical relics. Famous chestnut-beamed Barons Hall. Venture playground and nature trail. Toy museum.

Penshurst 870307

In Penshurst on B2176, 5 miles NW of Tunbridge Wells

Apr to early Oct daily (except Mon, but open Bank Hol. Mon) 12.30–5.30

Chartwell, Chiddingstone Castle, Hever Castle, Ightham Mote

Penshurst

## Port Lympne

*Lympne, near Hythe*

Mansion in Dutch colonial style built by Sir Herbert Baker before First World War. Excellent example of work of Rex Whistler in the Tent Room. Zoo park and gardens with many animals.

Hythe 60618

3 miles w of Hythe off A20

All year daily (except Dec 25) 10–5.30

Lympne Castle, Smallhythe Place

Sandling (3 miles)

## Quebec House

*Westerham, near Sevenoaks*

NT

Principally a 17th-C square brick house, the childhood home of General James Wolfe. On view are intimate relics of the general, also of Montcalm.

Westerham 62206

E of Sevenoaks at junction of A25 and B2026

Mar, Sun only; Apr to end Oct daily (except Thur and Sat) 2–6

Chartwell, Hever Castle, Ightham Mote, Knole, Squerryes Court

Sevenoaks (4 miles)

Not Sun

PATTYNDENNE MANOR

## Rochester Castle

*In Rochester*

Building started *c.* 1087. Keep still stands to provide fine panoramic view of town, cathedral, Medway and estuary.

Daily except public hols (DES)

Cobham Hall, Ightham Mote, Lullingstone Castle

Rochester

## Roydon Hall

*Roydon, near Maidstone*

16th-C manor house, with panelling.

Maidstone 813243

10 miles SW of Maidstone off B2016

All year Sun and Bank Hol. Mon, also Wed from mid-Mar to mid-Oct, 1–4.30

Old Soar Manor, Penshurst Place

Wateringbury (3 miles)

Price included with admission

## Saltwood Castle

*Saltwood, near Hythe*

Norman building with imposing gatehouse. Association with Henry II and Thomas à Becket.

Hythe 67190

2 miles NW of Hythe just s of A20

Late May to end Aug, Sun and Bank Hol. Mon, also Tues to Fri in Aug 2–5.30

Dover Castle, Lympne Castle, Port Lympne

Sandling (1½ miles)

## Sissinghurst Castle

*Near Tunbridge Wells*

This large Tudor mansion and beautiful gardens were lovingly restored after they had been bought in 1930 by Harold Nicolson and his wife the writer Victoria Sackville-West.

Cranbrook 712850

14 miles E of Tunbridge Wells, 1 mile NE from A262 at Sissinghurst

Apr to mid-Oct, Tues to Fri 1–6.30, Sat and Sun 10–6.30. Closed Mon, incl Bank Hol.

Boughton Monchelsea Place, Finchcocks

Staplehurst (5 miles)

(1 mile)

## Smallhythe Place

*Near Tenterden*

Timbered house *c.* 1480. Was owned by Ellen Terry from 1899 until her death in 1928. Contents include her personal and theatrical relics, and those of Mrs Siddons, Sir Henry Irving and others.

Tenterden 2334

2 miles s of Tenterden on B2082

Mar to end Oct daily (except Tues and Fri) 2–6

Bodiam Castle, Godinton Park, Lympne Castle

Appledore (10 miles)

Not Sun

## Squerryes Court

*In Westerham*

Good example of red-brick house of the Wren period, it was built by Sir Nicholas Crispe in 1681. Paintings, ceramics, furniture and tapestries, also items connected with General Wolfe. Woodland walks and lake.

Westerham 62345

W side of Westerham, just off A25

Mar to end Oct, Sat, Sun and Bank Hol. Mon, also Wed and Thur from May to Aug, 2–6

Chartwell, Hever Castle, Quebec House

Oxted (3½ miles)

## Stoneacre

*Otham, near Maidstone*

Late 15th-C half-timbered house with great hall and crown post.

In Otham, 3 miles SE of Maidstone, 1 mile s of A20

Apr to end Sept, Wed and Sat 2–6

Allington Castle, Boughton Monchelsea Place

Maidstone (4 miles)

## Tonbridge Castle

*In Tonbridge*

Mentioned in the Domesday Book, built by Richard de FitzGilbert. 12th-C curtain walls and 14th-C gatehouse. Nature trail and public gardens.

Tonbridge 353241

In town centre

May to end July, weekends and Bank Hol. only; Aug daily 10.30–4.30

Chiddingstone Castle, Hever Castle, Penshurst Place

Tonbridge

## Upnor Castle

*Near Rochester*

Built *c.* 1561 as a defensive fortress for the Medway. Queen Elizabeth I reviewed her fleet there in 1581. Interesting relics.

NE of Rochester off A228

Daily except Wed, Fri and public hols (DES)

Allington Castle, Lullingstone Castle, Old Soar Manor, Rochester Castle

Strood (2 miles)

## Walmer Castle

*In Walmer*

Dating from 1540, another work put up for coastal defence. Residence of the Lord Warden of the Cinque Ports. Contains Lucas collection of Wellingtoniana.

2 miles s of Deal off A258

All year daily (except Mon, but open Bank Hol. Mon) 9.30–5.30, Sun 2–5.30; winter 9.30–4, Sun, 2–4. Closed when Lord Warden is in residence

Deal Castle, Godinton Park, Lympne Castle, Port Lympne

Walmer ($1\frac{1}{2}$ miles)

# LANCASHIRE

## Astley Hall

*In Chorley*

Elizabethan manor reconstructed mid-17th C. Ceramics, furniture, paintings and tapestries.

Chorley 62166

In town centre on A6

All year daily, summer 12–6, winter 12.30–3.30

Browsholme Hall, Heaton Hall, Newton Hall

Chorley

Summer months

## Browsholme Hall

*Bashall Eaves, near Clitheroe*

Tudor house with Elizabethan façade, Queen Anne wing and Regency additions. Home of Parker family, Bowbearers of Forest of Bowland. Family portraits and silver.

Stonyhurst 330

Off B6243 at Bashall Eaves

Ring to ascertain dates and times

Astley Hall, Gawthorpe Hall

Blackburn ($12\frac{1}{2}$ miles)

## Gawthorpe Hall

*Padiham, near Burnley*

Early 17th-C manor house restored in 1860s. Jacobean long gallery, good panelling and moulded ceilings. Kay-Shuttleworth collections of embroidery and textiles, also Ryder collection of European furniture.

Nelson 66411

On E outskirts of Padiham on A671

Mid-Mar to end Oct, Wed, Sat, Sun and Bank Hol. Mon, also Tues in July and Aug 2–6

Browsholme Hall, Skipton Castle

Burnley (3 miles)

## Hoghton Tower

*Hoghton, near Preston*

Fortified mansion on hilltop, probably rebuilt *c.* 1565. Here it was that the Englishman's favourite joint became Sirloin, when James I knighted the loin of beef in 1617. Antique dolls and dolls' houses. Walled gardens and Old English roses.

Hoghton 2986

5 miles E of Preston on A675

Easter weekend, then Sun until end Oct, also Sat in July and Aug and Bank Hol. Mon 2–5.30

Browsholme Hall, Gawthorpe Hall

Preston ($5\frac{1}{2}$ miles)

## Leighton Hall

*Yealand Conyers, near Carnforth*

Was probably given its Neo-Gothic façade by Chester architect Harrison. Painters represented include Guardi and Copley Fielding. Weather permitting, eagles are flown every afternoon when property is open.

Carnforth 2729

2 miles W of A6 through village of Yealand Conyers

May to Sept, Wed, Thur, Sun and Bank Hol. Mon 2–5

Browsholme Hall, Leven Hall, Sizergh Castle

Carnforth (3 miles)

## Rufford Old Hall

*Rufford, near Ormskirk*

Late medieval half-timbered hall with plaster panels, also rare 15th-C screen. Ashcroft collection of relics of Lancashire life.

Rufford 821254

7 miles N of Ormskirk (A59)

Mar to Dec 23 daily except Mon (but open Bank Hol. Mon) 1–6. Closed Wed in Mar, Oct, Nov and Dec

Heaton Hall, Hoghton Tower

Rufford ($\frac{1}{2}$ mile)

RUFFORD OLD HALL

## Thurnham Hall

*Thurnham, near Lancaster*

13th-C house with additions and alterations from 16th and 19th C. Fine panelling and plasterwork.

Lancaster 751766

5 miles S of Lancaster off A588

Easter weekend, Apr to end Oct, Mon to Thur 2–5, Sun 11–5.30, also Fri from June to Aug

Browsholme Hall, Leighton Hall

Lancaster (5 miles)

## Ashby-de-la-Zouch Castle

*In Ashby-de-la-Zouch*

Largely 14th C. In 1474 Lord Hastings added Hastings tower. Royalist stronghold in Civil War.

All year daily except Wed and Thur (DES)

Prestwold Hall, Stapleford Park

## Belgrave Hall

*In Leicester*

Small Queen Anne House with 18th- and 19th-C furniture.

Leicester 554100

In N end of Leicester off A6

Daily all year (except Good Fri and Dec 25–26) 10–5.30, Sun 2–5.30

Ashby-de-la-Zouch Castle

Leicester (2 miles)

## Belvoir Castle

*Belvoir, near Grantham*

Family seat of Dukes of Rutland since Henry VIII. Formerly a fortress, rebuilt in early 19th C by James Wyatt. Noteworthy Gobelin tapestries and works by Gainsborough, Holbein, Poussin and Reynolds. Armoury of weapons and military museum. Special events most Sundays.

Knipton 262

7 miles SW of Grantham, $3\frac{1}{2}$ miles S of A52

Apr to early Oct, Wed, Thur and Sat 12–6, Sun 2–7; Bank Hol. Mon 11–7; Good Fri and Bank Hol. Tues 12–6; also Sun in Oct 2–6

Prestwold Hall, Woolsthorpe Manor

Grantham (7 miles)

## Langton Hall

*West Langton, near Market Harborough*

Small private house dating from medieval times. 18th-C Venetian lace in drawing rooms, also notable oriental furniture.

East Langton 240

$4\frac{1}{2}$ miles N of Market Harborough off A6

Easter to Oct, Thur, Sat, Sun and Bank Hol. Mon 2–6

Lamport Hall, Rushton Hall*, Stanford Hall

Market Harborough

## Manor House

*Donington-le-Heath, near Coalville*

13th-C house with some good furniture. Herb garden.

Coalville 31259

11 miles NW of Leicester off A50

Easter Sat to end Sept, Wed to Sun and Bank Hol. Mon and Tues 2–6

The Moat House*, Prestwold Hall, Stanford Hall

Leicester (11 miles)

## Oakham Castle

*Oakham, near Melton Mowbray*

Late 12th-C Norman great hall. Unique collection of horseshoes given by peers of the realm.

Oakham 3654

Near market place

All year daily, Sun and Mon 2–5.30, Tues to Sat and Bank Hol. Mon 10–1, 2–5.30. Nov to Mar close at 4. Closed Good Fri and Dec 25–26

Rockingham Castle, Stapleford Park, Woolsthorpe Manor

Oakham

## Prestwold Hall

*Near Loughborough*

19th-C house on site of many earlier buildings including a Gilbertine Priory. In 1843 reconstruction and rebuilding were carried out by William Burn. Interesting marbled plasterwork and fine English and European furniture. Large gardens.

2½ miles NE of Loughborough off B676

For parties only by appointment. Apply in writing to the Curator

Belvoir Castle, Melbourne Hall

Loughborough (3 miles)

## Quenby Hall

*Hungarton, near Leicester*

Jacobean mansion set in beautiful wooded park. Fine carving and panelling, ceilings and furniture. Magnificent cedars in park.

Hungarton 234

7 miles NE of Leicester, 2½ miles N of A47

June to end Sept, Sun, also Bank Hol. Mon 2–6

Belvoir Castle, Prestwold Hall

Leicester (7 miles)

## Stanford Hall

*Stanford-on-Avon, near Lutterworth*

Late 17th-C William-and-Mary house. On display full-size replica of 1898 Flying Machine of Percy Pilcher, and motor cycle and car museum. Family costumes. Walled rose garden and nature trail.

Swinford 250

7½ miles NE of Rugby off B5414

Easter Sun to end Sept, Thur, Sat and Sun 2.30–6, also Bank Hol. Mon and Tues

Kenilworth Castle

Rugby (8 miles)

If booked in advance

## Stapleford Park

*Stapleford, near Melton Mowbray*

Earliest parts date from *c.* 1500; restored *c.* 1633 and added to in 1670. Pictures, tapestries, furniture and Balston collection of Staffordshire portrait figures. Passenger-carrying miniature railway and model liners on lake.

Wymondham 245

5 miles E of Melton Mowbray, 1½ miles S of B676

Easter Sun to Thur following, then late Apr and May, Sun only; June to Aug, Sun, Tues, Wed and Thur; Sept, Sun, Wed and Thur, also Bank Hol. Mon and Tues 1.30–6

Prestwold Hall, Woolsthorpe Manor

Melton Mowbray (5½ miles)

STAPLEFORD PARK

# LINCOLNSHIRE

## Aubourn Hall

*Aubourn, near Lincoln*

Red-brick house of Tudor origin possibly by J. Smythson Jnr. Refaced and altered in mid-17th C. Fine staircase and panelling.

Bassingham 224

7 miles S of Lincoln, 3 miles E of A 46

July and Aug, Wed 2–6

Belton House, Doddington Hall, Thoresby Hall

Hykeham (5½ miles)

## Belton House

*Belton, near Grantham*

A truly outstanding house of the 17th C, attributed to Wren. Altered in 1776 by James Wyatt. Jeffry Wyatville built the orangery in 1811. Fine carvings probably by Grinling Gibbons, Aubusson carpets, souvenirs of Duke of Windsor. Amongst notable paintings is a version of the *Mona Lisa*. The Toy House has largest collection of die-cast models in the world. Museum of the Horse. Vintage cycles. 600-acre park with nature trail and largest children's adventure jungle in Europe. River trips and steam railway.

Grantham 66116

2 miles NE of Grantham off A607

Late Mar to early Oct daily 11–5.30

Aubourn Hall, Belvoir Castle, Tattershall Castle

Grantham (2½ miles)

## Doddington Hall

*Doddington, near Lincoln*

Elizabethan manor house by Robert Smythson with 3 octagonal cupolas; interior redecorated *c.* 1761 by William Lumby. Stuart and Georgian furniture, tapestries and ceramics. Pioneer schools project for use of historic houses in teaching.

Doddington 227

5 miles W of Lincoln off B1190

May to Sept, Wed, Sun and Bank Hol. Mon 2–6

Aubourn Hall, Tattershall Castle, Thoresby Hall

Lincoln (5½ miles)

## Fydell House

*South Square, Boston*

Erected in 1726 by William Fydell, 3 times Mayor of Boston. Now houses Pilgrim College.

Boston 51520

All year Mon to Fri 9–12, 2.30–4.30

Belton House, Gunby Hall, Tattershall Castle

Boston

## Gunby Hall

*Spilsby, near Skegness*

Built in 1700 in style of Wren, red brick with stone dressings. Portraits by Reynolds, oak staircase and contemporary wainscoting. Old walled garden.

7 miles W of Skegness on S side of A158

Apr to end Sept, Thur 2–6, Tues, Wed and Fri by prior written appointment only

Harrington Hall, Tattershall Castle

Skegness (7 miles)

## Harrington Hall

*Harrington, near Horncastle*

Site mentioned in Domesday Book, now a mid-17th-C manor house sited on medieval stone base. Panelling, paintings and ceramics. Terrace is the 'High Hall Garden' of Tennyson's *Maud*. She lived at the Hall with her guardian.

5 miles E of Horncastle, 2 miles N of A158

Easter to late Sept, Thur 2–5, also Bank Hol. Sun 2–6. Gardens mid-Apr to end Oct, Wed and Thur 12–8

Gunby Hall, Tattershall Castle

## Marston Hall

*Marston, near Grantham*

16th-C manor house. Some pictures of note, also furniture. Old garden with fine trees and Gothic gazebo.

Honington 225

6 miles NW of Grantham, 2 miles E of A1

On certain Sun for local charities, and at other times by appointment only

Aubourn Hall, Belton House, Belvoir Castle

Grantham ($6\frac{1}{2}$ miles)

## The Old Hall

*In Gainsborough*

15th- and 16th-C manor house with notable medieval kitchen. Rebuilt by Lord Burgh after earlier hall was ruined during Wars of the Roses. Richard III was a visitor, as was Henry VIII who met his 6th wife Katherine Parr here. First meeting place of the early Dissenters, later known as the Pilgrim Fathers. John Wesley was frequent preacher in Hall. Collections of bygones, china, dolls, period costumes, paintings and furniture.

Gainsborough 2669

In centre of Gainsborough

All year Mon to Sat 10–5; also Sun 2–5 from Easter to Oct

Conisborough Castle, Doddington Hall, Thoresby Hall

Gainsborough

If booked in advance

## Tattershall Castle

*Tattershall, near Horncastle*

Built *c.* 1440 by Ralph Cromwell, Treasurer of England, on site of medieval castle. Records quote brickmaker as supplying 322,000 'large tiles' for 'le Dongeon' (the keep); thickness of walls in basement is $6\frac{1}{2}$ m. Only the massive brick keep remains, and this looms up over the countryside 30 m high. Number of exhibits, including model of castle.

TATTERSHALL CASTLE

10 miles s of Horncastle, off A153

All year daily 11–6.30, Sun 1–6.30; Oct to end Mar, closed 1–2. Closed Dec 25–26

Aubourn Hall, Belton House, Gunby Hall

## Woolsthorpe Manor

*Colsterworth, near Grantham*

17th-C farmhouse where Sir Isaac Newton was born. Reputedly it was in the orchard that he observed an apple fall, leading him to study the laws of gravity.

7 miles s of Grantham, just off A1

Apr to end Oct, Mon, Wed, Fri and Sun 11–12.30, 2–6. Closed Good Fri

Belton House, Belvoir Castle, Stapleford Park

Grantham (7 miles)

# LONDON

## 100 Bayswater Road

*In Bayswater, W2*

Small Regency house where Sir James Barrie wrote *Peter Pan.*

N of Kensington Gardens

Selected days in Jan, Feb, Mar, Oct and Nov 2.30–5. Write for details

Lancaster House, Kensington Palace

Queensway

## Carlyle's House

*24 Cheyne Row, Chelsea, SW3*

18th-C town house where Thomas and Jane Carlyle lived from 1834. Contents include personal relics, books, portraits and furniture.

→ Just off Chelsea Embankment

Apr to end Oct, Wed to Sat 11–5, Sun 2–5. Closed Good Fri

Chiswick House, Hogarth's House

Sloane Square (1 mile)

## Chiswick House

*Burlington Lane, Chiswick, W4*

Possibly finest example of Palladian architecture in country, built in 1725 for Earl of Burlington to his own design, probably adapted from Palladio's Villa Capra. Some interior decoration by William Kent. Paintings by Kneller, Reni, Dobson and Sebastiano Ricci.

All year: Mar, Apr and Oct 9.30–5.30; May to Sept 9.30–7; Nov to Feb 9.30–4. Closed daily 1–2, also Mon and Tues from Oct to Mar, Maundy Thur, Good Fri, Dec 24–26 and Jan 1

Ham House, Hampton Court Palace, Syon House

Chiswick

Gunnersbury

## Dickens House

*48 Doughty Street, St Pancras, WC1*

Where Dickens finished *Pickwick Papers* and wrote *Nicholas Nickleby*. His study is on view as well as original manuscript pages, 1st editions, letters and reading desk used on his reading tours.

01-405 2127

→ Near Grays Inn Road

All year daily except Sun and Bank Hols 10–5

Carlyle's House, 100 Bayswater Road

Russell Square

## Eastbury Manor House

*In Barking*

Good example of medium-sized Elizabethan house.

→ 1 mile from Barking centre

All year, Tues 10–1, 2–5

Greenwich Royal Naval College Hall and Chapel, Queen's House (Greenwich)

Upney

## Eltham Palace

*In Eltham*

Fine great hall with 15th-C hammer-beam roof. Moat spanned by old bridge.

01-859 2112 ex 255

→ A20 from Lewisham

Nov to Mar, Thur and Sun 10.30–4; Apr to Oct, Mon, Thur, Fri, Sat and Sun 10.30–6

Greenwich Royal Naval College Hall and Chapel, Queen's House (Greenwich)

Eltham Well Hall

## Fenton House

*Windmill Hill, Hampstead, NW3*

Late 17th-C house with walled garden. Contains Benton–Fletcher collection of musical instruments and some fine porcelain.

→ 300 m N of underground station on W side of Hampstead Grove

Feb, Mar and Nov, Sat 11–5, Sun 2–5; Apr to end Oct daily (except Thur and Fri) 11–5, Sun 2–5

Keats House, Kenwood House

Hampstead

## Forty Hall

*Forty Hill, Enfield*

Built in 1629 for Sir Nicholas Raynton, Lord Mayor of London. Fine collection of paintings, ceramics, glass and furniture.

01-363 8196

→ 1 mile N of Enfield centre

All year: Easter to Sept, Tues to Fri 10–6, Sat and Sun 10–8; Oct to Easter daily (except Mon) 10–5

Fenton House, Hatfield House

Enfield Town ($1\frac{1}{2}$ miles)

Summer only

## Greenwich Royal Naval College Hall and Chapel

*In Greenwich*

Impressive group of buildings designed by Webb and later Wren; additions by Vanbrugh and Hawksmoor. In the Hall is an immense painting by Sir James Thornhill.

01-858 2154

All year daily (except Thur), 2.30–5

Eltham Palace, Queen's House, Tilbury Fort

Maze Hill

## Hall Place

*In Bexley*

Fine mansion built in 1540. Topiary in form of the Queen's Beasts. Specialist gardens: herb, peat, rock and water.

→ Near junction of A2 and A223

All year weekdays 10–5; Apr to Sept, Sun 2–6

Eltham Palace, Queen's House

Bexley

## Ham House

*Ham, Richmond*

OAP NT

Fine Stuart house built in 1610, redecorated and furnished in 1670s. Much of this furniture still stands in its original place. Portrait gallery. Restored 17th-C garden.

01-672 9414/01-393 4922

→ 1 mile S of Richmond

Daily except Mon (but open Bank Hol. Mon), Apr to end Sept 2–6, Oct to end Mar 12–4. Closed Dec 24–26, Jan 1 and Good Fri

Hampton Court Palace, Osterley Park House, Syon House

Richmond (1 mile)

Summer months

## Hampton Court Palace

*In Hampton Court*

OAP DoE

Built in 1514 by Cardinal Wolsey, some additions by Henry VIII, others by Wren for William III. Fine State apartments and banqueting rooms, Henry VIII's tennis court built in 1529, maze, great vine and orangery. Contents include many great treasures: Mantegna cartoons fortunately withdrawn from Cromwell's sale of Charles I collection; works by Grinling Gibbons, Laguerre, Verrio, Sir James Thornhill; and ornamental ironwork by Jean Tijou.

→ On N bank of Thames

All year daily: May to Sept 9.30–6, Sun 11–6; Mar, Apr and Oct 9.30–5, Sun 2–5; Nov to Feb 9.30–4, Sun 2–4. Closed Maundy Thur, Good Fri, Dec 24–26 and Jan 1

Ham House, Osterley Park House, Syon House

Hampton Court

HAMPTON COURT PALACE

## Hogarth's House

*Hogarth Lane, Chiswick, W4*

The painter's country house for 15 years. The site is a good illustration of the growth of Greater London.

01-994 6757

Great West Road (A4), Chiswick

Apr to Sept daily 11–6, Sun 2–6; Oct to Mar daily (except Tues) 11–4, Sun 2–4. Closed Good Fri, Dec 25–26 and Jan 1

Ham House, Hampton Court Palace, Syon House

Chiswick

Gunnersbury or Turnham Green

## Keats House

*Keats Grove, Hampstead, NW3*

Built in 1815–16. Poet John Keats wrote his famous odes here.

01-435 2062

s end of Hampstead Heath

All year daily 10–1, 2–6, Sun and Bank Hol. Mon 2–5. Closed Dec 25–26, Jan 1, Easter and May Day

Fenton House, Kenwood House

Hampstead Heath

Hampstead

## Kensington Palace

*In Kensington, W8*

Acquired by William III in 1689 and enlarged by Wren. Still a Royal Residence. Birthplace of Queen Victoria. State apartments have pictures and furniture from the Royal collection.

01-937 9561 ex 2

w of Kensington Gardens, w end of Hyde Park

All year daily: Mar to Sept 10–6, Sun 2–6; Oct and Feb 10–5, Sun 2–5; Nov to Jan 10–4, Sun 2–4. Closed Good Fri, Dec 25–26 and Jan 1

Carlyle's House, Lancaster House

Notting Hill Gate

## Kenwood House

*Hampstead Lane, Hampstead, NW3*

Outstanding Neo-Classical house, modelled by Robert Adam for 1st Lord Mansfield. Outstanding paintings by Gainsborough, Hals, Reynolds, Turner, Vermeer.

01-348 1286

All year daily 10–7 (dusk in winter). Closed Good Fri and Dec 24–25

Keats House, Fenton House

Hampstead Heath (1 mile)

Hampstead (1¼ miles)

## Kew Palace

*In Kew Gardens, Kew*

Built in 1631 with Dutch gabling. Mementoes of George III.

Apr to Mid-Oct daily 11–5.30. Closed Maundy Thur and Good Fri

Ham House, Syon House

Kew Gardens

Kew Gardens

Summer months only

## Lancaster House

*Stable Yard, St James's, SW1*

Built during early Victorian period for Duke of York and was originally 'York House'. State apartments on view.

Easter Eve to mid-Dec, Sat, Sun and Bank Hol. 2–6. Closed at times for official functions; also on Maundy Thur and Good Fri

Carlyle's House, Dickens House, Kensington Palace

Green Park

## Linley Sambourne House

*18 Stafford Terrace, W8*

Home of Linley Sambourne, chief political cartoonist of *Punch*. Works also by Kate Greenaway and Walter Crane. Interior shows décor of 1870–1910.

01-994 1019

Wed and Sun afternoon, by appointment only

Kensington Palace, Carlyle's House

High Street, Kensington

## Marble Hill House

*Richmond Road, Twickenham*

English Palladian villa with early Georgian furniture and paintings. Designed by Roger Morris and completed in 1729.

01-348 1286

Twickenham, Middlesex, off A305

All year daily (except Fri) 10–5, closes 4 pm Nov to Jan

Ham House, Osterley Park House, Syon House

St Margaret's (¾ mile)

## Marlborough House

*Pall Mall, SW1*

Built by Wren between 1709 and 1711 for Sarah Duchess of Marlborough. Fine murals by Laguerre showing the Duke's victories at Blenheim, Malplaquet and Ramillies. Became Royal residence in 1817, last Royal occupant being Queen Mary, widow of George V. Now a Commonwealth Conference Centre.

01-930 9249

Close to St James's Palace

Mon to Fri by appointment only. Closed when in use for conferences

Carlyle's House, Dickens House, Kensington Palace

Green Park

## The Old Palace

*In Croydon*

Seat of Archbishops of Canterbury since 871. Has an impressive banqueting hall, Norman undercroft, guardroom and Tudor chapel.

01-688 2027

Conducted tours for 5-day periods in Apr and May, also latter half of July daily (except Sun). Telephone for information

Chartwell, Down House, Knole

East Croydon

## Orleans House

*Riverside, Twickenham*

Superb Octagon erected in 1720 by James Gibbs. Fine example of distinguished baroque work, set in woodland garden.

01-892 0221

From Richmond road, A305

All year: Tues to Sat 1–5.30 (Oct to Mar 1–4.30), Sun and Bank Hols 2–5.30 (Oct to Mar 2–4.30). Closed Dec 25–26

Ham House, Marble Hill House

St Margaret's (¾ mile)

OSTERLEY PARK HOUSE

## Osterley Park House

*Syon Lane, Isleworth*

OAP NT

Quadrangular house built by Sir Thomas Gresham about 1577, refaced and redecorated internally by Robert Adam for Robert Child, the banker. Gobelins tapestry room, fine furniture and rare objects. Garden houses and stable block.

01-560 3918

→ Off A4 just N of Osterley underground station

⏲ All year daily except Mon (but open Bank Hol. Mon): Apr to end Sept 2–6; Oct to end Mar 12–4. Closed Good Fri, May Day, Dec 24–26 and Jan 1

Ham House, Hampton Court Palace, Syon House

⊖ Osterley

Summer months only

## The Queen's House

*In Greenwich*

Though designed by Inigo Jones for Anne of Denmark, wife of James I, completion did not take place until 1635, then for Charles I's wife, Henrietta Maria. Has great central galleried saloon, also well balanced façade. A model for many later houses.

→ From S bank of Thames at Greenwich

⏲ All year daily: summer 10–6, winter 10–5, Sun (all year) 2.30–6. Closed Good Fri, Dec 24–26 and Jan 1

Eltham Palace, Greenwich Royal Naval College Hall and Chapel

Maze Hill

## Syon House

*Park Road, Isleworth*

OAP

Adapted from 15th-C nunnery and most wonderfully redecorated internally by Robert Adam. Elegant furniture, portraits and historical associations. Landscaping by 'Capability' Brown.

☎ 01-560 0884

→ N bank of Thames between Brentford and Isleworth off A315

⏲ Good Fri to end Sept daily (except Fri and Sat) 12–5; Oct, Sun 12–5

Ham House, Hampton Court Palace, Osterley Park House

Syon Lane (1 mile)

⊖ Boston Manor (2 miles)

## Tower of London

*Near Tower Bridge*

OAP DoE

Massive group of fortified buildings begun by William the Conqueror in 11th C. Stands wreathed with probably more memories than any other place in England. Royal prisoners, villains, spies and the rest. Blood and torture were commonplace within these walls. The White Tower houses the Royal Armouries, one of the finest collections in the world. In the Jewel House are the Crown Jewels.

☎ 01-709 0765

⏲ All year: Mar to Oct 9.30–5, Sun 2–5; Nov to Feb 9.30–4, closed Sun. Closed Good Fri, Dec 24–26 and Jan 1

Dickens House, Greenwich Royal Naval College Hall and Chapel

⊖ Tower Hill

## Whitehall

*Malden Road, Cheam*

Timber-framed house *c.* 1500. Material associated with Henry VIII's Nonsuch Palace and medieval pottery on view. Cheam School.

☎ 01-643 1236

→ In Cheam village on A2043 immediately N of junction with A232

⏲ All year: Apr to Sept, Tues to Fri and Sun 2–5.30, Sat 10–5.30; Oct to Mar, Wed, Thur and Sun 2–5.30, Sat 10–5.30. Bank Hols as for Sat. Closed Dec 24–Jan 1

Chiswick House, Kew Palace, Osterley Park House, Syon House

Cheam ($\frac{1}{2}$ mile)

# MERSEYSIDE

## Speke Hall

*The Walk, Liverpool*

Fine half-timbered courtyard house built between 1490 and 1612 by succeeding members of Norris family. Interior is rich in carving, panelling and plasterwork, and fully furnished.

Liverpool 427 7231

7 miles SE of town centre on N bank of Mersey off A561

Apr to end Sept, Mon to Sat 10–5, Sun 2–7, Bank Hols 10–7; Oct to end Mar, Mon to Sat 10–5, Sun 2–5. Closed Good Fri, Dec 24–26 and Jan 1

Heaton Hall, Newton Hall, Platt Hall, Tatton Park

Garston (2 miles)

During summer

# NORFOLK

## Baconsthorpe Castle

*Baconsthorpe, near Cromer*

Semi-fortified house dating from late 15th C, with gatehouse, towers and some curtain walling.

6 miles SW of Cromer, 2 miles S of A148

Daily except public hols (DES)

Blickling Hall, Felbrigg Hall, Holkham Hall

Cromer (8 miles)

## Beeston Hall

*Beeston St Lawrence, near Wroxham*

18th-C house with external Gothic treatment but Georgian interiors.

2½ miles NE of Wroxham near junction of A1151 and A1062

Mid-Apr to mid-Sept, Fri, Sun and Bank Hols 2–5.30

Blickling Hall, Caister Castle

Wroxham (3 miles)

## Blickling Hall

*Blickling, near Aylsham*

Outstanding red-brick Jacobean house built for Sir Henry Hobart. Started in 1616 by Robert Lyminge, who earlier had worked at Hatfield House. Later Ivory family of architects worked on completion. Peter the Great room with Russian tapestry, and long gallery. Formal gardens, orangery, mausoleum and lake.

Aylsham 3084

Off A140 13 miles N of Norwich

Apr to mid-Oct daily except Mon and Fri (but open Bank Hol. Mon) 11–6 (Apr to mid-May and Oct 2–6)

Beeston Hall, Felbrigg Hall

North Walsham (7 miles)

BLICKLING HALL

## Burgh Castle
*Near Great Yarmouth*

Early massive walls date from 3rd C. Was an intermediate fort of the Saxon Shore system. Remains of 6 bastions.

➔ sw of Great Yarmouth, 3 miles w of junction of A12 and A143

Ⓞ Daily except public hols (DES)

Caister Castle, Somerleyton Hall

Great Yarmouth ($4\frac{1}{2}$ miles)

## Caister Castle
*West Caister, near Great Yarmouth*

Moated castle dating from mid-15th C, with 30-m high tower affording superb views. *Paston Letters*, which give lively look at 15th-C home life, were written here. Large collection of veteran and vintage motor cycles and cars.

☎ Great Yarmouth 720267

➔ 3 miles N of Great Yarmouth off A1064

Ⓞ Mid-May to end Sept daily (except Sat) 10.30–5

Beeston Hall, Burgh Castle, Somerleyton Hall

Great Yarmouth ($2\frac{1}{2}$ miles)

## Castle Rising
*Near King's Lynn*

Noteworthy Norman keep possibly built by Earl of Arundel; stands within large earthworks.

➔ 5 miles NE of King's Lynn off A149

Ⓞ Daily except public hols (DES)

Oxburgh Hall, Sandringham House

King's Lynn ($4\frac{1}{2}$ miles)

## Felbrigg Hall
*Felbrigg, near Cromer*

Exceptional 17th-C house, has original furniture and pictures. Books from Dr Johnson's collection. Walled garden and park with fine trees and lake.

☎ West Runton 444

➔ 2 miles sw of Cromer off B1436

Ⓞ Apr to mid-Oct, Tues, Wed, Thur, Sat, Sun and Bank Hol. Mon 2–6

Blickling Hall, Sheringham Hall

Cromer (2 miles)

## Holkham Hall
*Holkham, near Wells-next-the-Sea*

18th-C Palladian home of Thomas Coke of Norfolk, constructed from plans by William Kent, under supervision of Matthew Brettingham. Very fine collections of paintings, tapestries, furniture and statuary. Formal garden by Sir Charles Barry. Pottery.

☎ Fakenham 710227

➔ 2 miles w of Wells off A149

Ⓞ June and Sept, Thur; July and Aug, Mon, Wed and Thur; also Spring Bank Hol. Mon 11.30–5

Sandringham House, Sheringham Hall

## Houghton Hall
*Near King's Lynn*

18th-C mansion built for Sir Robert Walpole by Colen Campbell and Thomas Ripley, interior by William Kent. Stables with horses and ponies.

☎ East Rudham 247

➔ 13 miles E of King's Lynn off A148

Ⓞ Mid-Apr to end Sept, Thur and Bank Hols 11–5.30, Sun 1.30–5.30

Castle Rising, Holkham Hall, Sandringham House

King's Lynn ($13\frac{1}{2}$ miles)

## Oxburgh Hall
*Oxborough, near Swaffham*

Late 15th-C moated house with 24-m high gatehouse, little altered.

On view needlework panels by Mary Queen of Scots and Bess of Hardwick. French parterre garden.

☎ Gooderstone 258

➜ 7 miles SW of Swaffham

Apr to mid-Oct, Tues, Wed, Thur, Sat, Sun and Bank Hol. Mon 2–6

Castle Rising, Sandringham House

Downham Market (8½ miles)

Sat only

## Sandringham House

*Sandringham, near King's Lynn*

Bought by Queen Victoria for the Prince of Wales in 1862. Royal portraits, ceramics, sculpture, ornaments and furniture.

☎ King's Lynn 2675

➜ 8 miles NE of King's Lynn off B1440

Mid-Apr to late Sept, Mon to Thur 11–4.45, Sun 12–4.45. Always closed when Royal Family is in residence. Check times in advance

Castle Rising, Houghton Hall

King's Lynn (8½ miles)

## Sheringham Hall

*Sheringham, near Cromer*

Designed by Humphry Repton and erected in 1812, good example of Regency mansion. Outstanding rhododendron woods planted in 19th C.

☎ Sheringham 822074

➜ Just w of town

May to Sept, Fri 2–6, only on written application. Proceeds in aid of charity. Woods open May to end June

Felbrigg Hall, Holkham Hall, Houghton Hall

Sheringham (½ mile)

## Weeting Castle

*Weeting, near Thetford*

Ruined 11th-C fortified manor house with remains of 3-storeyed cross-wing and set in rectangular enclosure.

➜ NW of Thetford off B1106

Any reasonable time (DES)

Ixworth Abbey

Thetford (8 miles)

# NORTHAMPTONSHIRE

## Althorp

*Near Northampton*

Originally built by Sir John Spencer in 1508, altered by Henry Holland in 1790. Paintings by Lely, Lotto, Rubens and Van Dyck. Furniture by Weisweiler, Boulle and Saunier. Notable ceramics from Bow, Chelsea, Meissen and Sèvres.

☎ East Haddon 209

➜ 6 miles NW of Northampton on A428

All year: Tues, Thur, Sat (except June and July) and Sun; daily in Aug (except Mon) 2.30–5.30. Open Bank Hol. Mon 11.30–5.30

Lamport Hall

Northampton (6 miles)

## Aynhoe Park

*Aynho, near Banbury*

Original Jacobean house was burnt during Civil War, being rebuilt after the Restoration. Interior remodelled *c.* 1810 by Sir John Soane. Good furniture, ceramics and paintings.

☎ Croughton 810 659

➜ 6 miles SE of Banbury off A41

May to Sept, Wed and Thur 2–5

Broughton Castle, Sulgrave Manor

King's Sutton (2 miles)

## Boughton House

*Geddington, near Kettering*

15th-C monastic building gradually enlarged around 7 courtyards; French-style additions in 1695. Paintings by El Greco, Murillo, Caracci; 40 sketches by Van Dyck; armoury; tapestries; early carpets; French and English 17th- and 18th-C furniture. Large park with avenues and lakes.

Kettering 82248

3 miles N of Kettering off A43

Easter and Spring Bank Hol. weekends then late July to end Sept daily (except Fri); Oct, Thur, Sat and Sun 2–6

Lamport Hall, Lyveden New Bield, Rockingham Castle

Kettering ($3\frac{1}{2}$ miles)

## Burghley House

*Near Stamford*

One of the largest and grandest Elizabethan houses in country. Built by William Cecil, 1st Lord Burghley and Lord High Treasurer to Queen Elizabeth I. Ceiling and murals by Laguerre and Verrio, silver fireplaces, tapestries and fine furniture.

Stamford 52451

1 mile SE of Stamford off B1443

Apr to early Oct, Tues, Wed, Thur, Sat and Bank Hol. 11–5, Good Fri and Sun 2–5

Lyveden New Bield, Rockingham Castle

Stamford (1 mile)

## Castle Ashby

*Near Northampton*

Outstanding Tudor and early Stuart house, S wing attributed to Inigo Jones. Paintings, tapestries. Landscape by 'Capability' Brown.

Yardley Hastings 234

6 miles E of Northampton, $2\frac{1}{2}$ miles N of A428

July to end Aug daily 2–5, Sun and Bank Hol. 11–5

Boughton House, Lamport Hall, Stoke Park Pavilions

Northampton ($6\frac{1}{2}$ miles)

## Deene Park

*Deene, near Corby*

Mainly 16th-C house of considerable architectural importance. Large lake and park, rare trees and old-fashioned roses.

Bulwick 278361

$5\frac{1}{2}$ miles NE of Corby, $1\frac{1}{2}$ miles W of A43

Easter, Bank Hol. Sun and Mon, also Sun in June, July and Aug, 2–6

Burghley House, Lyveden New Bield

## Hinwick House

*Hinwick, near Wellingborough*

Distinguished Queen Anne house with pictures by Kneller, Lely and Van Dyck. Mortlake tapestries.

Rushden 53624

6 miles SE of Wellingborough, $2\frac{1}{2}$ miles E of A509 at Wollaston

Easter, Spring and Summer Bank Hol. Mon 2–5. Other times by appointment

Boughton House, Lamport Hall, Stoke Park Pavilions

Wellingborough (6 miles)

By arrangement

## Kelmarsh Hall

*Kelmarsh, near Market Harborough*

£

Designed by Gibbs, is noteworthy example of Palladian style.

5 miles s of Market Harborough on A508

Apr daily, also certain days at end of Aug 2–5.30. Other times by appointment

Althorp, Castle Ashby, Lamport Hall

Market Harborough (5 miles)

## Lamport Hall

*Lamport, near Northampton*

£

Present house dates mainly from 17th and 18th C. sw front is rare example of work of John Webb, pupil and son-in-law of Inigo Jones. Notable music hall, and plasterwork by John Woolston.

Maidwell 272

8 miles N of Northampton near junction of A508 and B576

Easter to mid-Sept, Sun and Bank Hol. Mon; late July to end Aug, Wed, Thur and Fri 2.15–5.15

Boughton House, Rockingham Castle, Stoke Park Pavilions

Northampton ($8\frac{1}{2}$ miles)

Not Sun

School and private parties by appointment

## Lyveden New Bield

*Near Oundle*

Shell of unusual Renaissance building erected by Sir Thomas Tresham *c.* 1600 to symbolize the Passion. Never finished as he became involved in Gun Powder Plot. 7 emblems of the Passion on a frieze.

4 miles sw of Oundle via A427. Property approached across two fields

All year daily

Boughton House, Burghley House, Rockingham Castle

(3 miles)

## Priest's House

*Easton-on-the-Hill, near Stamford*

Pre-Reformation priest's lodge, of specialist architectural interest. Small museum of village bygones.

Stamford 2616

2 miles sw of Stamford off A43

By prior appointment only

Boughton House, Burghley House, Rockingham Castle

Stamford (2 miles)

## Rockingham Castle

*Rockingham, near Corby*

£

Royal castle built on site of earlier fortification by William the Conqueror. King John used it when hunting in Rockingham Forest. Towering above village, it offers views over 5 counties. Stands in 12 acres of formal and wild gardens. 400-year-old hedge shaped like elephants.

Rockingham 240

2 miles N of Corby off A6003

Easter Sun to end Sept, Sun, Thur and Bank Hol. Mon and Tues 2–6

Boughton House, Burghley House, Southwick Hall

Kettering (8 miles)

## Southwick Hall

*Cotterstock, near Oundle*

£ OAP

Oldest parts date from 1300; some Tudor rebuilding has left a manor house of charm.

Cotterstock 213

3 miles N of Oundle, 1 mile w of A605

Easter Mon to following Thur 2.30–5.30, then May to

mid-Sept, Thur 2.30–4.30 and Bank Hol. Mon 2.30–5.30

Burghley House, Rockingham Castle

Peterborough (10 miles)

## Stoke Park Pavilions

*Stoke Bruerne, near Towcester*

Colonnade and 2 pavilions built in 1630 by Inigo Jones. Remains of Stoke Park burnt out in 1884 and subsequently rebuilt.

Roade 862172

$4\frac{1}{2}$ miles E of Towcester off A508

June to Aug, Sat, Sun and Bank Hol. Mon 2–6

Althorp, Lamport Hall, Sulgrave Manor

Northampton (9 miles)

## Sulgrave Manor

*Sulgrave, near Banbury*

Manor house built *c.* 1560 by Lawrence Washington, ancestor of George Washington. Fine contemporary furniture, portraits of George Washington and some of his possessions. Great kitchen with much antique equipment.

Sulgrave 205

8 miles NE of Banbury off B4252

All year (except Jan) daily (except Wed) Apr to Sept, 10.30–1, 2–5.30; Oct to Mar, 10.30–1, 2–4

Aynhoe Park, Edgcote

Banbury (7 miles)

# NORTHUMBERLAND

## Alnwick Castle

*In Alnwick*

Norman Border stronghold of Percy family. In 19th C 4th Duke of Northumberland had interior converted into likeness of magnificent Italian Renaissance Palazzo by Director of the Capitoline Museum in Rome. An outstanding private collection: paintings by Claude, Titian, Tintoretto, del Piombo, Canaletto, Dobson, Van Dyck, del Sarto, Nicholas Poussin, Palma Vecchio; furniture; ceramics; and other treasures of equal quality.

Alnwick 602722

Early May to end Sept daily (except Sat) 1–5

Callaly Castle, Dunstanburgh Castle, Warkworth Castle

Alnmouth ($3\frac{1}{2}$ miles)

## Bamburgh Castle

*Bamburgh, near Belford*

Impressive 12th-C Norman keep; remainder largely restored. Fine hall with armoury and large collection of weapons.

Bamburgh 208

5 miles E of Belford on B1342

Easter to end Oct daily, opens 1; for closing times ask Custodian

Dunstanburgh Castle, Lindisfarne Castle

Chathill (6 miles). Not Sun

## Berwick-upon-Tweed Castle

*In Berwick-upon-Tweed*

DoE

Remains of 12th-C stronghold, with 3 towers. Town walls re-erected during Elizabethan times.

Daily except public hols (DES)

Lindisfarne Castle

Berwick-upon-Tweed

## Callaly Castle

*Whittingham, near Alnwick*

17th-C mansion incorporating pele tower, with additions from Georgian and Victorian times. Good plasterwork.

ALNWICK CASTLE

☎ Whittingham 663

➔ 2 miles W of Whittingham and A697

◷ May to end Sept, Sat, Sun and Bank Hol. Mon 2.15–5.30

Alnwick Castle, Dunstanburgh Castle, Warkworth Castle

## Cragside

*Rothbury, near Alnwick*

£ NT

Designed by Richard Norman Shaw for 1st Lord Armstrong and built between 1864 and 1895. Pre-Raphaelite paintings and experimental scientific apparatus. First house in world to be lit by electricity generated by water power. Country park is noted for rhododendrons and lakes.

☎ Rothbury 20333

➔ ½ mile N of Rothbury off B6341

◷ Mid-Apr to end Sept daily except Mon (but open Bank Hol. Mon and closed following Tues) 1–6; Oct and early Apr, Wed, Sat and Sun 2–5. Park open all year daily

Callaly Castle, Warkworth Castle

Acklington (15 miles). Not Sun

## Dunstanburgh Castle

*Craster, near Alnwick*

£ OAP NT DoE

Ruins of castle begun in 1316 by Thomas, Earl of Lancaster, and strengthened by John of Gaunt. Its walls enclose an area of 11 acres.

➔ From Craster on coast 2½ miles E of B1339

◷ All year daily: mid-Mar to mid-Oct, 9.30–6.30 (Sun in Mar and Oct 2–6.30); mid-Oct to mid-Mar, 9.30–4, Sun 2–4. Closed Dec 24–26 and Jan 1

Alnwick Castle, Bamburgh Castle

Chathill (8½ miles). Not Sun

(1½ miles)

## George Stephenson's Cottage

*Wylam-on-Tyne, near Newcastle*

£ NT

Birthplace, in 1781, of the great inventor.

☎ Wylam 3457

➔ 8 miles W of Newcastle, 1½ miles S of A69

◷ Apr to end Oct, Wed, Sat and Sun 2–5

Seaton Delaval Hall

Wylam (½ mile)

## Lindisfarne Castle

*On Holy Island*

£ NT

Erected *c.* 1550 on a cone of dolerite rock on Holy Island as protection against marauding Scots. In 1903 was greatly restored and converted into private dwelling by Sir Edwin Lutyens. Early oak furniture and noteworthy collection of prints.

➔ From A1 to Beal then 5 miles E across causeway

◷ First half of Apr, Wed, Sat and Sun 2–5, then daily to end Sept except Fri (but

LINDISFARNE CASTLE

open Good Fri) 11–1, 2–5; Oct, Sat and Sun 2–5

Bamburgh Castle, Berwick-upon-Tweed Castle

Berwick (14 miles)

## Norham Castle

*Norham, near Berwick-upon-Tweed*

DoE

Very strong 12th-C keep built to oversee the Tweed by Bishop Hugh le Puiset; later alterations.

sw of Berwick-upon-Tweed off B6470

Daily except public hols (DES)

Berwick-upon-Tweed Castle, Lindisfarne Castle

Berwick (8 miles)

## Prudhoe Castle

*Prudhoe, near Newcastle-upon-Tyne*

DoE

Extensive remains of 12th-C castle and keep, curtain wall and gatehouse. Passed to the Percys in 1381.

s bank of the Tyne, ½ mile from Prudhoe off A695

Daily all year except Wed, Fri and public hols (DES)

Seaton Delaval Hall, Wallington Hall

Prudhoe

## Seaton Delaval Hall

*Seaton Delaval, near Whitley Bay*

OAP

This splendid baroque house is one of Sir John Vanbrugh's masterpieces. There have been several bad fires since it was begun in 1718 for Admiral George Delaval, but restorations have been largely successful. Paintings, ceramics and furniture. Medieval banquets are held regularly in the Great Kitchen.

Seaton Delaval 481493

Between Blyth and Whitley Bay off A190

May to end Sept, Wed, Sun and Bank Hol. Mon 2–6

Prudhoe Castle, Warkworth Castle

Newcastle-upon-Tyne (11½ miles)

## Wallington Hall

*Cambo, near Morpeth*

NT

Built in 1688, altered in 18th C and again in 19th. Some decorations and designs by Ruskin and William Bell Scott. Pictures and ceramics. Walled garden with conservatory containing outstanding fuchsias.

Scots Gap 283

12 miles w of Morpeth on B6342

Mid-Apr to end Sept daily (except Tues) 1–6; Oct and early Apr, Wed, Sat and Sun 2–5. Grounds all year

Prudhoe Castle, Seaton Delaval Hall

Morpeth (12½ miles)

## Warkworth Castle

*Warkworth, near Amble*

DoE

Earliest parts date from 12th C. Came into possession of Percys in

14th C and they built magnificent keep.

➔ 7½ miles SE of Alnwick on A1068

⏲ All year except public hols (DES)

Cragside, Callaly Castle

Acklington (5½ miles).

# NORTH YORKSHIRE

## Bedale Hall

*Bedale, near Northallerton*

Fine Georgian house with ballroom and museum of arts and crafts.

➔ 7½ miles SW of Northallerton off A684

⏲ Mar to Sept, Tues 2–4.30

Newby Hall, Norton Conyers

Northallerton (7 miles)

## Beningbrough Hall

*Shipton-by-Beningbrough, near York*

Built *c.* 1716, has now been reopened after extensive restoration. 100 portraits on permanent loan from the National Portrait Gallery. Victorian laundry. Gardens.

☎ Beningbrough 666 or 715

➔ 8 miles NW of York midway between A19 and A59

⏲ Apr to end Oct daily 12–6. Closed Good Fri

Castle Howard, Sutton Park

York (8 miles)

(1 mile)

## Braithwaite Hall

*East Witton, near Leyburn*

17th-C hall, now a working farmhouse.

➔ 1½ miles SE of Middleham off A6108

⏲ By arrangement with the tenant

Markenfield Hall, Newby Hall, Ripley Castle

(2 miles)

## Broughton Hall

*Broughton, near Skipton*

Original construction 1597. Now with Georgian front. Alterations carried out in 1756, 1810 and 1840. Italian garden by W. A. Nesfield.

☎ Skipton 2267

➔ 3½ miles W of Skipton off A59

⏲ June weekdays 2–5 and Bank Hols 2–5. Other times by appointment

Gawthorpe Hall, Skipton Castle

Gargrave (2 miles). Not Sun

## Carlton Towers

*Goole, near Selby*

Impressive Victorian Gothic exterior by A. W. Pugin and State rooms by John Francis Bentley, architect of Westminster Cathedral. On view are paintings collected by Prince Henry Benedict, Cardinal York. Priest's hole to be seen. Costumes and uniforms.

☎ Goole 860243

➔ 6 miles S of Selby off A1041

⏲ Easter Sat to Tues, then Sun and Bank Hol. Mon to mid-May (Spring Bank Hol. Sat to Wed), thereafter Sat, Sun, Mon and Wed to end Sept, 1–5

Harewood House, Temple Newsam

Selby (6 miles)

## Castle Howard

*Coneysthorpe, near York*

Earliest and most spectacular example of Vanbrugh's creative imagination, begun in 1699 and finished by Hawksmoor. Great hall surmounted by a painted and gilded dome, long gallery and chapel. Outstanding collections of ceramics, furniture, paintings and tapestries. Costume galleries in the stables. Grounds are extensive and contain Vanbrugh's Temple of the Four Winds and Hawksmoor's Mausoleum, a fountain and lakes.

- Coneysthorpe 333
- 15 miles NE of York, 4 miles W of A64
- Good Fri to Oct daily 11.30–5
- Beningbrough Hall, Gilling Castle
- Malton (5 miles)
- (3 miles)

CASTLE HOWARD

## Fountains Abbey

*Near Ripon*

Founded *c.* 1132 by the Cistercian Brotherhood. Damaged by fire started by those disliking abbot; reconstructed between 1148 and 1179. Entire ground plan is intact and there are interesting survivals of medieval waterworks and drainage. John Aislabie laid out gardens in 1720.

- 4 miles SW of Ripon on unclassified road 1½ miles S of junction with B6265
- All year daily: Mar, Apr and Oct 9.30–5.30; May and Sept 9.30–7; June to Aug 9.30–9; Nov to Feb 9.30–4, Sun 2–4. Closed Maundy Thur, Good Fri, Dec 24–26 and Jan 1
- Markenfield Hall
- Harrogate (9½ miles)

## Gilling Castle

*Gilling East, near Thirsk*

£

Elizabethan house with 18th-C front. Great Chamber has ceiling built up from columns and arches. Panelling and original stained glass.

- Ampleforth 238
- 13 miles E of Thirsk, 5 miles S of Helmsley off B1363
- All year daily (except Sun) 10–12, 2–4. Gardens July to Sept
- Castle Howard, Nunnington Hall
- Thirsk (13 miles)

## Helmsley Castle

*Helmsley, near Thirsk*

£ OAP DoE

Keep, curtain wall and towers were begun at end of 12th C by Robert de Roos. Besieged during Civil War. Fine earthworks.

- In Helmsley on A170
- Daily except public hols (DES)
- Gilling Castle, Pickering Castle
- Thirsk (16 miles)

## Jervaulx Abbey

*Near Masham*

£

Cistercian abbey ruins in magnificent setting.

- 4 miles NW of Masham
- All year
- Summer months, 3–5

## Markenfield Hall

*Near Ripon*

£

Good example of manor house; 14th-, 15th- and 16th-C buildings surrounded by moat.

3 miles s of Ripon, 2 miles w of A61

May to Sept, Mon 10–12.30, 2.15–5.

Fountains Abbey, Newby Hall, Ripley Castle

Ripon (4 miles)

(1 mile)

## Newburgh Priory

*Coxwold, near Thirsk*

Original remains of Augustinian priory founded in 12th C; 17th- and 18th-C additions and alterations. Interesting wild water garden.

Coxwold 435

9 miles SE of Thirsk, 5½ miles s of A170

July to end Aug, Wed 2–5

Gilling Castle, Newby Hall, Shandy Hall

Thirsk (9 miles)

## Newby Hall

*Skelton, near Ripon*

Early 18th-C Robert Adam house. Gallery showing William Weddell's classical sculpture. Large gardens.

Boroughbridge 2583

4 miles SE of Ripon, 3 miles w of A1

Apr, May and Sept, Wed, Thur, Sat, Sun and Bank Hol. Mon; June to Aug daily except Mon (open Bank Hol. Mon) 1.30–5.30

Markenfield Hall, Ripley Castle

Ripon (5 miles)

## Norton Conyers

*Wath, near Ripon*

Jacobean house with family pictures and furniture. Collections of toys, Victorian dresses, children's costumes, family manuscripts and mementoes of Charlotte Brontë.

Melmerby 333

3½ miles N of Ripon, 2 miles w of A1

Mid-May to mid-Sept, Sat, Sun and all Bank Hols (plus odd days in Aug and Sept) 2–5. Check in advance

Fountains Abbey, Markenfield Hall

Ripon (4 miles)

Sun and Bank Hols only

## Nunnington Hall

*Nunnington, near Helmsley*

Elizabethan manor house, enlarged in late 17th C. Good staircase, tapestries and ceramics.

Bilsdale 283

4½ miles SE of Helmsley, 2 miles N of B1257

Apr to end Oct, Wed to Sun and Bank Hol. Mon 2–6. Closed Good Fri

Gilling Castle, Shandy Hall

Malton (10 miles)

## Pickering Castle

*Pickering, near Scarborough*

Late 11th- and 12th-C castle with shell keep on a fine motte. Curtain walls and towers are later.

N of Pickering on A170

Daily except public hols (DES)

Castle Howard, Nunnington Hall

Malton (8 miles)

## Richmond Castle

*In Richmond*

Built in 11th C with commanding position over Swaledale. Fine keep is 12th C.

s of Richmond on A6136

Daily except public hols (DES)

Barnard Castle, Bedale Hall

Darlington (12 miles)

## Rievaulx Terrace and Temples

*Rievaulx, near Thirsk*

Grass terrace and woodlands with view over to Rievaulx Abbey. Two mid-18th-C temples, one with ceilings decorated in tempera. Exhibition of English 18th-C landscape work.

Bilsdale 340

10 miles E of Thirsk, 2½ miles NW of Helmsley off B1257

Apr to end Oct daily 10.30–6. Closed Good Fri

Helmsley Castle, Nunnington Hall, Shandy Hall

Thirsk (10 miles)

## Ripley Castle

*Ripley, near Harrogate*

Home of the Ingilby family since early 14th C. Visitors have included James I and Cromwell. In late 18th C Gothic and Classical alterations were made. Paintings, chandeliers, furniture, mantlepieces, arms and armour plus recently discovered Priest's hole. Grounds landscaped by 'Capability' Brown with specimen trees from many parts of world.

Harrogate 770186

In Ripley on A61

Easter weekend to end May, Sat and Sun; June to Aug, Tues (except June), Wed, Thur, Sat and Sun; Sept, Sat and Sun 2–6. Good Fri and Bank Hol. Mon 11–6

Markenfield Hall, Newby Hall

Harrogate (4½ miles)

## Scarborough Castle

*In Scarborough*

OAP DoE

Remains of 12th-C castle with keep which dominates town. Besieged twice and taken twice by Parliamentarians in 1643 and 1648. George Fox, the Quaker, was imprisoned here in 1655. Damaged by shell-fire in 1914–18 War.

On high cliff to E of town

Daily except public hols (DES)

Burton Agnes Hall, Pickering Castle

Scarborough

## Shandy Hall

*Coxwold, near Thirsk*

Good medieval house altered in 17th and 18th C. Laurence Sterne wrote *A Sentimental Journey* here, also large part of *Tristram Shandy*. Memorabilia of the author.

Coxwold 465

8½ miles SE from Thirsk, 5 miles S of A170

June to Sept, Wed 2–6

Newburgh Priory, Nunnington Hall

Thirsk (8½ miles)

## Skipton Castle

*In Skipton*

Fully roofed 12th-C and later building. Massive gatehouse and 6 solid towers. Besieged for 3 years during Civil War.

Skipton 2442

In centre of town on A65

All year daily (except Dec 25 and Good Fri) 10–6, Sun 2–6

East Riddlesden Hall, Gawthorpe Hall

Skipton (½ mile)

## Spofforth Castle

*Spofforth, near Harrogate*

DoE

Early 14th-C building with some interesting details, remains of a solar wing and hall. Note how one wall of the ground floor was hewn from living rock.

5 miles SE of Harrogate on A661

Daily except public hols (DES)

Beningbrough Hall, Harewood House, Ripley Castle

Harrogate (5 miles)

## Stockeld Park

*Wetherby, near Harrogate*

Palladian-style small country mansion by James Paine. Fine hall and staircase. Pleasant grounds and gardens.

Wetherby 62376

3 miles N of Wetherby off A661

Open to groups only by prior appointment

Harewood House, Ripley Castle

Harrogate ($7\frac{1}{2}$ miles)

By arrangement

## Sutton Park

*Sutton-on-the-Forest, near York*

Built in 1730, mansion has notable contents: excellent Chippendale, Sheraton and French furniture; paintings; ceramics; plasterwork by Cortese. Georgian ice house. Delightful gardens, temple, woodland walks and nature trail.

Easingwold 810249

8 miles to N of York off B1363

Good Fri, Easter Sun and Mon, then early May to late Sept, Tues, Wed, Thur, Sun and Bank Hol. Mon 2–6

Beningbrough Hall, Castle Howard

York (9 miles)

## Treasurer's House

*Chapter House Street, York*

There has been a building on this site since Roman times. Present building dates from 17th C. To be seen are collections of good furniture and also paintings by Etty, Riley, Hudson and Bueckelaer. Small formal garden.

York 24247

Behind York Minster

Apr to end Oct daily (except Good Fri) 10.30–6

Beningbrough Hall, Sutton Park

York ($\frac{1}{2}$ mile)

TREASURER'S HOUSE, YORK

# NOTTINGHAMSHIRE

## Carlton Hall

*Carlton-on-Trent, near Newark*

Notable Georgian house by celebrated architect Carr of York.

7 miles N of Newark off A1

Apr to Oct by prior appointment only

Thoresby Hall, Newstead Abbey

Newark Castle or Northgate (7 miles)

## Clumber Chapel

*Clumber Park, near Worksop*

Built between 1886 and 1889, a noteworthy example of Victorian architecture by G. F. Bodley. Set in a vast park of 3,800 acres with the longest lime avenue in Europe. Lake with bridge and temple.

Worksop 476592

5 miles SE of Worksop off A57

Apr to end Sept, Sat, Sun and Bank Hol. Mon 12–7, Mon to Fri 2–7; Oct to end Mar daily 1–4

Bolsover Castle, Thoresby Hall

Worksop (5 miles)

## Holme Pierrepont Hall

*Radcliffe-on-Trent, near Nottingham*

Early Tudor manor house with regional oak furniture. Courtyard garden with box parterre.

Radcliffe-on-Trent 2371

5 miles SE of Nottingham, 1½ miles N of A52

Easter Sun, Mon and Tues, Spring and Summer Bank Hol. Mon and Tues, then June to Aug, Sun, Tues, Thur and Fri, also Sun in Sept 2–6

Belvoir Castle, Wollaton Hall

Radcliffe-on-Trent (1½ miles)

(1 mile)

## Newstead Abbey

*Linby, near Nottingham*

Home of Byron family from 1540 to 1817 when Lord Byron, the poet, had to sell it to relieve his debts. Original priory was bought by Sir John Byron who converted it to a private dwelling. Byron relics. Fine and extensive gardens.

Blidworth 3557

11 miles N of Nottingham

Good Fri to end Sept daily 2–6

Hardwick Hall, Thoresby Hall, Wollaton Hall

Nottingham (10 miles)

## Thoresby Hall

*Near Ollerton*

Third house to be erected on the site, it was designed by Anthony Salvin. Impressive 3-storeyed great hall with hammerbeam roof, and fine entrance tower which Salvin modelled on that of Burghley.

Mansfield 823210

4 miles N of Ollerton, 1½ miles W of A614

May to Aug, Sun (not in May), Wed and Thur 2–5. Also Bank Hol. Mon

Bolsover Castle, Clumber Chapel, Doddington Hall

Worksop (9½ miles)

## Thrumpton Hall

*Thrumpton, near Nottingham*

Built *c.* 1610 by Gervase Pigot. His son added very fine Caroline staircase in 1665. Byron portraits and quality furniture.

Nottingham 830333

7 miles S of Nottingham off A453

Only to parties by prior appointment

Belvoir Castle, Melbourne Hall

Long Eaton (4 miles)

By arrangement

## Wollaton Hall

*Wollaton Park, Nottingham*

Elizabethan Renaissance building put up *c.* 1585 by Sir Francis Willoughby under supervision of Robert Smythson. Interior altered by Jeffry Wyatville *c.* 1805. Natural history museum.

Nottingham 281333

SW of city off A609

All year daily: Apr to Sept 10–7, Sun 2–5; Oct to Mar 10–dusk, Sun 1.30–4.30. Closed Dec 25–26

Holme Pierrepont Hall, Thrumpton Hall

Nottingham (2 miles)

## Ardington House

*Near Wantage*

Grey brick house with red brick dressings *c*. 1720. Fine hall, double staircase and painted ceiling.

East Hendred 244

12 miles s of Oxford, $2\frac{1}{2}$ miles E of Wantage

May to Sept daily 2–5 (by appointment)

Milton Manor House, Greys Court

Didcot

By arrangement

## Ashdown House

*Lambourn, near Swindon*

Built in late 17th C by 1st Lord Craven for Elizabeth of Bohemia. Large staircase ascends from hall to attics. Craven family portraits. Contemporary box parterre.

$2\frac{1}{2}$ miles s of Ashbury off B4000

Apr, Wed only, May to Sept, Wed and 1st and 3rd Sat in these months, 2–6

Kelmscott Manor, Uffington Castle

Swindon (10 miles)

## Blenheim Palace

*Woodstock, near Oxford*

Nation's gift to 1st Duke of Marlborough and justly considered to be supreme masterpiece of Sir John Vanbrugh. Henry Wise, Queen Anne's gardener, worked out designs for the gardens, following principles of Le Nôtre employed at Versailles: elaborate scrolling patterns with low box hedges and flower plantings. Much of this was changed later by 'Capability' Brown who also created the famous lake spanned by Vanbrugh's fine causeway. Good collection of pictures and tapestries. Room in which Sir Winston Churchill was born, plus Churchill memorabilia. 4,000 model soldiers. Narrow gauge steam railway and boat trips.

Woodstock 811325

From Woodstock 8 miles N of Oxford on A34

Mid-Mar to end Oct daily 11.30–5.

Ditchley Park, Rousham House

Handborough (3 miles)

In summer months

## Broughton Castle

*Broughton, near Banbury*

Moated Tudor mansion with earlier nucleus. During Civil War secret meetings were held there by some Parliamentary leaders; after Battle of Edgehill castle was besieged and captured by Royalists. Notable plaster ceilings, furniture and arms and armour.

Banbury 62624

2 miles sw of Banbury off B4035

BLENHEIM PALACE

June to mid-Sept, Wed, Sun and Bank Hol. Mon, also Thur in July and Aug 2–5

Aynhoe Park, Rousham House

Banbury (3 miles)

## Buscot Old Parsonage

*Near Faringdon*

£ NT

Early 18th-C house of Cotswold stone beside the Thames. Small garden.

2 miles SE of Lechlade on A417

Wed 2–6, only by prior appointment in writing

Arlington Mill, Blenheim Palace, Kelmscott Manor

Swindon (11 miles)

(2 miles)

## Buscot Park

*Near Faringdon*

18th-C house with park and lake. Water gardens by Harold Peto. Burne Jones Room. Faringdon collection of furniture and paintings.

3 miles NW of Faringdon off A417

Apr to end Sept, Wed, Thur and Fri, also 2nd and 4th Sat and immediately following Sun in these months, 2–6

Blenheim Palace, Kelmscott Manor, Milton Manor House

Swindon (12 miles)

## Chastleton House

*Chastleton, near Chipping Norton*

Unspoilt example of early 17th-C building by Walter Jones. Fine plasterwork and panelling. Period furniture and tapestries. Famous topiary garden laid out *c.* 1700.

Barton-on-the-Heath 355

4 miles SE of Moreton-in-Marsh, 1½ miles W of A44

All year daily (except Wed) 10.30–1, 2–5.30, Sat and Sun 2–5

Blenheim Palace, Ditchley Park, Snowshill Manor

Moreton-in-the-Marsh (4½ miles)

Closed in winter

## Ditchley Park

*Charlbury, near Chipping Norton*

£

18th-C mansion by James Gibbs with interior decoration by William Kent and Henry Flitcroft. For 350 years owned by family of General Robert E. Lee, who commanded the South in American Civil War. In Second World War Sir Winston Churchill used it as a weekend headquarters. Now equipped as Anglo-American conference centre.

Enstone 346

1½ miles W of A34 at Kiddington

For about 10 days at end of July, 2–5. Phone for details

Blenheim Palace, Chastleton House. Rousham House

Charlbury (2 miles)

## Great Barn

*Great Coxwell, near Faringdon*

£ NT

13th-C monastic barn, interesting timber roof and fine proportions.

2 miles SW of Faringdon between A420 and B4019

Daily at reasonable hours

Arlington Mill, Kelmscott Manor, Milton Manor House

Swindon (10 miles)

(1 mile)

## Greys Court

*Rotherfield Greys, near Henley-on-Thames*

£ NT

Jacobean manor house standing amidst ruined walls and towers of 14th-C fortified house. Tudor donkey wheel for raising water from a well.

Rotherfield Greys 529

At Rotherfield Greys, 3 miles NW of Henley-on-Thames on road to Peppard

Apr to end Sept, Mon, Wed and Fri 2.15–6. Closed Good Fri

MAPLEDURHAM HOUSE

Cliveden, Mapledurham House

Henley ($3\frac{1}{2}$ miles)

Bank Hols and Sat

## Mapledurham House

*Mapledurham, near Reading*

Late 16th-C mansion in pleasant parklands beside Thames. Alexander Pope was a frequent visitor and among the portraits are those of 2 sisters with whom he was in love. Fine moulded plasterwork on ceilings, and a great oak staircase. Family Chapel built in 1789 is reminiscent of Strawberry Hill Gothic. Restored watermill nearby.

Kidmore End 3350

4 miles NW of Reading, 1 mile W of A4074. River service from Promenade, Reading, 2.15 daily when house is open

Easter to end Sept, Sat, Sun and Bank Hol. 2.30–5.30

Cliveden, Hughenden Manor, Milton Manor House

Reading ($4\frac{1}{2}$ miles)

## Milton Manor House

*Milton, near Didcot*

17th-C house with Georgian wings reputedly work of Inigo Jones. Lake, walled garden and attractive grounds.

Abingdon 831287

4 miles S of Abingdon in Milton village just off A34

Easter weekend, then late Apr to mid-Oct, Sat, Sun and Bank Hol. Mon 2–5.30

Ashdown House, Blenheim Palace, Uffington Castle

Didcot (3 miles)

By arrangement

## Rousham House

*Steeple Aston, near Bicester*

Jacobean house enlarged by William Kent who also planned landscape garden, designed much of furniture and decorated some of the ceilings. Some elaborate plasterwork by Roberts of Oxford *c.* 1765. Portraits and miniatures.

12 miles N of Oxford, $1\frac{1}{2}$ miles from junction of A423 and B4030

Apr to end Sept, Wed, Sun and Bank Hol. Mon 2–5.30

Aynhoe Park, Blenheim Palace, Ditchley Park

Heyford (1 mile)

## Stonor Park

*Near Henley-on-Thames*

Built over many centuries, it is home of Lord and Lady Camoys and has been the Stonor family's home for 800 years. A centre of Catholicism throughout the Recusancy Period; Mass still celebrated in its own Chapel today. Many interesting details of domestic architecture from the various periods of its history. Stained glass, drawings, tapestries, pictures and furniture.

Turville Heath 587

5 miles N of Henley-on-Thames off B480

Mid-Apr to end Sept, Wed, Thur and Sun 2–5.30, Bank Hol. Mon 11–5.30

Cliveden, Hughenden Manor, Mapledurham House

Henley-on-Thames (5½ miles)

## Uffington Castle

*Whitehorse Hill, near Swindon*

Defensive Iron Age hill fort set on the ancient Ridgeway at a height of some 210 m. Below, cut in the chalk, is the celebrated White Horse which is thought by some to be contemporary with castle.

6 miles W of Wantage off B4507

At any reasonable time

Ashdown House, Kelmscott Manor, Milton Manor House

Swindon (9 miles)

# SHROPSHIRE

## Acton Burnell Castle

*Acton Burnell, near Shrewsbury*

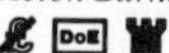

Ruined 13th-C fortified manor house. By repute the meeting place of 1st English Parliament in 1283.

8 miles S of Shrewsbury midway between A49 and A4580

At any reasonable time (DES)

Acton Round Hall, Attingham Park, Benthall Hall

Shrewsbury (8½ miles)

## Acton Round Hall

*Acton Round, near Bridgnorth*

Dower house for Aldenham Park, built by Smith Brothers of Warwick in early 18th C. Structure little altered.

6 miles W of Bridgnorth on unclassified road between A458 and B4368

Mid-May to mid-Sept, Thur 2.30–5.30

Attingham Park, Upton Cressett Hall

Church Stretton (14 miles)

## Adcote

*Baschurch, near Shrewsbury*

Outstanding country mansion by Norman Shaw. Now administered by Adcote School Educational Trust.

Baschurch 260202

7 miles NW of Shrewsbury via B5067

Late Apr to mid-July, except certain days in May, then Sept daily 2–5

Attingham Park, Powis Castle

Shrewsbury (7 miles)

## Attingham Park

*Atcham, near Shrewsbury*

Built in 1785 by George Steuart for 1st Lord Berwick. In 1805 John Nash added fine picture gallery and circular staircase. Notable interior decoration, particularly in boudoir. Park is fine example of work of Humphry Repton.

Upton Magna 203

4 miles SE of Shrewsbury off A5

Easter Sun to end Sept, Tues, Wed, Thur, Sat, Sun and Bank Hol. Mon 2–5.30

Acton Burnell Castle, Benthall Hall, Boscobel House

Shrewsbury (5 miles)

## Benthall Hall

*Broseley, near Wellington*

16th-C stone house with mullioned windows and moulded brick chimneys. Later exquisitely carved staircase, decorated plaster and panelling. Small garden.

Telford 882254

➔ 4 miles NE of Much Wenlock off B4375

Ⓟ Easter Sat to Sept, Tues, Wed, Sat and Bank Hol. Mon 2–6

Attingham Park, Boscobel House

Wellington (8 miles)

## Boscobel House

*Tong, near Shifnal*

£ OAP DoE

17th-C building preserving spot where Charles II hid in 1651. In the grounds is a descendant of the celebrated Royal oak tree.

➔ 4½ miles N of Albrighton off A41

Ⓟ Mar, Apr and Oct, Tues to Sat 9.30–5.30, Sun 2–5.30; May to Sept, Tues to Sat 9.30–7, Sun 2–7; Nov to Feb, Tues to Sat 9.30–4, Sun 2–4

Benthall Hall, Weston Park

Shifnal (7 miles)

## Dudmaston

*Quatt, near Bridgnorth*

£ NT

Late 17th-C house with noteworthy furniture, also flower paintings which belonged to Francis Darby of Coalbrookdale.

☎ Upton Magna 649

➔ 4 miles SE of Bridgnorth on A442

Ⓟ Apr to end Sept, Wed and Thur only, 2.30–5.30

Benthall Hall, Shipton Hall, Wilderhope Manor

## Ludlow Castle

*In Ludlow*

£

Part dates from 11th C. Many additions include late Norman circular chapel, decorated period State rooms, and details in Perpendicular and Tudor styles. Castle granted by Edward IV to his 2 sons, and by Henry VII to Prince Arthur who died there in 1502. In 1634 Milton's *Comus* was performed there as *A Masque presented at Ludlow Castle*. In 1646 castle was dismantled.

Ⓟ All year daily (except Sun and Dec 25, 26, Jan 1). Times from the Custodian

Berrington Hall, Eye Manor, Stokesay Castle

Ludlow

## Mawley Hall

*Cleobury Mortimer, near Bewdley*

£

18th-C house with notable plasterwork and panelling, possibly by Smith of Warwick.

➔ 1 mile S of Cleobury Mortimer off A4117

Ⓟ By written appointment only

Ludlow Castle, Wilderhope Manor

Kidderminster (12 miles)

## Shipton Hall

*Shipton, near Much Wenlock*

£

Elizabethan manor house with fine interior plasterwork by T. F. Pritchard. Georgian stable block. Medieval dovecote and garden.

☎ Brockton 225

➔ In Shipton on A4378

Ⓟ May to Sept, Thur, also Sun in July and Aug and Bank Hol. Mon 2.30–5.30

Benthall Hall, Ludlow Castle, Wilderhope Manor

Church Stretton (9 miles)

STOKESAY CASTLE

## Stokesay Castle

*Craven Arms, near Ludlow*

£

Dating from 13th C, a fine example of moated and fortified

manor house. Rebuilt in 1280 by Lawrence of Ludlow, a rich wool merchant.

- 8 miles NW of Ludlow just off A49
- Apr to end Sept daily except Mon and Tues (open Mon in July and Aug) 10–6; Mar and Oct, Wed to Sun 10–5
- Ludlow Castle, Shipton Hall, Wilderhope Manor
- Craven Arms ($1\frac{1}{2}$ miles)

## Tyn-y-Rhos Hall

*Near Oswestry*

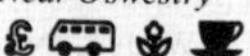

Small, ancient building where reputedly the Prince of North Wales slept in 1164 after Battle of Crogen. Good oak staircase, 2 carved fireplaces.

- Chirk 7898
- 4 miles N of Oswestry, W of A5
- May to mid-Sept, Wed, Thur, Sat, Sun and Bank Hol. Mon 2.30–6
- Chirk Castle
- Chirk ($2\frac{1}{2}$ miles)

## Upton Cressett Hall

*Upton Cressett, near Bridgnorth*

£

Late Tudor manor and gatehouse. Interior has commendable plasterwork and panelling. Great hall dates from 14th C.

- Morville 307
- 4 miles W of Bridgnorth on road off A458
- May to end Oct, Thur, also Summer Bank Hol. Mon 2.30–5.30
- Benthall Hall, Shipton Hall, Stokesay Castle

## Weston Park

*Weston-under-Lizard, near Shifnal*

£

Fine example of Restoration period, built in 1671 by Lady Wilbraham. Outstanding collection of paintings by Bassano, Gainsborough, Holbein, Hoppner, Lely, Reynolds and Van Dyck. Gobelin tapestries. Terraced gardens, stable block and Temple of Diana by James Paine. Three lakes, 'Capability' Brown wooded parkland with herds of deer and rare sheep. Woodland adventure playground, aquarium, miniature railway, pony rides.

- Weston-under-Lizard 207
- From A5 at Weston-under-Lizard
- Mid-Apr to end July daily except Fri, Aug daily, Sept, weekends only 2–6
- Benthall Hall, Boscobel House
- Oakengates (6 miles)

## The White House

*Aston Munslow, near Ludlow*

£

Late Saxon site with 13th-C undercroft, Cruck Hall dated 1335, half-timbered 16th-C crosswing and Norman dovecote. Implements, bygones, tools, domestic and dairy utensils, horse-drawn vehicles.

- Munslow 661
- $9\frac{1}{2}$ miles N of Ludlow off B4368
- Easter to end Oct, Sat 11–5 and Wed 2–5.30. Good Fri, 2–5.30; Bank Hol. weeks daily 11–5.30 (except Fri and Sun)
- Ludlow Castle, Stokesay Castle
- Craven Arms ($6\frac{1}{2}$ miles)

## Wilderhope Manor

*Longville, near Church Stretton*

£ NT

16th-C house of limestone with 17th-C plaster ceilings. Let as a Youth Hostel.

- Longville 363
- $7\frac{1}{2}$ miles E of Church Stretton off B4371
- Apr to end Sept, Wed and Sat 2–4.30; Oct to Mar, Sat 2–4.30
- Attingham Park, Benthall Hall, Shipton Hall
- Church Stretton (8 miles)
- ($1\frac{1}{2}$ miles)

# SOMERSET

## Barford Park

*Enmore, near Bridgwater*

Good example of early 18th C mansion for study of style and manner. Garden.

- Spaxton 269
- 5 miles w of Bridgwater via Durleigh
- May to Sept, Wed, Thur and Bank Hol. Mon 2–6
- Coleridge Cottage, Lytes Cary Manor
- Bridgwater ($5\frac{1}{2}$ miles)

## Barrington Court

*Barrington, near Ilminster*

Built between 1514 and 1520 in pure Gothic style by 2nd Lord Daubeny. An 'E' ground plan and one of earliest long galleries in country. Gardens laid out in 1920s by Gertrude Jekyll. Late 17th-C stable block.

- 3 miles NE of Ilminster, 1 mile E of B3168
- All year, Wed 10.15–12.15, 2–6 (except Oct to Easter 2–4)
- East Lambrook Manor, Forde Abbey, Montacute House
- Taunton (15 miles)

BARRINGTON COURT

## Bishop's Palace

*In Wells*

Built between 13th and 15th Cs and enclosed by 14th-C fortifications with moat; access through 14th-C gatehouse. Ruins of banqueting hall (late 13th C). Early part of palace has undercroft and contains former State rooms. Long gallery has portraits of Bishops of Bath and Wells. Moat is fed by St Andrew's Well – from which Wells derives its name. Gardens contain some unusual trees.

- Wells 78691
- Easter to end Oct, Sun and Thur, also daily in Aug 2–6
- Lytes Cary, Nunney Castle

## Brympton d'Evercy

*Brympton, near Yeovil*

Mansion with late 17th-C s front, and Tudor w front. State rooms. Felix dress collection. Priest house museum. Zingari Cricket Club collection. Large garden and vineyard.

- West Coker 2528
- 2 miles w of Yeovil just off A30
- Good Fri to Easter Mon, then May to end Sept daily (except Thur and Fri) 2–6
- Barrington Park, Montacute House
- Yeovil

## Coleridge Cottage

*35 Lime Street, Nether Stowey, Bridgwater*

Coleridge's home from 1797 to 1800, where he wrote *The Ancient Mariner* and part of *Christabel.*

- Nether Stowey 732662
- 8 miles w of Bridgwater
- Apr to end Sept daily (except Fri and Sat) 2–5
- Gaulden Manor, Barford Park
- Bridgwater ($8\frac{1}{2}$ miles)

## Dunster Castle Mill

*Dunster, near Minehead*

Fortified home of Luttrell family for 600 years. Early castle remodelled in 19th C by Anthony Salvin. Paintings include work by Eworth, Reynolds, Bower and Downman. Notable painted leather hanging panels, also carving and plasterwork. In conservatory and gardens grow rare specimens: cork oak, date palm, lemon and olive trees. Deer park.

Dunster 314

From Dunster, 3 miles SE of Minehead on A396

Apr to end Sept daily (except Fri and Sat), 11–5; Oct, Tues, Wed and Sun 2–4

Coleridge Cottage, Gaulden Manor

## East Lambrook Manor

*South Petherton, near Ilminster*

15th-C house with 16th-C additions. Good plasterwork and panelling. Noteworthy cottage-style garden with rare plants.

South Petherton 40328

2½ miles N of South Petherton

Mar to Oct, Thur 2–5

Barrington Court, Montacute House

Taunton (11 miles)

## Farleigh Castle

*Farleigh Hungerford, near Trowbridge*

Late 14th-C ruined castle with 2 courts defended by moat, towers and walls. Chapel in outer court with fine tomb of Sir Thomas Hungerford, builder of castle.

3½ miles W of Trowbridge on A366

Daily except public hols (DES)

Claverton Manor, Great Chalfield Manor

Trowbridge (4 miles)

## Gaulden Manor

*Tolland, near Wiveliscombe*

Dating from 12th C, this red sandstone house was seat of Turberville family immortalized by Thomas Hardy. Great hall with fine plasterwork ceiling and oak screen to room known as the chapel. Interesting bog garden with primulas and other moisture-loving plants. Herb garden.

Lydeard St Lawrence 213

9 miles NW of Taunton off B3188

Easter Sun and Mon, May to early Sept, Thur and Sun, also Bank Hol. Mon 2–6

Barrington Court, Coleridge Cottage, Dunster Castle Mill

## Hatch Court

*Hatch Beauchamp, near Taunton*

Bath stone mansion in Palladian style, designed in 1755 by Thomas Prowse of Axbridge. Fine stone staircase, china room. Small Canadian military museum. Deer park.

Hatch Beauchamp 480208

6 miles SE of Taunton on A358

July to Sept, Thur 2.30–5.30. Parties by prior appointment only

Barrington Court, East Lambrook Manor, Montacute House

Taunton (6 miles)

By arrangement

## Lytes Cary Manor

*Charlton Mackerell, near Somerton*

Manor house with 14th-C chapel, 15th-C hall and 16th-C great chamber. Home of Henry Lyte, writer of *Niewe Herball* in 1598.

2½ miles NE of Ilchester bypass A303, signposted from junction of A303 with A37

Mar to end Oct, Wed and Sat 2–6

Barrington Court, East

LYTES CARY MANOR

Lambrook Manor, Montacute House

Castle Cary (8 miles)

## Midelney Manor

*Drayton, near Langport*

16th- to 18th-C manor house originally island manor of Abbots of Muchelney. Falcon's Mews, Heronry and gardens.

- 11 miles E of Taunton, 2 miles from A378 at Langport
- Bank Hol. Mon, also June to Oct, Wed 2–5.30
- Barrington Court, East Lambrook Manor
- Taunton (11 miles)

## Montacute House

*Montacute, near Yeovil*

Beautiful late 16th-C house built by Edward Phelips and probably designed by William Arnold, a Somerset mason. Tudor style entrance front on W added in 1786 by a later Edward Phelips, the 5th Edward to live at Montacute, the materials being purchased from Clifton Maybank, a Dorset house that was being pulled down. In 55-m long gallery are Elizabethan and Jacobean portraits from National Portrait Gallery; also heraldic glass, panelling and fine furniture. Formal gardens.

- Martock 823289
- In village 4 miles W of Yeovil on A3088
- Apr to end Oct daily except Tues 12.30–6
- Barrington Court, East Lambrook Manor
- Yeovil ($4\frac{1}{2}$ miles)
- Apr to Sept 3–5.30

## Nunney Castle

*Nunney, near Frome*

DOE

Small but complete building modelled on French 'Bastille', compact tower with round towers at angles and standing in moat. Built by Sir John de la Mare in 1373. Fell to Parliamentarians in 1645 on 2nd day of siege.

- $3\frac{1}{2}$ miles SW of Frome, 1 mile N of A361
- Daily except public hols (DES)
- Longleat House, Lytes Cary
- Frome (4 miles)

## Stoke-sub-Hamdon Priory

*Stoke-sub-Hamdon, near Yeovil*

NT

14th- and 15th-C stone buildings, once residence of the priests of Chantry of St Nicholas. Only Great Hall of Chantry house is open to public. Of architectural interest.

- Between A303 and A3088, 2 miles W of Montacute
- All year daily 10–6
- Montacute House
- Yeovil (6 miles)

## Treasurer's House

*Martock, near Yeovil*

NT

Small house dating from 13th C with medieval hall and kitchen. Of architectural interest.

- 1 mile NW of A303, opposite Martock Church
- Only by prior written appointment
- Barrington Court, East Lambrook Manor, Montacute House
- Yeovil (8 miles)

## SOUTH YORKSHIRE

### Cannon Hall
*Cawthorne, near Barnsley*

17th-C mansion rebuilt in 18th C by Carr of York. Furniture, glassware and William Harvey bequest of Dutch and Flemish paintings. Regimental museum of the 13th/18th Royal Hussars.

Barnsley 790270
5 miles W of Barnsley
All year daily 10.30–5, Sun 2.30–5. Closed Good Fri, Dec 25–26 and Jan 1
Oakes Park, Redhouse
Denby Dale (2 miles)

### Conisbrough Castle
*Conisbrough, near Doncaster*

Round keep built by Hamelin Plantagenet, Henry II's half-brother, *c.* 1185. Keep stands 27 m tall, almost its original height.

4½ miles SW of Doncaster on A630
Standard (DES), but Sun, Apr to Sept, from 9.30
Bolsover Castle, Thoresby Hall
Conisbrough

### Oakes Park
*Norton, near Sheffield*

First house on site built during 15th C. Rebuilt *c.* 1673 and altered again in 19th C. Fine furniture, tapestries, paintings and collection of dolls. Gardens and long lake.

Sheffield 746468
4 miles S of Sheffield on B6054
By arrangement for parties only
Bolsover Castle, Thoresby Hall
Sheffield (5 miles)

## STAFFORDSHIRE

### Chillington Hall
*Near Wolverhampton*

Home of Giffards since 1178, existing house was partly erected by Francis Smith in 1724 and completed by Sir John Soane in 1785. Notable saloon. Grounds and lake by 'Capability' Brown.

Brewood 850236
9 miles NW of Wolverhampton
May to mid-Sept, Thur, also Sun in Aug, Easter Sun and Sun prior to Bank Hol. Mon 2.30–5.30
Boscobel House
Wolverhampton (9 miles)

### Hanch Hall
*Near Lichfield*

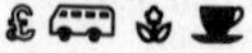

Interesting combination of architecture. Original house was built in reign of Edward I, and there are also elements of Tudor, Jacobean, Queen Anne and Georgian. Notable strapwork staircase, oak panelling, collection of needlework, costumes, baby clothes, dolls, teapots, seashells and 17th-C parchments. Landscaped gardens, trout pool and waterfowl.

4 miles NW of Lichfield off B5014
Early Apr to early Oct, Sun and Wed, also Easter, Spring and Summer Bank Hol. Mon and Tues 2.30–6
Chillington Hall, Shugborough
Lichfield (4½ miles)

### Hoar Cross Hall
*Hoar Cross, near Burton-on-Trent*

Built in 1871 in Elizabethan style and modelled in part on Temple

Newsam, Leeds. Good plasterwork in Chapel and on some ceilings. Gardens with fine trees and shrubs, ponds.

Hoar Cross 224

From A515 at Newchurch, 7 miles w of Burton-on-Trent

Ring for details

Hanch Hall, Shugborough

Burton-on-Trent ($7\frac{1}{2}$ miles)

## Moseley Old Hall

*Fordhouses, near Wolverhampton*

Small Elizabethan manor house, formerly half-timbered, and with secret hiding places. Charles II took refuge here after Battle of Worcester in 1651; the bed in which he slept can be seen.

Wolverhampton 782808

4 miles N of Wolverhampton off A449

Mar to end Oct, Wed, Thur, Sat, Sun and Bank Hol. Mon; Nov, Wed and Sun 2–5.30

Boscobel House, Chillington Hall, Weston Park

Codsall (3 miles). Not Sun

(1 mile)

## Shugborough

*Milford, near Stafford*

Impressive country house begun in late 17th C, added to *c.* 1750 and enlarged by Samuel Wyatt between 1790 and 1806. Fine plasterwork by Vassali and Joseph Rose, pictures, furniture and memorabilia of Admiral Anson. In grounds a Chinese garden house in neo-Grecian style by James 'Athenian' Stuart. Estate buildings contain: brewhouse, laundry, farm equipment, bygones of domestic life, costumes.

Little Haywood 881388

$5\frac{1}{2}$ miles SE of Stafford off A513

Mid-Mar to late Oct, Tues to Fri and Bank Hol. Mon 10.30–5.30; weekends 2–5.30

Boscobel House, Chillington Hall, Weston Park

Stafford (6 miles)

## Tamworth Castle

*In Tamworth*

Normans raised their motte on site of Saxon fortress erected by Ethelfleda, daughter of Alfred the Great. Within the massive walls is a medieval banqueting hall and 17th-C apartments with fine heraldic frieze and good period furniture. Keep now houses a museum; exhibits include collection of early English coins from Tamworth Mint.

Tamworth 3561 ex 294

In Tamworth, 15 miles NE of Birmingham on A453

Apr to Sept 10–6, Sun 2–6; Oct to Mar weekdays (except Fri) 10–5, Sun 2–5. Closed Dec 25–26

Kenilworth Castle, Melbourne Hall

Tamworth ($\frac{3}{4}$ mile)

# SUFFOLK

## Angel Corner

*8 Angel Hill, Bury St Edmunds*

Queen Anne house containing Gershom-Parkington collection of clocks and watches.

Bury St Edmunds 63233

Daily except Sun 10–1, 2–5 (Nov to Mar 2–4). Closed Good Fri, Easter Sat, May Day, Dec 25–26 and Jan 1

Haughley Park, Ickworth, Ixworth Abbey

Bury St Edmunds

## Badingham

*Badingham, near Saxmundham*

Main house, built 1727 as rectory, is noteworthy example of

Georgian domestic architecture. Large grounds; lake with boat rides. Walled kitchen garden.

Badingham 222

6 miles NW of Saxmundham, off A1120

Early Apr to late Sept, Thur 2–6

Glenham Hall, Haughley Park

Saxmundham (6 miles)

## Christchurch Mansion

*Christchurch Park, Ipswich*

Built *c.* 1550 by Edmund Withipoll, reconstructed in 1675 after fire. Period furniture. Museum with variety of exhibits of local interest.

Ipswich 53246

All year daily 10–5, Sun 2.30–4.30. Closed on some public hols

Melford Hall, Orford Castle

Ipswich (2 miles)

## Euston Hall

*Euston, near Thetford*

18th-C house with fine display of paintings by such as Kneller, Lely, Stubbs and Van Dyck. Pleasure grounds are work of John Evelyn and William Kent.

Thetford 3281

3 miles SE of Thetford off A1088

Early June to late Sept, Thur, 2.30–5.30

Angel Corner, Ixworth Abbey

Thetford (3½ miles)

## Framlingham Castle

*Framlingham, near Saxmundham*

Erected between 1177 and 1215 by Roger Bigod. Good curtain walls and 13 towers. Almshouses built inside walls in 1639 by Pembroke College, Cambridge.

Daily except public hols (DES)

Glenham Hall, Haughley Park, Orford Castle

Wickham Market (6½ miles)

Not Sun

## Gainsborough's House

*46 Gainsborough Street, Sudbury*

Here the great painter was born. Houses some of his works; furnishing in accord with building.

Sudbury 72958

All year, Tues to Sat 10–12.30, 2–5, Sun 2–5. Closed Dec 25–26

Gosfield Hall, Melford Hall

Sudbury

## Glemham Hall

*Little Glemham, near Woodbridge*

Elizabethan house in red brick, altered early in 18th C. Fine staircase, panelling and Queen Anne furniture. Walled garden with specimen trees.

Wickham Market 746219

4½ miles SW of Saxmundham off A12

Easter Mon to end Sept, Sun, Wed and Bank Hol. 2–5.30

Framlingham Castle, Haughley Park, Orford Castle

Wickham Market (3 miles)

## Haughley Park

*Haughley, near Stowmarket*

Built *c.* 1620 on 'E' plan, and recently restored. Octagonal chimneys. Park and gardens.

Elmswell 40205

4 miles NW of Stowmarket off A45

May to Sept, Tues 3–6

Ickworth, Ixworth Abbey

Elmswell (2 miles)

## Ickworth

*Horringer, near Bury St Edmunds*

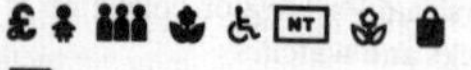

Elegant house begun *c.* 1794 and finished in 1830. Basic idea conceived by eccentric 4th Earl of

Bristol, Bishop of Derry, using architect Francis Sandys. Notable contents include very fine silver, late-Regency and 18th-C furniture and paintings. Formal gardens, herbaceous borders and woodland walk.

- ☎ Horringer 270
- ➔ 3 miles SW of Bury St Edmunds off A143
- ⌚ Apr to mid-Oct, Tues, Wed, Thur, Sat, Sun and Bank Hol. Mon 2–6
- Angel Corner, Haughley Park
- Bury St Edmunds ($3\frac{1}{2}$ miles)
- Not Sun

ICKWORTH

## Ixworth Abbey

*Ixworth, near Bury St Edmunds*

£

17th/18th-C house containing parts of 12th-C crypt of original abbey and sundry alterations and additions in between. Abbey documents and manuscripts on view.

- ☎ Pakenham 30374
- ➔ 6 miles NE of Bury St Edmunds, junction of A143 and A1088
- ⌚ May to mid-Aug, Tues, Sun and Spring Bank Hol. 2.30–5. Ring to confirm
- Euston Hall, Haughley Park, Ickworth
- Bury St Edmunds (6 miles)
- Not Sun

## Kentwell Hall

*Long Melford, near Sudbury*

£ OAP

Fine red-brick Tudor house with broad moat. Neglected for many years, restoration began in 1971 and is still proceeding. Provides interesting look at process actually being carried out. Gothic dining room, great hall and quantities of early painted and heraldic glass. Display of bygones. Gardens with $\frac{3}{4}$-mile avenue of lime trees.

- ☎ Long Melford 207
- ➔ In Long Melford, 3 miles N of Sudbury on A134
- ⌚ Good Fri to end Sept, Wed, Thur and Sun, also Fri and Sat from July and Bank Hol. weekends 2–6
- Gainsborough's House, Melford Hall
- Sudbury (3 miles)
- Not Sun

## Little Hall

*Lavenham, near Bury St Edmunds*

£

Interesting example of 15th-C house in charming and well-cared-for town. Gayer Anderson collection of antiques and books.

- ➔ 11 miles SW of Bury St Edmunds off A1141
- ⌚ Easter to mid-Oct, Sat, Sun and Bank Hol. 2–6
- Haughley Park, Melford Hall
- Bury St Edmunds (11 miles)

## Melford Hall

*Long Melford, near Sudbury*

£ NT

Distinguished Tudor house with elegant turrets erected between 1554 and 1578 by Sir William Cordell, Speaker of the House of Commons in reign of Queen Mary and Master of the Rolls to Elizabeth I. Original panelled banqueting hall, 18th-C drawing room, Regency library and Beatrix Potter room. On display celebrated Hyde Parker collection of Chinese porcelain.

- ➔ 3 miles N of Sudbury on A134

Apr to end Sept, Wed, Thur, Sun and Bank Hol. Mon 2–6

Gainsborough's House, Kentwell House

Sudbury (3 miles)

Not Sun

## Orford Castle

*Orford, near Woodbridge*

Built by Henry II between 1165 and 1173, was of importance and intended by the King to be part of his successful attempt to re-assert royal power in East Anglia. Today only the keep survives; this is circular inside with a polygonal exterior.

12 miles E of Woodbridge off B1084

Daily except public hols (DES)

Framlingham Castle

Wickham Market ($7\frac{1}{2}$ miles)

## Somerleyton Hall

*Somerleyton, near Lowestoft*

Glorious piece of extravagance built in early part of 19th C round an earlier 16th/17th-C house. Style is robust Anglo-Italianate. Works by Landseer, Wright of Derby and Stanfield adorn the walls, also carvings by Grinling Gibbons from the earlier house. Stable clock made by Vulliamy in 1847 is original model for Big Ben. 12 acres of grounds with famous maze and glass houses.

Lowestoft 730224

5 miles NW of Lowestoft off B1074

Mid-Apr to early Oct, Sun, Thur and Bank Hol. Mon, also Tues and Wed in July and Aug 2–6

Burgh Castle, Caister Castle

Haddiscoe (3 miles)

# SURREY

## Albury Park

*Albury, near Guildford*

House dates from Queen Anne period. Interior changed by Sir John Soane in 1802 and A. W. Pugin rebuilt exterior in Gothic style in 1846, adding some 48 decorative chimneypots. Grounds partly laid out by John Evelyn, famous diarist, in 17th C.

4 miles SE of Guildford, $1\frac{1}{2}$ miles E of Albury

May to Sept, Wed and Thur 2–5

Clandon Park, Loseley House

Chilworth (1 mile)

## Clandon Park

*West Clandon, near Guildford*

Built in early 1730s for Onslow family, this Palladian house was work of Giacomo Leoni; one successful device he used was to hide roof behind a balustrade. Ceiling in the hall is well worth studying. Amongst the many fine paintings, stop and examine subtle composition by Daniel Gardner with his oval of a game of chess. Also Mrs Gubbay's collection of furniture and porcelain. 19th-C kitchen in basement. Landscape by 'Capability' Brown.

Guildford 222482

3 miles E of Guildford on A247, just N of junction with A246

Apr to mid-Oct daily (except Mon and Fri) 2–6; open Bank Hol. Mon but closed Tues following

Albury Park, Loseley House

Clandon (1 mile)

## Detillens

*Limpsfield, near Oxted*

Medieval manor house erected *c.* 1450, with huge king post and tie beam. Georgian front added early in 18th C. Excellent display of furniture, china and militaria. Large collection of Orders of Chivalry of all nations. Large walled garden.

- Oxted 3342
- 9 miles E of Reigate on A25
- May to June, Sat; July to Sept, Wed and Sat; also Bank Hol. Mon 2–5
- Knole, Quebec House, Squerryes Court
- Oxted (1½ miles)

## Farnham Castle

*In Farnham*

Built originally by Henry of Blois, Bishop of Winchester, between 1129 and 1171. Additions in Tudor and Jacobean periods. Great hall remodelled during Restoration.

- N side of town
- Daily except public hols (DES)
- Albury Park, Loseley House
- Farnham

## Hatchlands

*East Clandon, near Guildford*

Built *c.* 1756 for the victor of Louisberg, Admiral Boscawen. Superb interior decoration by Robert Adam.

- Guildford 222787
- 4 miles E of Guildford on A246
- Apr to end Sept, Wed and Sun 2–6
- Hampton Court Palace, Polesden Lacey
- Clandon (2 miles)

## Loseley House

*Littleton, near Guildford*

Fine Elizabethan mansion built in 1562 by Sir William More, relation of Sir Thomas More. Elizabeth I stayed here 3 times. Notable chimney piece, panelling from Henry VIII's Nonsuch Palace. Famous Jersey herd.

- Guildford 71881
- 2½ miles SW of Guildford between A3 and A3100
- June to end Sept, Wed, Thur, Fri and Sat, also Summer Bank Hol. 2–5
- Albury Park, Clandon Park
- Guildford (2 miles)

## Polesden Lacey

*Near Dorking*

Originally a Regency villa that was remodelled in 1906 by Hon. Mrs Ronald Greville, celebrated Edwardian hostess. Outstanding collection of paintings including works by Lely, Raeburn, Reynolds, Lawrence, Matsys, Ghirlandaio, Van Orley, Baptiste Monnoyer, Salomon van Ruysdael, William van de Velde, Cuyp, Fabritius, De Hooch, Bakhuysen, David Teniers and Metsu. Also fine silver, porcelain and furniture. Extensive grounds.

- Bookham 52048
- 3 miles NW of Dorking, 1½ miles S of Great Bookham, off A246
- Mar and Nov, Sat and Sun 2–5; Apr to end Oct daily (except Mon and Fri) 2–6. Open Bank Hol. Mon, closed following Tues
- Clandon Park, Hatchlands
- Bookham (2½ miles)
- (1½ miles)

POLESDEN LACEY

# TYNE AND WEAR

## Gibside Chapel and Avenue

*Burnopfield, near Newcastle-upon-Tyne*

£ NT

Notable piece of Georgian architecture built in Classical style of James Paine *c.* 1760 and restored in 1965. Delicate plasterwork, panelled pews and a rare mahogany 3-tier pulpit. Terrace and oak avenue.

Rowlands Gill 2255

6 miles SW of Gateshead off B6314

Apr to end Sept daily except Tues 2–6; Mar and Oct, Wed, Sat and Sun 2–5

Tynemouth Priory and Castle, Washington Old Hall

Newcastle Central (6 miles)

## Hylton Castle

*South Hylton, near Sunderland*

£ OAP DoE

Basically a keep-gatehouse, dating from early 15th C and erected by William de Hylton. Good examples of medieval heraldry. Considerably changed in the 18th and 19th Cs.

$3\frac{3}{4}$ miles W of Sunderland off A19

Exterior only accessible (DES)

Finchale Priory, Gibside Chapel

Sunderland ($3\frac{3}{4}$ miles)

## Tynemouth Priory and Castle

*In Tynemouth*

£ OAP DoE

Earliest monastic foundation here was destroyed by the Danes in 865 and abandoned in 1008. In 1090 it was refounded as a Benedictine priory. In 14th C a curtain wall with towers and a gatehouse-keep were erected for defence. After the Dissolution fortress was maintained as part of coastal defences.

8 miles E of Newcastle on coast just N of Tynemouth

Daily except public hols (DES)

Gibside Chapel, Hylton Castle, Washington Old Hall

Tynemouth

## Washington Old Hall

*The Avenue, Washington*

£ NT

From 1183 to 1613 home of George Washington's ancestors. Largely rebuilt *c.*1610. In 1936 it narrowly escaped demolition. Washington relics and Delft ware.

Washington 466789

5 miles W of Sunderland

Mar to end Oct daily (except Tues) 1–6; Nov to end Feb, Sat and Sun 2–4

Hylton Castle

Newcastle Central (7 miles)

# WARWICKSHIRE

## Arbury Hall

*Astley, near Nuneaton*

£

First building on site was an Augustinian priory; in 1580 a private dwelling was erected. During 18th C remains were rebuilt and given Gothic treatment by Sanderson Miller, Henry Keene and Couchman of Warwick. Contents include good paintings; furniture; china and glass; also excellent plasterwork. Stable block with designs by Wren. Extensive grounds. George Eliot (Mary Ann Cross, *née* Evans) was born on the estate in 1819. Arbury Hall was her *Cheverel Manor*.

Nuneaton 347478

2 miles SW of Nuneaton off B4102

Easter Sun to early Oct, Sun and Bank Hol. Mon and Tues 2.30–6

Kenilworth Castle, Tamworth Castle

Nuneaton (3½ miles)

1 mile

Summer months

## Charlecote Park

*Wellesbourne, near Stratford-upon-Avon*

Built by Lucy family in 1558, has frequently been altered since, particularly during early part of 19th C, hence the Victorian-Elizabethan-Gothic Revival decoration and furniture. Brewhouse, kitchen and carriages. Large park with deer and Jacob sheep. Legend has it that William Shakespeare was arraigned before Sir Thomas Lucy for poaching Charlecote deer and subsequently lampooned him as Mr Justice Shallow.

Stratford-upon-Avon 840277

5 miles E of Stratford-upon-Avon off B4086

Apr and Oct, Sat and Sun; May to end Sept daily except Mon (but open Bank Hol. Mon) 11–6

Coughton Court, Warwick Castle

Stratford-upon Avon (5½ miles)

## Coughton Court

*Coughton, near Alcester*

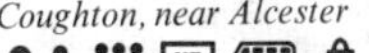

Main part of building is Elizabethan originally moated. Throckmorton family owned property from 1409 until it was presented to NT in 1946. Has been distinguished through centuries by tenacious allegiance to Roman Catholicism. Family was not directly involved in Gunpowder Plot, but Mr Throckmorton, who was abroad, lent house to Sir Everard Digby, and in the gatehouse on that 5th November Lady Digby and others awaited news of the plot, eventually brought to them at dead of night. Jacobite relics.

Alcester 762435

2 miles N of Alcester on A435

Apr and Oct, Sat and Sun; Easter week daily (except Good Fri); May to end Sept, Wed, Thur, Sat, Sun, Bank Hol. Mon and Tues following, 2–6

Shakespeare's Birthplace Trust Properties, Warwick Castle

Stratford-upon-Avon (9 miles)

## Farnborough Hall

*Farnborough, near Banbury*

Mainly 18th-C stone-built house, good plasterwork. Grass terrace walk with 2 temples.

6 miles N of Banbury off A423

Apr to end Sept, Wed and Sat 2–6

Snowshill Manor, Upton House

Banbury (6 miles)

## Harvard House

*High Street, Stratford-upon-Avon*

Built in 1596. Here lived mother of John Harvard, founder of Harvard University in USA.

Stratford-upon-Avon 4507

Apr to Sept daily 9–1, 2–6, Sun 2–6; Oct to Mar daily except Sun 10–1, 2–4. Closed Dec 24–26

Shakespeare's Birthplace Trust Properties

Stratford-upon-Avon (½ mile)

## Honington Hall

*Honington, near Stratford-upon-Avon*

Originally built in 1680, has fine quality 18th-C plasterwork.

Shipston-on-Stour 61434

10 miles S of Stratford-upon-Avon, ½ mile E of A34

May to end Sept, Wed, Thur and Bank Hol. Mon 2.30–5.30

Shakespeare's Birthplace Trust Properties, Upton House

Moreton-in-Marsh (7 miles)

## Kenilworth Castle

*In Kenilworth*

At height of its greatness Kenilworth was most important of all the lake-fortresses. Stretch of water was made by damming streams on S and W. Geoffrey de Clinton was given estate by Henry I *c.* 1122. Keep erected between 1150 and 1175 by either Geoffrey's son or grandson. John of Gaunt, a builder and lover of the castle, added great hall and State apartments. Henry VIII put up the block termed King Henry's Lodgings. Castle passed through many hands: in 1553 to John Dudley, Duke of Northumberland, but he was soon executed; then to Mary I, on to Elizabeth I, who restored it to Robert Dudley, later the Earl of Leicester. Elizabeth paid several visits to the castle. On one occasion she must have witnessed one of history's greatest parties, which went on for 19 days, cost Leicester £100,000 (this would need several more noughts after it today) and during which 320 hogsheads of beer alone were drunk. In 1649 Cromwellians 'slighted' the castle: its walls were breached, the keep damaged; but still today the rich spirit of this most knightly place lives on.

Daily except public hols (DES)

Packwood House, Warwick Castle

Coventry (5 miles)

## Kinwarton Dovecote

*Kinwarton, near Alcester*

Circular 14th-C dovecote with good ogee doorway.

$1\frac{1}{2}$ miles N of Alcester off B4089

All year daily till sunset. Key from Glebe Farm next door

Charlecote Park, Coughton Court, Ragley Hall

Stratford-upon-Avon (6 miles)

## Packwood House

*Lapworth, near Solihull*

Timber-framed Tudor house with additions from 17th C. Notable collections of tapestry, needlework and furniture. Outside is John Fetherston's Yew Garden, symbolizing the Sermon on the Mount.

Lapworth 2024

2 miles E of A34 at Hockley Heath, off B4439

May to end Sept daily (except Mon and Tues), also Bank Hol. Mon 11–6; Oct to Apr, Wed, Sat and Sun 2–5. Closed Dec 25 and Jan 1

Kenilworth Castle, Warwick Castle

Lapworth (2 miles)

(2 miles)

KENILWORTH CASTLE

## Ragley Hall

*Arrow, near Alcester*

Built in 1680. Portico and interiors by James Wyatt added 100 years later. Noteworthy collection of antiques including important library. 500-acre park and lake, landscaping by 'Capability' Brown. Adventure woodland.

☎ Alcester 2090

→ 2 miles sw of Alcester near junction of A422 and A435 at Arrow

Ⓞ Apr to early Oct daily (except Mon and Fri, but open Bank Hol. Mon) 1.30–5.30

Kinwarton Dovecote, Shakespeare's Birthplace Trust Properties

Stratford-upon-Avon (8½ miles)

## Shakespeare's Birthplace Trust Properties

*In Stratford-upon-Avon*

An inclusive ticket is available for all 5 properties.

**Anne Hathaway's Cottage**

*Shottery*

Her thatched home before she married Shakespeare.

→ 1 mile w of centre off A422

Ⓞ Apr to Oct daily 9–6 (9–7 on Thur, Sat and all weekdays from June to Sept), Sun 10–6; Nov to Mar daily 9–4.30, Sun 1.30–4.30

**Hall's Croft**

*Old Town*

Fine Tudor house with period furniture and walled garden. Shakespeare's daughter and Dr John Hall lived here.

Ⓞ Apr to Oct daily 9–6, Sun 2–6; Nov to Mar, weekdays only 9–12.45, 2–4

**Mary Arden's House**

*Wilmcote*

Tudor farmhouse where Shakespeare's mother lived. Interesting dovecote.

→ 5 miles NW of Stratford, off A34

Ⓞ As for Hall's Croft

**New Place**

*Chapel Street*

Foundations of Shakespeare's last home, preserved in an Elizabethan garden with Nash's house adjoining.

Ⓞ As for Hall's Croft

**Shakespeare's Birthplace**

*Henley Street*

Half-timbered house, containing many exhibits.

Ⓞ As for Anne Hathaway's Cottage

## Upton House

*Edge Hill, near Banbury*

NT

Late 17th-C house on site and core of earlier building. Outstanding contents: Brussels tapestries; Sèvres; Chelsea figures; 18th-C furniture; impressive hanging of paintings of principal European Schools. Large garden with lakes.

☎ Edge Hill 266

→ 7 miles NW of Banbury off A422

Ⓞ Apr to end Sept, Mon, Tues, Wed and Thur, also certain Sat and Sun in May and Aug, 2–6

Farnborough Hall, Honington Hall

Banbury (7 miles)

Thur and Sat only

## Warwick Castle

*In Warwick*

On pre-Norman site, perched above River Avon and looking down on 'Capability' Brown landscape, One of finest of great medieval castles still inhabited. First fortifications set up more than 1,000 years ago by Ethelfleda, daughter of King Alfred. State apartments display many great treasures, with paintings by Rubens and Van Dyck. Pieces in the armoury rank with best in the country.

☎ Warwick 45421

Ⓞ All year daily: Mar to end Oct 10–5.30; Nov to end Feb 10–4.30

Charlecote Park

Warwick (½ mile)

## Asbury Cottage

*Newton Road, Great Barr, near West Bromwich*

Between 1746 and 1771 this was the home of Francis Asbury, 1st Bishop of the American Methodist Church. Furnished in period style.

Birmingham 569 2308

3 miles NE of centre of West Bromwich

All year, Mon to Fri 2–4

Hagley Hall, Wightwick Manor

Hamstead ($1\frac{1}{2}$ miles)

## Aston Hall

*Frederick Road, Birmingham*

OAP

Built by Sir Thomas Holte between 1618 and 1635. Great staircase goes up to 2nd floor. Important marble chimney pieces, plaster friezes and panelling in the long gallery. Quality paintings and furnishings. Visitors in stiletto-heeled shoes will be asked to remove them.

Birmingham 327 0062

$2\frac{1}{2}$ miles N of city centre, $\frac{1}{2}$ mile from M6 exit 6

Easter to Oct, Mon to Sat 10–1, 2–5; Sun 2–5

Asbury Cottage, Hagley Hall

Witton (1 mile). Not Sun

## Hagley Hall

*Hagley, near Stourbridge*

OAP

Outstanding house of English rococo period with somewhat severe exterior but richly handled interior. Designed by Sanderson Miller for 1st Lord Lyttleton and finished *c.* 1760. Fine plasterwork by Vassali. Arabesque tapestries by Joshua Morris and notable furniture and pictures.

Hagley 882408

Just off A456 6 miles NE of Kidderminster

Mid-Apr to early Sept daily 12.30–5

Asbury Cottage, Aston Hall

Hagley (1 mile). Not Sun

## Oak House

*Oak Road, West Bromwich*

Tudor yeoman's house with unusual lantern tower. Quality carving, panelling and furniture.

Birmingham 553 0759

Near centre of West Bromwich

May to Sept, weekdays 10–5 (except Thur 10–1), Sun 2.30–5; Oct to Apr, weekdays 10–1

Aston Hall, Hagley Hall

Hamstead (2 miles). Not Sun

## Wightwick Manor

*Wightwick Bank, near Wolverhampton*

NT

Begun in 1887, house and contents reflect influence of William Morris. Examples of his wallpapers; works by the Pre-Raphaelites, Rossetti, Millais, also Burne-Jones and Maddox-Brown; tiles by de Morgan; stained glass by Kempe. Gardens with yew hedges.

Wolverhampton 761108

3 miles W of Wolverhampton off A454

All year (except Feb), Thur, Sat, Bank Hol. Sun and Mon 2.30–5.30; also May to end Sept, Wed 2.30–5.30. Closed Dec 25–26 and Jan 1–2

Asbury Cottage, Aston Hall

Wolverhampton (3 miles)

## Arundel Castle

*In Arundel*

££

Home of Dukes of Norfolk and their ancestors for over 700 years, castle was begun in time of Edward the Confessor. Damaged by Cromwellians and largely reconstructed in 18th C, the great 12th-C keep being preserved. Fine paintings by Gainsborough, Reynolds and Van Dyck. Early furniture.

- Arundel 883136
- 10 miles E of Chichester
- End Mar to Mid-Apr and early Sept to end Oct, Mon to Fri 1–5; mid-Apr to late May, Sun to Fri, 1–5; end May to end Aug, Sun to Fri 12–5
- Goodwood House, Parham, Petworth House
- Arundel (¾ mile)

## Danny

*Hassocks, near Burgess Hill*

£

Elizabethan house built *c.* 1593 by George Goring, a wing being added in 1728 by Henry Campion. Family portraits and historical associations.

- Between Hurstpierpoint and Hassocks on B2116
- May to Sept, Wed and Thur 2–5
- Firle Place, Glynde Place, Parham
- Hassocks (½ mile)

## Goodwood House

*Goodwood, near Chichester*

£

Originally a hunting-box of 1st Duke of Richmond, reconstructed about 1800 by James Wyatt, the stables by Chambers. Paintings by Canaletto, Stubbs, Van Dyck; fine furniture and porcelain. Specimen trees in grounds.

- Chichester 527107
- 3½ miles NE of Chichester, 1½ miles W of A285 at Halnake
- Easter Sun and Mon, then early May to mid-Oct, Sun and Mon (except some special days), also Tues, Wed and Thur in Aug 2–5
- Arundel Castle, Parham, Petworth House
- Chichester (5½ miles)

## Newtimber Place

*Newtimber, near Burgess Hill*

£

Moated and dating from 17th/18th Cs. Wall paintings in Etruscan style.

- Hurstpierpoint 833104
- 7 miles N of Brighton off A23
- May to Aug, Thur 2–5
- Arundel Castle, Danny
- Hassocks (1½ miles)

## Parham

*Cootham, near Pulborough*

£

'E' shaped house built by Sir Thomas Palmer *c.* 1577. Hall and

ARUNDEL CASTLE

gallery have survived and there is noteworthy collection of Elizabethan, Jacobean and Georgian portraits, also good examples of early needlework.

Storrington 2021

4 miles S of Pulborough off A283

Easter Sun to early Oct, Sun, Wed, Thur and Bank Hol. Mon 2–5.30

Arundel Castle, Goodwood House

Pulborough (4 miles)

## Petworth House

*Petworth, near Pulborough*

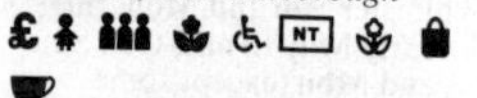

Rebuilt towards end of 17th C by 6th Duke of Somerset, later altered by Salvin. Apart from examples of work of Grinling Gibbons this is very much house for those wishing to study and enjoy paintings. One of largest and finest collections in country, works by such as: David Teniers, Lely, Mytens, Snyders, West, Hobbema, Cuyp, Claude, Brill, Millet, Van Dyck, Reynolds, Kneller, Dahl, Titian, Gaspard Poussin, Van der Weyden, Eworth, Opie, Blake, Turner, Gainsborough, Fuseli and Wilkie. Park and pleasure grounds are by 'Capability' Brown. Deer park.

Petworth 42207

In Petworth 5 miles NW of Pulborough on A283

Apr to end Oct daily except Mon and Fri (but open Bank Hol. Mon and closed Tues following) 2–6

Goodwood House, Parham, Uppark

Pulborough (4 miles)

Not Sun

## St Mary's

*Bramber, near Shoreham-by-Sea*

Good example of 15th-C timber-framed house with unusual panelling. Apart from good furnishings, rare books and bygones, it houses one of largest collections of butterflies in world. Dioramas and artificial jungle.

Steyning 813158

4 miles N of Shoreham on A283

All year daily (except Dec 25–26) 10–5

Arundel Castle, Danny, Parham

Shoreham-by-Sea (4 miles)

## Standen

*Turner's Hill, near East Grinstead*

Built in 1894 to designs by Philip Webb, it is only one of his major house projects to have stayed untouched. Textiles and wallpapers by William Morris. Hillside garden and views across Medway.

East Grinstead 23029

$1\frac{1}{2}$ miles SW of East Grinstead off B2028

Apr to end Oct, Wed, Thur and Sat 2–5.30

Chiddingstone Castle, Penshurst Place

East Grinstead (2 miles)

Not Sun

## Uppark

*South Harting, near Petersfield*

Dates from *c.* 1690. Mid-18th-C furnishings, with original wallpapers and curtains. Queen Anne dolls' house, Victorian kitchen. Garden landscape by Humphry Repton.

Harting 317

5 miles SE of Petersfield off B2146

Apr to end Sept, Wed, Thur, Sun and Bank Hol. Mon 2–6

Goodwood House, Petworth House

Petersfield (6 miles)

($1\frac{1}{4}$ miles). Not Sun

## Bolling Hall

*Bowling Hall Road, Bradford*

Of interest architecturally: evolution of house from 15th to late 18th C.

- Bradford 23057
- All year daily except Mon (but open Bank Hol. Mon) 10–5. Closed Good Fri and Dec 25–26
- Brontë Parsonage, Redhouse
- Bradford

## Bramham Park

*Bramham, near Leeds*

Queen Anne house built for Robert Benson, 1st Lord Bingley, possibly designed by Thomas Archer. Collections of noteworthy paintings, porcelain and furniture. Grounds treated in the manner of Le Nôtre.

- Boston Spa 844265
- 9 miles NE of Leeds at junction of A1 and A64
- Easter weekend (Good Fri to Tues), then Tues, Wed, Thur, Sun and Bank Hol. Mon till end Sept, 1.15–5.30. Closed during Horse Trials
- Harewood House, Temple Newsam
- Garforth (5½ miles)

## Brontë Parsonage

*Haworth, near Keighley*

House is preserved as nearly as possible to state it was in when the sisters wrote their novels and poems. Manuscripts, dresses, furniture and relics of the family.

- Haworth 42323
- 4 miles SW of Keighley off A6033
- All year weekdays 11–5.30 (Oct to Mar 11–4.30), Sun 2–5.30 (Oct to Mar 2–4.30). Closed last 3 weeks in Dec
- Bolling Hall, East Riddlesden Hall
- Keighley (3 miles)

## East Riddlesden Hall

*Bradford Road, Keighley*

17th-C manor house with strange wheel windows, typical of certain West Riding manors. Associated with house were Murgatroyds of Riddlesden, who in their time were profane and wild living, collecting fines, imprisonment and excommunication. Good plasterwork, panelling, pewter, pictures and furniture. Outside a fine example of a tithe barn and a fishpond.

- Keighley 607075
- 1 mile NE of Keighley off A650
- Apr to Oct, Wed to Sun, Bank Hol. Mon and following Tues 2–6; June, July, Aug, 10.30–6. Closed Good Fri
- Bolling Hall, Brontë Parsonage
- Keighley (2 miles)

## Harewood House

*Harewood, near Leeds*

Exterior of house begun in 1759 was designed by John Carr of York; interior completed later by Robert Adam, with 19th-C

BRONTË PARSONAGE

alterations by Sir Charles Barry. Outstanding Chippendale furniture, also paintings and Chinese and Sèvres porcelain. Park by 'Capability' Brown and there is now a 4-acre bird garden with species from all over world.

Harewood 886225

7 miles s of Harrogate off A61

Apr to end Oct daily; Nov, Feb and Mar, Sun, Tues, Wed and Thur, from 10

Bramham Park, Lotherton Hall

Horsforth (6 miles)

(1 mile)

## Lotherton Hall

*Aberford, near Leeds*

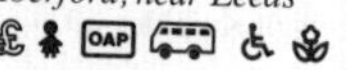

Edwardian house erected round earlier building from mid-18th C. Gascoigne collection of quality antiques. Costume gallery.

Leeds 645535

1 mile E of A1 at Aberford, 10 miles E of Leeds

All year Tues to Sun 10.30–6.15; Thur from May to Sept, 10.30–8.30. Open Bank Hol. Mon

Bramham Park, Temple Newsam

Micklefield (3½ miles)

## Manor House

*Castle Yard, Ilkley*

Built on site of Roman Fort with some Roman walls visible in grounds. Roman relics.

Ilkley 600066

All year daily except Mon (but open Bank Hol. Mon) 10–5. Closed Good Fri and Dec 25–26

Broughton Hall, East Riddlesden Hall

Ilkley

## Nostell Priory

*Nostell, near Wakefield*

On original site of a priory, in 1733 James Paine began work of erecting this Palladian house; Robert Adam added a wing in 1766. Plasterwork by Rose and panels by Zucchi; fine furniture, particularly Chippendale. Motor cycle and aviation museums.

Wakefield 863892

6 miles SE of Wakefield off A638

Apr, May and Oct, Thur, Sat and Sun 2–6; June to end Sept daily except Fri 2–6; open Bank Hol. Sun, Mon and following Tues 11–6

Oakwell Hall, Shibden Hall

Wakefield (6 miles)

## Oakwell Hall

*Birstall, near Batley*

Elizabethan moated manor house built *c.* 1583, with Civil War and Brontë connections. It was 'Fieldhead' of Charlotte's novel *Shirley*.

Batley 474926

From Birstall near M62 exit 27

Apr to Oct, Tues to Sat 10–6, Sun 1–5; Nov to Mar, Tues to Sat 10–5

Redhouse, Shibden Hall

Batley (2 miles)

## Redhouse

*Gomersal, near Bradford*

Built *c.* 1660 of red brick, thus its name. Associations with Charlotte Brontë who used it in her novel *Shirley* under name of 'Briarmains'.

Cleckheaton 872165

3½ miles SE of Bradford

Apr to Oct, Tues to Sat 10–6, Sun 1–5; Nov to Mar, Tues to Sat 10–5

Oakwell Hall, Temple Newsam

Batley (3½ miles)

## Shibden Hall

*Hipperholme, near Halifax*

Early 15th-C half-timbered house, altered in 19th C. Now a folk museum. Large park and terrace gardens.

Halifax 52246

1 mile E of Halifax near junction of A58 and A6036

Apr to Sept, weekdays 11–7, Sun 2–5; Oct, Nov and Mar, weekdays 11–5, Sun 2–5; Feb, Sun only, 2–5

Redhouse, Oakwell Hall

Halifax (1½ miles)

### Temple Newsam

*Colton, near Leeds*

Once a preceptory of Knights Templar of Jerusalem, altered by Sir Thomas D'Arcy and later largely rebuilt by Sir Arthur Ingram. During reign of Queen Elizabeth I was centre of Anglo/Scottish intrigue. Birthplace of Lord Darnley. Outstanding displays of furniture, pictures, ceramics and silver.

Leeds 647321

4 miles E of Leeds, just S of A63

All year daily except Mon (but open Bank Hol. Mon) 10.30–6.15; Wed from May to Sept, 10.30–8.30. Closed Dec 25–26

Lotherton Hall, Redhouse

Garforth (2½ miles)

## WILTSHIRE

### Avebury Manor

*Avebury, near Marlborough*

Charming Elizabethan manor house with pleasant gardens and dovecote standing just outside the greatest Megalithic circle in Europe. Good plasterwork, panelling and furniture. Herb border and topiary. Model railway in landscaped garden.

Avebury 203

7 miles W of Marlborough on A361

May and Sept, Sat and Sun 2–5; June to Aug daily 2–5, also Easter weekend (Fri to Mon) and Bank Hol. Mon 10–6

Littlecote, Lydiard Mansion

Swindon (12 miles)

### Bowood

*Calne, near Chippenham*

Original house was bought unfinished by 1st Earl of Shelburne in 1754; he and his successors employed some of greatest designers to work there: Keene, Adam, Dance, Cockerell, Smirke and Barry. The Big House was pulled down in 1955, leaving the present building as fine example of 18th-C architecture. Rooms open include the 'laboratory' where Dr Joseph Priestley discovered oxygen in 1774, picture and sculpture gallery. Park by 'Capability' Brown extends over 100 acres with such delights as: the Hermit's Cave, a Doric Temple, and a Rococo Cascade. Adventure playground.

Calne 812102

2½ miles W of Calne off A4

Good Fri to end Sept, Tues to Sat 2–6; Sun and Bank Hol. Mon 12–6

Claverton Manor, Great Chalfield Manor, Lydiard Mansion

Chippenham (4½ miles)

### Chalcot House

*Westbury, near Warminster*

Small Palladian manor.

2 miles W of Westbury off A3098

Aug daily 2–5

Badminton House, Lydiard Mansion

Westbury (2½ miles)

## Corsham Court

*Corsham, near Chippenham*

Elizabethan manor with additions by 'Capability' Brown, Nash and Repton. Fine Georgian State rooms and an outstanding collection of Old Masters and furniture.

Corsham 712214

$4\frac{1}{2}$ miles SW of Chippenham, off A4 at Corsham

All year (except mid-Dec to mid-Jan), Tues, Wed, Thur, Sat, Sun and Bank Hol. Mon 2–4 (June to Sept 2–6)

Bowood, Lacock Abbey

Chippenham ($4\frac{1}{2}$ miles)

## Great Chalfield Manor

*Great Chalfield, near Melksham*

NT

Built *c.* 1480, example of moated house of architectural interest. Great hall and screen. Carefully restored in early 20th C.

$2\frac{1}{2}$ miles NE of Bradford-on-Avon, $1\frac{3}{4}$ miles E of B3109 at Bradford Leigh

Mid-Apr to 3rd week in Sept, Wed 12–1, 2–5

Claverton Manor, Westwood Manor

Bradford-on-Avon (4 miles)

($1\frac{1}{2}$ miles)

GREAT CHALFIELD MANOR

## Lacock Abbey

*Lacock, near Chippenham*

NT

Augustinian convent consecrated in 1232. After Dissolution in 1539 it was converted into private residence by Sir William Sharington. Some of the Tudor Renaissance work can still be seen including octagonal tower and stables. 18th-C 'Gothick' entrance hall by Sanderson Miller. It was here in 1835 that Fox-Talbot made the first photographic negative. Museum to his work is in village. Fine trees in grounds.

3 miles S of Chippenham, off A350

Apr, May and Oct, Wed to Sun 2–6 (closed Good Fri); June to end Sept daily 2–6. Open Bank Hol. Mon 2–6

Corsham Court, Great Chalfield Manor

Chippenham (3 miles)

## Littlecote

*Hungerford, near Marlborough*

Tudor manor built *c.* 1490–1520. Has unique Cromwellian armoury, antique furniture, ceramics and carpets. Also famous haunted bedroom, Cromwellian chapel and long gallery. 6-acre walled garden with trout stream.

Hungerford 2170

$2\frac{1}{2}$ miles W of Hungerford off A419

Apr to June, Sat, Sun and Bank Hol. Mon 2–6; July to Sept, Mon to Fri 2–5, Sat, Sun and Bank Hol. Mon 2–6

Avebury Manor, Lydiard Mansion

Hungerford ($2\frac{1}{2}$ miles)

(1 mile)

## Longleat House

*Near Warminster*

OAP

This important Elizabethan house was built in Renaissance style between 1566 and 1580. In early 19th C modernization was carried out by Wyatville. Some rooms redecorated in Italian style by 4th Marquess of Bath in 1860. Contents include fine furniture, paintings and objets d'art. Victorian kitchens open during summer. Wall hanging by Amanda Richardson and the Royal School of Needlework. New display of rare books. Park by 'Capability' Brown. Separate admission charge to safari park with famous lions.

- ☎ Maiden Bradley 551 and 328
- ➔ 4 miles SW of Warminster via A362
- ⏱ Daily all year (except Dec 25) 10–6; Oct to Easter 10–4
- Philipps House, Stourhead
- Frome ($4\frac{1}{2}$ miles)
- ($2\frac{1}{2}$ miles)

## Luckington Court

*Luckington, near Chipping Sodbury*

£

Interesting group of old buildings, mainly Queen Anne. Delightful formal garden with ornamental trees and flowering shrubs.

- ☎ Sherston 205
- ➔ 6 miles SW of Malmesbury off B4040
- ⏱ All year, Wed 2–6 outside only; inside view by prior appointment
- Badminton House, Little Sodbury Manor

## Ludgershall Castle

*Ludgershall, near Andover*

£ DoE

Norman castle with extensive earthworks and complex but ruined series of buildings.

- ➔ N side of Ludgershall on A342, 7 miles NW of Andover
- ⏱ Any reasonable time (DES)
- Lydiard Mansion, Uffington Castle
- Andover (7 miles)

## Lydiard Mansion

*Purton, near Swindon*

£ OAP

House has medieval core and was reconstructed *c.* 1745 by 2nd Viscount St John, possibly to designs of Roger Morris. Fine mid-Georgian decoration.

- ☎ Purton 770401
- ➔ 5 miles W of Swindon just N of M4 exit 16
- ⏱ All year daily (except Dec 25–26) 10–1, 2–5.30, Sun 2–5.30
- Ashdown House, Ludgershall Castle
- Swindon ($5\frac{1}{2}$ miles)

## Mompesson House

*53 The Close, Salisbury*

£ NT

Dignified early 18th-C house in Salisbury Cathedral Close, built in style of Wren. Refurnished in 1977 as town house of an English gentleman of 18th C. Notable collection of drinking glasses.

- ⏱ Apr to end Oct daily except Thur and Fri 12.30–6
- Wardour Castle, Wilton House
- Salisbury ($\frac{1}{2}$ mile)

## Newhouse

*Redlynch, near Salisbury*

£

Centre part dates from *c.* 1619, 2 Georgian wings being added in 1742 and 1760. One of rare houses to be built in shape of 'Y', probably to design of John Thorpe. Nelson relics.

- ☎ Downton 20055
- ➔ 9 miles SE of Salisbury just off B3080
- ⏱ Easter Mon then early May to early Sept, Sun and Bank Hol. Mon 2–6
- Mompesson House, Mottisfont Abbey, Wilton House
- Salisbury (9 miles)

## Philipps House

*Dinton, near Salisbury*

£ NT

Neo-Grecian house by Jeffry Wyatville completed in 1816. Let to YWCA as conference centre.

- ➔ 9 miles W of Salisbury off B3089

Apr to Sept, Wed 2.15–5.30
Pyt House, Wilton House
Tisbury (4 miles)

## Pyt House

*Tisbury, near Shaftesbury*

Georgian mansion in Palladian style.

Tisbury 870210
4½ miles N of Shaftesbury, 2½ miles SE of A350 at East Knoyle
May to Sept, Wed and Thur 2–5
Stourhead, Wardour Castle, Wilton House
Tisbury (2½ miles)

## Sheldon Manor

*Near Chippenham*

Plantagenet manor with porch added in 13th C, also detached chapel erected in 15th C. Delightful garden with old-fashioned roses and terraces.

Chippenham 3120
2 miles W of Chippenham between A4 and A420
Early Apr to late Sept, Thur, Sun and Bank Hol. Mon 2–6
Bowood, Lacock Abbey
Chippenham (2 miles)
Not Sun

## Stourhead

*Stourton, near Frome*

NT

Palladian house begun in 1722 by Colen Campbell; contents include fine paintings, also furniture by the younger Chippendale. Famous landscaped gardens laid out between 1741 and 1772 with rare trees and plants, a large lake and numerous buildings such as: Bristol Cross, Temple of Flora, Paradise Well, Temple of the Sun, Pantheon and Rustic Cottage.

Bourton 348
9½ miles S of Frome on B3092 at Stourton
Apr, Sept and Oct, Mon, Wed, Sat and Sun; May to Aug daily (except Fri) 2–6
Longleat, Pyt House, Wardour Castle
Gillingham (5 miles)

## Wardour Castle

*Tisbury, near Shaftesbury*

Outstanding Palladian style house designed by James Paine in 1768. Fine rooms and staircase with 2 semi-circular flights.

Tisbury 464
5 miles NE of Shaftesbury, from A30 at Milkwell
Mid-July to early Sept, Mon, Wed, Fri and Sat 2.30–6
Longleat, Pyt House, Stourhead, Wilton House
Tisbury (2 miles)

## Westwood Manor

*Near Bradford-on-Avon*

NT

15th-C stone manor house altered in late 16th C. Late Gothic and Jacobean windows, also good plasterwork. Topiary in garden.

1½ miles SW of Bradford-on-Avon off B3109
Apr to end Sept, Wed 2.30–6
Claverton Manor, Great Chalfield Manor
Bradford-on-Avon (2 miles)

## Wilton House

*Wilton, near Salisbury*

Early parts by Inigo Jones *c.* 1650, later additions by James Wyatt in 1810. Famous collection of paintings, Kent and Chippendale furniture, also illustrious sundries including lock of Elizabeth I's hair and Napoleon's despatch case. Display of model soldiers, set in Diorama scenes. 20 acres of lawns with great Cedars of Lebanon. Palladian bridge.

Wilton 3115
On A30 2½ miles W of Salisbury
Apr to early Oct, Tues to Sat and Bank Hol. Mon 11–6, Sun 2–6
Pyt House, Wardour Castle
Salisbury (2½ miles)

# IRELAND

## CO ANTRIM (NI)

### Ballygally Castle

*Carncastle, near Larne*

Unique example of 17th-C plantation castle. Built by James Shaw in 1625. Note pepperpot bartizans and curvilinear dormer-gables. In 1814 was residence of the Rev Thomas Alexander. Today a hotel.

➔ Near Larne

⏱ Normal hours by permission

▦ Belfast Castle, Dunluce Castle, Templetown Mausoleum

### Belfast Castle

*In Belfast*

Original castle built at beginning of 17th C by the Lord Deputy, Sir Arthur Chichester, its gardens and orchards reaching down to River Lagan. In 1708 destroyed by fire 'caused through carelessness of a female servant'. It was not rebuilt and ruins were demolished. In the 1860s 3rd Marquess of Donegal built a Scottish baronial style castle, with a tower not unlike Balmoral, on opposite side of the city. This was also named Belfast Castle and is now owned by City of Belfast.

➔ Cave Hill, Belfast

⏱ Enquiries should be made at Castle

▦ Ballygally Castle, Carrickfergus Castle, Dunluce Castle, Templetown Mausoleum

### Carrickfergus Castle

*Carrickfergus, near Newtownabbey*

£

Key to Anglo-Norman hold on Ulster. Started by John de Courcy between 1180 and 1204. Curtain walls follow natural lines of basalt rock peninsula. Fine keep, still strong enough to be air-raid shelter in last war. Two cannons surviving from the 16th C, and 6 from 1811, these being made in the cannon foundry, Edinburgh.

⏱ Daily all year except public hols. Enquire at castle for opening times

▦ Belfast Castle, Dunluce Castle, Templetown Mausoleum

### Dunluce Castle

*Near Portrush*

£

Earliest parts date from 14th C: 2 E towers and S wall. In 16th C in hands of the MacQuillans, a 'brave, hospitable and improvident' family. Castle was virtually impregnable before arrival of efficient artillery. The English Lord Deputy, by repute a son of Henry VIII, sadly savaged it with 'a culverin and two shakers of brass'. Today it stands a romantic ruin on the cliff tops.

➔ 3 miles E of Portrush

⏱ Daily all year except public hols. Enquire at castle for opening times

▦ Ballygally Castle, Belfast Castle, Carrickfergus Castle, Templetown Mausoleum

### Templetown Mausoleum

*Templepatrick, near Ballyclare*

£ NT

Built in 1783 to design of Robert Adam. Memorial to Hon Arthur Upton.

☎ Saintfield 510721 (NT Regional Office)

➔ Castle Upton graveyard, Templepatrick

⏱ All year daily at any time

▦ Ballygally Castle, Belfast Castle, Dunluce Castle

# CO ARMAGH (NI)

## Ardress House

*Charlemont, near Portadown*

17th-C farmhouse with main front and garden façades added in 18th C by owner-architect George Ensor. Good plasterwork in drawing room by Michael Stapleton of Dublin after Robert Adam. Display of farm implements. Woodland walks.

Saintfield 510721 (NT Regional Office)

7 miles W of Portadown

Apr to end Sept daily (except Fri, but open Good Fri) 2–6

Benburb Castle, Derrymore House, Kirkistown Castle

## Derrymore House

*Bessbrooke, near Newry*

Simple thatched single-storeyed manor house built *c.* 1787 by Isaac Corry, last Chancellor of Irish Exchequer. Act of Union is said to have been drafted in drawing room.

Saintfield 510721 (NT Regional Office)

$1\frac{1}{2}$ miles NW of Newry

By appointment with National Trust, Rowallane, Saintfield, Ballynahinch, Co Down

Ardress House, Kirkistown Castle

# CO CARLOW (EIRE)

## Ballymoon Castle

*Ballymoon, near Carlow*

This castle without a keep is of a unique, almost square plan. Has 2 square towers facing each other across quadrangle and dates from early part of 14th C, a period from which there are few surviving buildings in Ireland.

On L33 to E of Muine Bheag

At any reasonable time

Castletown, Johnstown Castle, Nenagh Castle

# CO CLARE (EIRE)

## Bunratty Castle

*In Bunratty*

One of the finest 15th-C castles in Ireland, it stands on side of small tidal creek of Shannon estuary. An ancient stronghold of the O'Briens of Thomond. Crenellations are modern, the whole castle and particularly the interior being restored in period 1956–60. Today filled with Lord Gort's furniture, tapestries, and works of art. In the grounds are re-erected farmhouses, displays of Irish life.

From Limerick-Ennis road

All year daily, 9.30–5

Knappogue Castle, Lemanagh Castle, Urlanmore Castle

## Knappogue Castle

*Near Quin*

Built in 1467 by John Maccon MacNamara, Lord of Clancullen and High Chieftain of the DalgCais. Elaborate edifice of late Georgian and Regency periods added to original Norman structure in mid-19th C. In 1922 was used as Army HQ under General Michael Brennan.

Recently much restoration work carried out not only inside, but also to stables and workshops.

- Apr to end Oct, 10–5
- Bunratty Castle, Lemanagh Castle, Urlanmore Castle

### Lemanagh Castle

*Near Lisdoonvarna*

£

Fine sturdy old castle of the O'Briens. Consists of tower built about 1480, joined to a 4-storeyed gabled house of 17th C. Has rather blood-stained history; battered by Cromwell's soldiers.

- From L53 between Corofin and Kilfenora
- All year at any reasonable time
- Bunratty Castle, Dunguaire Castle, Knappogue Castle

### Urlanmore Castle

*Near Newmarket-on-Fergus*

13th-C stronghold of the McMahons. Has 3-storeyed tower, in an upper room of which there are still some outlines of paintings.

- SW of Newmarket-on-Fergus
- All year at any reasonable time
- Bunratty Castle, Knappogue Castle, Lemanagh Castle

## CO CORK (EIRE)

### Ballincollig Castle

*Near Cork*

Massive keep of this 14th-C building stands on lofty outcrop. Formerly the seat of the Barretts.

- W of Cork
- All year at any reasonable time
- Bantry House, Blarney Castle, Riverstown House

### Ballynacarriga Castle

*Near Dunmanway*

Built in 1585. In thickness of walls is spiral staircase leading to battlements, and in stonework of windows are some curiously carved stones representing Jesus on the Cross between 2 thieves.

- On an unclassified road off T65 SE of Dunmanway
- All year at any reasonable time
- Ballincollig Castle, Blarney Castle, Riverstown House

### Bantry House

*In Bantry*

Original house dates from *c.* 1740, with wing added *c.* 1770. Greatly enlarged and remodelled in 1845 by Richard White, Viscount Berehaven, later 2nd Earl of Bantry. Building is beautifully situated overlooking bay and has some fine rooms, notably the library, drawing room and hall. There is much to admire: Flemish tapestries, Venetian glass, Spanish leather, Dutch marquetry, Russian icons, needlework, Chippendale, Sheraton and Derby and Chelsea wares. Gardens.

- Bantry 47
- Mid-Feb to mid-Dec daily 10–6 (open until 8 in summer)
- Ballincollig Castle, Blarney Castle, Riverstown House

### Barry's Court Castle

*Near Cork*

Early fortification with quadrangular keep with square towers surrounded by a bawn. Stands near inner reaches of Cork harbour in a position that would once have given it considerable command over area.

- All year at any reasonable time
- Blarney Castle, Mallow Castle, Riverstown House

## Blarney Castle

*Blarney, near Cork*

£ ♣ 🔒

Present building is third to be erected on site. The earliest, *c.* 10th C, was of wood: this was followed by a stone structure later demolished. On the foundations, Dermot MacCarthy, King of Munster, built third castle in 1446. The keep remains, standing 37 m high. On N side are dungeons and escape tunnel which had outlet near Blarney Lake. It was down this that a garrison escaped during siege by Cromwell's men. Up by battlements is famous 'Blarney Stone'. One legend says that this was once known as Jacob's Pillow, being brought to Ireland by returning crusaders. To those who kiss it, the stone is said to give the gift of oratory.

➔ 5 miles to W of Cork

⏱ All year daily, summer 9–8, winter 9 to dusk

🏰 Ballincollig Castle, Barry's Court Castle

## Liscarrol Castle

*Near Cork*

£

Early Anglo-Norman building dating from 13th C; possibly foundation of the de Barrys. Massive keep flanked by 2 square and 4 round towers.

⏱ All year at any reasonable time

🏰 Ballincollig Castle, Blarney Castle, Mallow Castle

## Mallow Castle

*In Mallow*

£

Originally fortified house of Sir Thomas Norreys, dates from 1590. Stands in park surrounding present house. Ruins are impressive with 3 towers on W side and one central tower on E. Castle was burnt in 1689 by order of James II.

⏱ By appointment

🏰 Ballincollig Castle, Blarney Castle, Liscarrol Castle

## Riverstown House

*Near Cork*

£ ♣

Building started *c.* 1602, and formerly seat of Dr Jemmett Browne, Bishop of Cork, who rebuilt it in 1745, adding fine plasterwork by the Francini Brothers.

➔ About 4 miles outside Cork on Dublin road

⏱ May to Sept, Thur to Sun 2–6

🏰 Barry's Court Castle, Blarney Castle, Mallow Castle

# CO DONEGAL (EIRE)

## Buncrana Castle

*In Buncrana*

£

Massive keep of old castle of the O'Doherty's was built in 1430 and stands to N of town. The more modern castle was built in early part of 18th C by Sir John Vaughan. In 1798 Wolfe Tone was brought here from the French ship *Hoche*.

⏱ At any reasonable time

🏰 Boom Hall, Donegal Castle, Mussenden Temple

## Donegal Castle

*In Donegal*

£

Dates from *c.* 1474 and was seat of the O'Donnells. The tall tower and 2 turrets incorporated by Sir Basil Brooke into the gabled Jacobean house he built in 1623. Noteworthy carving in chimneypiece with arms of Brooke impaling Leicester of Toft.

⏱ Enquire at castle

🏰 Buncrana Castle, Lissadell House

## CO DOWN (NI)

### Castle Ward
*Strangford, near Downpatrick*

Built by 1st Lord Bangor in 1765. He wanted a strictly Classical house, thus SW front and rooms were in Palladian style. Lady Bangor wanted Strawberry Hill Gothic, so this appeared on NE front. Good plasterwork and fan vaulting. The grounds landscaped in 18th C have recently been redesigned by Mr Lanning Roper; interesting collection of wildfowl on the Temple Water. Victorian laundry and summerhouse. Grounds run down to Strangford Lough.

Strangford 204

7 miles NE of Downpatrick

Apr to end Sept daily (except Fri, but open Good Fri) 2–6

Dundrum Castle, Kirkistown Castle, Mount Stewart

### Dundrum Castle
*Dundrum, near Downpatrick*

£

May originally have been site of early Christian fort. First reference to castle is 1205; it was captured in 1210. Slighted by Cromwell in 1652. Since 1954 is in State care and being restored. Keep is circular which is unusual for Ireland.

Daily all year except public hols. Enquire at castle

Castle Ward, Kirkistown Castle, Mount Stewart

### Kirkistown Castle
*Near Kircubbin*

£

Erected by member of Savage family in early part of 17th C. Massive keep within square bawn, southern wall of which is flanked by circular tower at each corner.

Close to Cloghy

Enquire at castle

Castle Ward, Dundrum Castle, Mount Stewart

### Mount Stewart
*Clay Gate, near Newtownards*

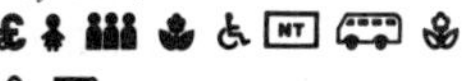

Bought in 1744 by Alexander Stewart, grandfather of famous Lord Castlereagh. Some 80 acres of formal and informal gardens designed by Edith 7th Marchioness of Londonderry. Many rare plants and shrubs. Temple of the Winds modelled on that at Athens and built here in 1783.

Greyabbey 387

On E shore of Strangford Lough, 5 miles SE of Newtownards

Apr to end Sept daily (except Fri, but open Good Fri) 2–6

Castle Ward, Dundrum Castle, Kirkistown Castle

## CO DUBLIN (EIRE)

### Dublin Castle
*In Dublin*

Built at beginning of 13th C. The Record, or Wardrobe, Tower remains with a machicolated parapet of 1813. Red-brick buildings of Upper Castle Yard and Bedford Tower (heraldic museum) contain State apartments, including the Throne Room and St Patrick's Hall. Fine paintings.

Centre of Dublin

All year daily except public hols: Mon to Fri 10–12.15, 2–5; Sat and Sun 2–5

James Joyce's Tower, Malahide Castle

### James Joyce's Tower

*Sandycove, near Dublin*

£

Martello tower at Sandycove is one of series of such towers on coast of Ireland, built as late 18th-C defence system against possible forays by Napoleon. This one was once temporary home of James Joyce. Now a Joyce museum showing memorabilia.

→ On sea front at Sandycove

May to Sept daily 10–1, 2.30–5.15, Sun 2.30–6

Dublin Castle, Malahide Castle

### Malahide Castle

*Malahide, near Dublin*

One of Ireland's oldest and most historic buildings. Estate founded in 12th C by Richard Talbot and the family was in occupation until 1976. Castle houses fine examples of Irish period furniture, a unique display of Irish historical portraits and many other works of art.

→ NE of Dublin

All year except public hols Mon to Fri 10–5, Sat and Sun 2–5

Dublin Castle, James Joyce's Tower

## CO FERMANAGH (NI)

### Castle Caldwell

*Belleek, near Lower Lough Erne*

£

18th-C 2-storeyed house over basement on shores of Lough Erne. In Georgian Gothic manner, façade had pointed and quatrefoil windows. Also little projecting turrets and battlemented pediment-gable at either end. Octagonal temple near water's edge. This romantic house passed to the Bloomfields through the marriage of Francis, daughter of Sir John Caldwell, Bart, to John Bloomfield. Sadly, house began to decline by the end of 19th C, but is still an impressive ruin. Recently Forestry Division has encouraged preservation and planting of parkland hardwoods.

Enquire locally

Castle Coole, Florence Court

### Castle Coole

*Near Enniskillen*

£ NT

Outstanding late Georgian house by James Wyatt who adapted earlier designs by Richard Johnston. Also demonstrates that Wyatt was influenced by Stuart and Revett's *Antiquities of Athens*, as at Castle Coole he produced a near perfect example of late 18th-C Hellenism. Plasterwork by Joseph Rose. Portland stone used came by sea to Ballyshannon and thence by bullock cart. When the joiners had finished on the house they made large part of the furniture, most of which remains in its original position in house. Flock of greylag geese nests on shores of Lough Coole.

Saintfield 510721 (NT Regional Office)

→ 1½ miles SE of Enniskillen

Apr to end Sept daily (except Fri, but open Good Fri) 2–6

Castle Caldwell, Florence Court

### Florence Court

*Near Enniskillen*

£ NT

Fine 18th-C house built by John Cole, and named after his wife, Florence. Probably completed by 1764. Outstanding plasterwork in manner of Robert West; its perfection may be noted in the Venetian Room where in high relief are eagles and other birds of prey with swirls of foliage.

☎ Saintfield 510721 (NT Regional Office)

➔ 8 miles sw of Enniskillen

Apr to end Sept daily (except Fri, but open Good Fri) 2–6

Castle Caldwell, Castle Coole

## CO GALWAY (EIRE)

### Athenry Castle

*Athenry, near Galway*

£

Built *c.* 1238–40 by Meiler de Bermingham, has 3-storey tower surrounded by remains of strong outer wall. Gables are later, probably 17th-C addition. Good early Gothic doorway with elaborate capitals.

➔ From town

Enquire on site

Dunguaire Castle

### Dunguaire Castle

*Near Kinvara*

£

16th-C building on shores of Galway Bay. Site was 7th-C stronghold of Kings of Connacht.

May to end Sept daily 9.30–5.30

Athenry Castle, Lough Cutra Castle

### Lough Cutra Castle

*Near Gort*

£

Bold castle that stares down on to a lough. Designed by John Nash; he was asked by his client, 2nd Viscount Gort, to make it like Nash's own house at Cowes, Isle of Wight. To watch over work, Nash sent to site 2 of his pupils James and George Richard Pain, who afterwards settled in Ireland and built up an extensive practice.

Sporadically open, enquire locally

Athenry Castle, Dunguaire Castle

### Portumna Castle

*Portumna, near Lough Derg*

£

At one time among most sophisticated houses of fortified Jacobean style in Ireland. Ruins of this once noble building hold themselves as a jagged backcloth against the soft Galway light. Demesne is now a Government Forestry centre. Those who have held Portumna include 1st owner 2nd Earl of Clanricarde and later 6th Earl of Harewood.

Enquire locally

Dunguaire Castle, Lough Cutra Castle

### Thoor Ballylee

*Near Gort*

£

16th-C tower house, summer home of W. B. Yeats. Inscription reads: 'I the poet William Yeats, With old mill boards and sea green slates And smithy work from the Gort forge, Restored this tower for my wife George'. On view are relics and mementoes of the poet.

Apr to end Oct daily 10–6 (July to Aug 10–9)

Dunguaire Castle, Lough Cutra Castle

THOOR BALLYLEE

## CO KERRY (EIRE)

### Muckross House

*Near Killarney*

£ ♣ ♣♣♣ ✿ 🔒 ☕

Gabled Victorian mansion built in 1843 by William Burn, standing wreathed in the misty magic of the Killarney Lakes. Porch added *c.* 1870 by William Atkins of Cork. Hall dominated by antlers of the great prehistoric Irish deer; glittering chandeliers; some Irish Chippendale; family portraits. In surrounding buildings much craft activity: pottery, weaving, blacksmithing, basket-making, candle-making. In 1932 the house and 11,000-acre estate were presented to nation for use as a national park, the largest in Ireland.

◷ Daily Easter to end June, Sept to end Oct 10–7; July and Aug 9–9; Nov to Easter, Tues to Sun 10–5

 Bantry House, Glin Castle, Ross Castle

### Ross Castle

*Near Killarney*

£

16th-C tower surrounded by bawn with rounded turrets. Built by one of the O'Donoghue Ross chieftains, and during Cromwellian wars was held by Royalists. Finally taken by Cromwellian assault from lake, Ludlow, the Puritan commander, having had a large boat carried overland. Fine views across lakes.

◷ At all reasonable hours

▦ Bantry House, Glin Castle, Muckross House

## CO KILDARE (EIRE)

### Belan House

*Near Ballitore*

£

Large 18th-C gable-ended house, built in 1743 for 1st Earl of Aldborough to the plans of Richard Castle working with Francis Bindon. House is ruined but a domed Doric rotunda and 2 obelisks survive in park.

◷ At any reasonable time. Enquire with local farmer

 Carton, Castletown, Kilkea Castle

### Carton

*Maynooth, near Dublin*

£ ♣ 🚌 ☕

This magnificent house, just 14 miles from Dublin, forms part of Manor of Maynooth, granted to Maurice Fitzgerald before his death in 1176. He had come to Ireland with Strongbow to fight in name of Henry II of England. In 1739 a start on the present building was made working from plans of German architect Richard Cassels. Attempts were made to persuade 'Capability' Brown to undertake landscaping, but despite offer of £1,000 on top of other costs, the genius refused, saying 'he had not finished England'. On banks of lake is Shell Cottage which displays an amazing feat of decoration with shells of all shapes and colours. In house a Telford organ, fine plasterwork, carved marble chimneypieces, and great elegance in handling of many of the rooms.

◷ Easter to end Sept, Sun and Bank Hol. Mon 2–6

▦ Belan House, Castletown

### Castletown

*Near Celbridge*

£ ♣ 🚌

Largest of great Irish Palladian houses, begun in 1722 by William Conolly, Speaker of Irish House of Commons, to plans of Alessandro Galilei, who designed façade of St John Lateran, Rome. Interior has some fine plasterwork, famous long gallery painted in Pompeian manner and hung with Venetian chandeliers, an 18th-C print room, and quality Irish furniture of period. Mile-long avenue of lime trees leading up to house. $1\frac{3}{4}$ miles to NW of house is Conolly's Folly, a large obelisk-crowned triumphal arch erected in 1740 by William Conolly's widow. Castletown is headquarters of the Irish Georgian Society.

Apr to end Sept daily (except Tues) 11–6, Sun 11–5

Belan House, Carton, Jigginstown House

Summer weekends

## Jigginstown House

*Near Naas*

One of largest mansions ever built in Ireland. Erected *c.* 1636 by Thomas Wentworth, later Earl of Strafford, when he was Lord Deputy of Ireland. Probably designed by John Allen, Wentworth intended it for his own use, but in view of grandiose treatment, he could have hoped that it would house Charles I who was proposing to visit Ireland. Now that much of the ivy has been cleared from remains, it is possible to gain an idea of the grandeur once there.

All year at any reasonable time

Belan House, Carton, Castletown

## Kilkea Castle

*Mageny, near Kildare*

Medieval castle of the FitzGeralds; particularly associated with the 11th Earl of Kildare, the 'Wizard Earl'. After a fire in 1849 was sympathetically restored by 3rd Duke of Leinster. Has been a hotel since 1960.

Kilkea 45156

At any reasonable time

Carton, Castletown

# CO KILKENNY (EIRE)

## Kilkenny Castle

*In Kilkenny*

Ancestral seat of the Ormonde Butlers, it rides high over town beside River Nore. First built in 1192 by Strongbow's son-in-law, Earl of Pembroke. By 1307 had more or less acquired form seen today, 4 massive round towers, of which 3 are still there; these were joined by curtain walls or ranges of buildings to enclose a courtyard. In 17th C 1st Duke of Ormonde made alterations. Later in 1826 William Robertson gave castle a thorough reconstruction, back to the medieval. Fine Classical gateway in W wall from 1684 has been retained. In old stables is the Kilkenny Design Workshop, an interesting experiment in design using traditional influences fluxed with modern thinking.

July to Sept daily 10–1, 2–6.30; Oct to June (not Mar) Tues to Sat 10.30–1, 2–5

Ballymoon Castle, Nenagh Castle, Rothe House

## Rothe House

*Near Kilkenny*

£

Elizabethan building erected by John Rothe in 1594. Ground floor is arcaded, 1st and 2nd floors have mullioned windows. Vaulted passage leads from street into courtyard. Well-preserved example of a typical well-to-do merchant's house in an Irish town of the period. Costumes, pewter, folkware, prehistoric weapons.

May to Sept, weekdays 10.30–12.30, 3–5; Oct to Apr, Tues, Fri and Sat 3–5

Ballymoon Castle, Kilkenny Castle, Nenagh Castle

# CO LAOIS (EIRE)

## Dunamase Castle

*Near Port Laoise*

Rock of Dunamase looms up conspicuously in a gap of West Leinster Hills. On its peak are impressive ruins of the large and complicated castle destroyed in 1650 by the Cromwellians. Originally site of early Christian fort, but with arrival of Normans, fell into hands of Strongbow. One of first mentions of castle comes in 1215 when King John ordered Geoffrey Luttrel to hand it over to William Marshall. Earthworks of outer defences may still be picked out, also gateway, with double turrets and curtain walling.

All year at any reasonable time

Birr Castle, Cloghan Castle, Lea Castle

## Lea Castle

*Near Monasterevin*

Remains of great Norman fortress built either by the Fitzgeralds or Marshalls in 12th or 13th C. Has a rough story: O'More burned it in 1346; O'Dempsey battled it away from the Earl of Kildare in 1422; 30 years later the Earl of Ormonde snatched it from them. The Confederates used it as a Mint before Cromwell's men took it and carried out usual slighting. Basic plan was square with three-quarter round towers at corners.

From Port Laoise, through farmyard and across a field, signposted

All year at any reasonable time

Birr Castle; Cloghan Castle, Dunamase Castle

# CO LIMERICK (EIRE)

## Adare Castle

*Near Limerick*

Near-square keep was surrounded by inner bailey, a gatehouse and a fosse. Castle has 2 great halls alongside river, larger dating from 13th C. Stronghold of the Fitzgeralds. Slighted by Cromwell.

SW from Limerick

Enquire locally

Askeaton Castle, Glenstal Castle, Glin Castle

## Ash Hill Towers

*Near Kilmallock*

Classical house, pedimented, built *c.* 1781, possibly to design of James and George Richard Pain. Back rebuilt *c.* 1833 in Gothic Revival style. Good plasterwork in the Wyatt manner.

By prior appointment

Adare Castle, Glin Castle, Muckross House

## Askeaton Castle

*In Askeaton*

Sited on small island in River Deel *c.* 1199, probably by William de Burgo. One of chief castles of the Fitzgeralds. Most interesting feature is 15th-C great hall with bold decorated windows. Slighted in 1652. Early 18th-C building near tower is reputed to have housed a 'Hell-Fire Club'.

Enquire locally; normally all year at any reasonable time

Adare Castle, Carrigogunell Castle, Glin Castle

## Ballygrennan Castle

*Near Kilmallock*

Was once a fine 15th-C 4-storeyed tower. 2nd floor is vaulted and there are some mullioned

ADARE CASTLE

windows. Originally held by Gerald, Earl of Kildare.

➔ 2 miles S of Lough Gur, along private avenue

By permission of the farmer

Adare Castle, Ash Hill Towers

## Carrigogunell Castle

*Near Limerick*

Massive stronghold of the O'Briens sited on high volcanic rock. The remains are a shattered keep, bawn and chapel. Well worth rugged climb up to this fierce place, as there is quite a superb view taking in Bunratty on N side of Shannon to Limerick city and beyond, the mountains to the E and S, and the S bank of river.

➔ Turn off Limerick-Askeaton road and struggle up a narrowing track for 2 miles

All year at any reasonable time

Askeaton Castle, Glin Castle

## Glenstall Castle

*Near Moroe*

Massive Norman-Revival castle by William Bardwell of London, begun in 1837. Medieval-style gatehouse is re-creation of that at Rockingham Castle, Northamptonshire, England. Elaborately carved stone Celtic-Romanesque doorway between 2 of the receptions copied from Killaloe Cathedral. Now a Benedictine Abbey and well-known boys' public school.

Enquiries to School Secretary

King John's Castle, Nenagh Castle

## Glin Castle

*In Glin*

Romantic white castellated house overlooking Shannon, built in 1780s by 24th Knight of Glin. Richly decorated with Neo-Classical plasterwork, hall ceiling possibly by Michael Stapleton. Unique double flying staircase and notable collection of mid-18th-C Irish furniture and family portraits.

Glin 34173

Contact Madam FitzGerald; an appointment is essential

Adare Castle, Askeaton Castle

By prior arrangement

## King John's Castle

*Near Limerick*

Building started by Normans *c.* 1200. 5-sided with one wall lapped by waters of Shannon. Fortified by 4 strong towers, one of which was replaced by a bastion in 1611. Has seen 3 surrenders: in 1641 to Confederate Catholics, in 1651 to General Ireton and in 1691 to Williamite forces.

Mon to Fri 2–5. Key from Office of Public Works in Mallow Street, Limerick

Adare Castle, Askeaton Castle, Glenstall Castle

# CO LONDONDERRY (NI)

## Boom Hall

*Near Derry*

Built *c.* 1770 for 1st Earl of Caledon, its name coming from boom which the English put across River Foyle to stop supply ships reaching Derry during the 105-day siege of 1689.

Only for reasons of special interest and after making appointment

Hezlett House, Mussenden Temple, Springhill

## Hezlett House

*Castlerock, near Coleraine*

Thatched cottage with unusual and important cruck-truss construction for roof.

Saintfield 510721 (NT Regional Office)

4 miles NW of Coleraine

Apr to end Sept daily (except Fri, but open Good Fri) 2–6

Boom Hall, Mussenden Temple, Springhill

## Mussenden Temple

*Castlerock, near Coleraine*

Built by Earl of Bristol, Bishop of Derry, in 1783, with Downhill Castle (now in ruins). A great eccentric, he arranged Saturday steeplechases for clergy of all denominations. A keen continental traveller, it is likely that many of the overseas 'Bristol' hotels took their name from him.

Saintfield 510721 (NT Regional Office)

1 mile W of Castlerock

Apr to end Sept daily (except Fri, but open Good Fri) 2–6

Boom Hall, Hezlett House, Springhill

## Springhill

*Moneymore, near Cookstown*

House dates from late 17th C and was built by 'Good Will' Conyngham who played leading part in defence of Derry during siege. Fine oak and yew staircase, good furniture and paintings. In dining room, added *c.* 1850 by William Lennox-Conyngham, there is chimneypiece of yellow marble brought back from Herculaneum by Earl of Bristol, Bishop of Derry, and given by him to the family. Costume museum and a cottar's kitchen.

Moneymore 210

1 mile from Moneymore

Apr to end Sept daily (except Fri, but open Good Fri) 2–6

Ardress House, Castle Coole, Florence Court, Hezlett House

# CO LOUTH (EIRE)

## Ardee Castle

*Ardee, near Dundalk*

Built by Roger de Peppard in 1207, additions in 15th C. In 15th and 16th Cs used for assaults on Ulster, and 2 English Lord Deputies died on such affrays, Stanley in 1414 and the White Earl of Ormonde in 1452. Both James II and William III came here at time of Battle of the Boyne.

Only between 7–8, Wed and Sun in June, but every evening in July and Aug, 7–8. Key from Mr O'Flynn, chemist about 7 shops up street on opposite side of road

Ardress House, Castleward House

# CO MAYO (EIRE)

## Rockfleet Castle

*Near Newport*

Also Carrigahowley Castle, it dates from 16th C, with possibly some earlier parts. Standing beside inlet of Clew Bay, has 4 storeys and corner turret. Mainly of interest as home of Grainne Mhaille. In 1574 she defeated English seaborne attack against Carraig an Chabhlaigh Castle. 19 years later she was apparently presented to Elizabeth I and received licence to attack the Queen's enemies. She retired to the castle with 'all her own followers and 1,000 head of cows and mares'.

Daily but may be locked; enquire at nearby house. Approach is down 1 mile of unmetalled road

Westport House

## Westport House

*In Westport*

Built in 1730 to design of Richard Castle for John Browne, later 1st Earl of Altamont. Three further sides followed in 1778, probably to design of Thomas Ivory. Dining room designed by Wyatt is enriched by stucco ornament executed by Michael Stapleton. Two columns fronting the library are replicas of those from Treasury of Atreus at Mycenae, brought back by 2nd Marquess after journey to Greece with his friend Byron. Interesting paintings of Irish origin, silver, Chinese wallpaper, furniture and historical mementoes. Zoo park.

Apr to early Oct daily 2–6 (May to early Sept 10.30–6.30)

Rockfleet Castle

WESTPORT HOUSE

# CO MEATH (EIRE)

## Donore Castle

*Near Trim*

In 1429 Henry VI promised a grant of £10 to every subject who erected a castle on a plan of 20 feet by 16 feet and 40 feet high before 1439 in the counties of Dublin, Kildare, Louth and Meath. This may be one of the bargain castles.

sw of Trim

Any reasonable time. Key from cottage opposite. Access across field

Castletown, Trim Castle, Tullynally Castle

## Trim Castle

*In Trim*

Largest Anglo-Norman castle in Ireland covering an area of 3 acres; bounded on one side by Boyne. First built in 1172 by Hugh de Lacy, but additions made *c.* 1190 to bring to present form. The irregular bailey has towers with an unusual plan of a 'D', sally ports and a barbican.

Any reasonable time. Collect key from restaurant opposite

Castletown, Tullynally Castle

# CO OFFALY (EIRE)

## Birr Castle

*Birr, near Roscrea*

Built around ruined medieval keep in 1620 by Sir Laurence Parsons. It had some importance during 17th C. Two sieges, in Civil War and during period before Battle of the Boyne. Appearance of the castle today largely due to Laurence, 2nd Earl of Rosse. His son William, 3rd Earl, was world-famous as builder of the Great Telescope, the structure of which can still be seen in museum. Lake and arboretum in grounds.

Birr 56

Grounds, telescope site and museum: all year daily 9–1, 2–6 (or dusk if earlier). Castle not open

Cloghan Castle, Dunamase Castle

## Cloghan Castle

*In Cloghan*

Probably dates from *c.* 1249, thence to the O'Maddens until 1595 when Lord Deputy Sir William Russell with English troops from Birr stormed the castle and left it slighted. In mid-19th C Dr Graves from Dublin bought it. Unlike so many of ragged ruined castles, this one is still lived in and cared for. Notable collections of paintings, furniture, armour and carpets.

→ N of Birr

Enquire locally

Birr Castle, Dunamase Castle

# CO ROSCOMMON (EIRE)

## Clonalis House

*Near Castlerea*

Seat of the O'Conor Don, senior descendant of last High Kings of Ireland. Built in mid-19th C, it stands on terraced site in extensive park. Replaced a 17th-C house occupied in penal times when Catholics in Ireland were only allowed single-storeyed buildings. Furniture, paintings and a fascinating collection of Irish manuscripts. Woodland and garden walks.

May, June and Sept, Sat, Sun and Mon, 2–6. July and Aug daily (except Tues) 2–6

Roscommon Castle

## Roscommon Castle

*In Roscommon*

Large keep-less castle built *c.* 1269 by Robert de Ufford, Lord Justice of Ireland; 7 years later it was taken by Hugh O'Conor, King of Connacht. O'Kellys grabbed it in 1308, the O'Conors reclaimed it in 1341. Cromwellians took it in 1652. Quadrangular in shape with rounded bastions at corner and a double-towered entrance gate.

All year at any reasonable time

Clonalis House

# CO SLIGO (EIRE)

## Ballinafad Castle

*Near Boyle*

Known as Castle of the Curlews, built *c.* 1590 to protect pass over Curlew Hills. Small keep with 4 massive cylindrical towers.

→ NE of Boyle

All year at any reasonable time

Ballymote Castle, Lissadell House

### Ballymote Castle
*In Ballymote*

One of strongest castles in Connacht, probably built by Richard de Burgo in 1300. Keep-less with cylindrical angle-towers and 'D' shaped towers in the centres of E and W walls.

From town, by permission through St John of God's Nursing Home

At any reasonable time

Ballinafad Castle, Lissadell House

### Lissadell House
*Near Sligo*

Late Georgian Italian-styled mansion built by Francis Goodwin in 1830–35 for Sir Robert Gore Booth, 4th Baronet. Here lived Eva Gore-Booth and Constance Markievicz; it is still home of the family. Associations with W. B. Yeats.

8 miles N of Sligo, off Sligo–Bundoran road

Easter week, then May to end Sept 2.30–5.15 (except Sun)

Ballinafad Castle, Ballymote Castle

## CO TIPPERARY (EIRE)

### Cahir Castle
*In Cahir*

Built early in 14th C probably by son of James Butler, Earl of Ormonde. Thought to be impregnable but Earl of Essex took it after only 10-day siege in 1599. One of most extensive castles in Ireland, it has recently been restored.

Oct to mid-June, Tues to Sat 10–6 or dusk, Sun 2–4; mid-June to end Sept daily 10–7

Damer House, Loughmore Castle, Nenagh Castle

NENAGH CASTLE

### Damer House
*Near Roscrea*

Fine early 18th-C house erected within walls of Old Butler castle, Scroll pedimented doorway and notable carved staircase. Has been leased by Irish Georgian Society and is being restored.

Easter to end Sept, Thur to Mon 2–6

Cahir Castle, Loughmore Castle, Nenagh Castle

### Loughmore Castle
*Near Templemore*

Tower at S end dates from 15th C. 17th-C additions including fine fireplace bearing initials and armorials; also mullioned windows.

N of Thurles, across fields

All year at any reasonable time

Cahir Castle, Damer House, Nenagh Castle

### Nenagh Castle
*In Nenagh*

Present massive, rather splendid, tower of donjon, was originally one of 3 towers spaced into curtain wall of very strong Norman castle; there were also 2 semi-circular towers and a gatehouse. Building erected in early 13th C by Theobald Walter (nephew of Thomas à Becket). Tower now remaining looms up 30 m high, dwarfing most of town.

Any reasonable time; obtain key from Tourist Information Office in Kickham Street

Cahir Castle, Damer House, Loughmore Castle

## CO TYRONE (NI)

### Benburb Castle

*Benburb, near Dungannon*

The ruined castle stands on edge of cliff beside River Blackwater. Of original 4 towers, 3 remain. The castle was built in 1615 by Sir Richard Wingfield on site of older fortress. Scene in 1646 of battle between Irish under Owen O'Neill and Scottish army under Munro. This ended in total victory for the Irish, 32 colours being taken.

6 miles s of Dungannon

At any reasonable time

Printing Press (Strabane)

### Gray's Printing Press

*49 Main Street, Strabane*

18th-C printing shop with particular associations for Americans through John Dunlap, printer of the Declaration of Independence. Legend claims he learned his profession here.

Saintfield 510721 (NT Regional Office)

Apr to end Sept, daily (except Thur and Sun) 2–6

Ardress House, Wellbrook Beetling Mill

### Wellbrook Beetling Mill

*Corkhill, near Cookstown*

18th-C water-powered mill with modifications made during 19th C. Pleasant woodland walks.

4 miles from Cookstown

Apr to end Sept daily (except Fri, but open Good Fri) 2–6

Ardress House, Gray's Printing Press

## CO WATERFORD (EIRE)

### Reginald's Tower

*In Waterford*

Norsemen first settled in Waterford in middle of 9th C. For 3 centuries they worked to establish port on s bank of the Suir. Walls and fortification went round some 15 acres of city, traces of which are still to be seen. By repute the massive 25-m high Reginald's Tower was erected in 1003 by Reginald the Dane. In 1463 it served as a Mint, in 19th C a prison and today a museum displaying City Regalia.

All year: summer daily 9–9, Sun 2–8; winter, Mon to Fri 9–5.30

Johnstown Castle

## CO WESTMEATH (EIRE)

### Killua Castle

*Near Clonmellon*

Among most romantic of all Ireland's homes; 3-storeyed house was built *c.* 1780 and transformed in 1830 into a castle of seeming strength, probably to designs of James Shiel. Entrance door gave on to octagonal hall with decorative plasterwork. The estate was large with a lake and follies, including an obelisk bearing the message that Sir Walter Raleigh planted the first potato in Ireland!

Not officially open but a judicious enquiry could produce an entry

Tullynally Castle

**Tullynally Castle**
*Near Castlepollard*

17th-C garrison house given Classical treatment by Myers in 1775. Home of Earls of Longford for 200 years, and transformed into a full-blown Gothic Castle by Frank Johnston between 1803 and 1806. Further additions and alterations made by James Shiel in 1825 and Sir Richard Morrison in 1842. Set in beautifully wooded demesne with woodland walks and walled gardens. The huge Victorian kitchen is open as a 'life below stairs' museum. Period costumes.

1 mile outside Castlepollard on Granard road

June to end Sept, Sat, Sun and Bank Hol. Mon 2.30–6

Killua Castle

## CO WEXFORD (EIRE)

**Johnstown Castle**
*Near Wexford*

Impressive group of buildings with numerous towers. Designed and built between 1830 and 1843 by Daniel Robertson of Kilkenny working in Gothic and Norman Revival manners. Stands in fine grounds complete with lake. Now an agricultural institute.

sw of Wexford

Grounds only, daily 9–5

Kilkenny Castle

## CO WICKLOW (EIRE)

**Avondale**
*Near Rathdrum*

Square house built in 1779 for Samuel Hayes, an amateur architect, who may have designed it himself. Good plasterwork, Bossi chimneypiece. Birthplace and home of Charles Stewart Parnell.

sw of Wicklow

By prior appointment only

Russborough House

**Russborough House**
*Russborough, near Blessington*

Outstanding Palladian house; work started in 1740 to design of Richard Castle; interior decoration supervised by Francis Bindon. Francini Brothers' plasterwork at its best. Furniture outstanding and many notable items of great worth. Splendid picture collection founded at turn of century by the uncle of the present owner of Russborough, Sir Alfred Beit, who has generously placed the house and collection in trust for the nation. On the walls are master works by such hands as Gainsborough, Goya, Hals, Rubens, Velazquez and Vermeer. Woodland garden.

Naas 65239

Easter to end Oct, Sun and Bank Hol, Mon, also Wed from June to Sept and Sat from July to Aug 2.30–5.30

Avondale

# SCOTLAND

## BORDERS REGION

### Abbotsford House

*Near Melrose, Roxburghshire*

Home of Sir Walter Scott. He bought property in 1811 and rebuilt much of house and also planted many trees in garden. On view Scott memorabilia and his collection of weapons.

Galashiels 2043

3 miles w of Melrose off B6360

Late Mar to end Oct, weekdays 10–5, Sun 2–5

Bowhill, Floors Castle, Mellerstain

Easter to Sept

### Bowhill

*Bowhill, near Selkirk, Selkirkshire*

Border home of Scots of Buccleuch, an 18th/19th-C house set in delightful natural park with fine trees. Outstanding collection of paintings by Canaletto, Claude, Gainsborough, Leonardo da Vinci and Reynolds. Fine silver, porcelain and French furniture. Rare relics of Duke of Monmouth. English portrait miniatures. Restored Victorian kitchen. Adventure woodland play area.

Selkirk 20732

3 miles w of Selkirk off B7039

Easter weekend (Mon to Fri); May, June and Sept, Wed, Thur, Sat and Sun; July and Aug daily (except Fri) 12.30–5, Sun 2–6

Abbotsford House, Floors Castle, Mellerstain

### Floors Castle

*Near Kelso, Roxburghshire*

Built by William Adam in 1721, this huge mansion has 365 windows; later added to by Playfair. Celebrated collection of paintings by Canaletto, Claude, Gainsborough, Guardi, Lely, Raeburn and Reynolds. Fine French furniture and porcelain.

Kelso 3333

From A6089, 2 miles NW of Kelso

Easter weekend, then May to Sept daily (except Mon and Sat, but open Bank Hol. Mon) 11–5.30

Abbotsford House, Manderston, Mellerstain

(1 mile)

### Hermitage Castle

*Hermitage, Roxburghshire*

Staunch and resolute 13th-C castle, stronghold of de Soulis family, later of the Douglases. It was to here that Mary Queen of Scots made her exhausting ride from Jedburgh to meet Bothwell in 1566. From outside appears almost perfect. 4 towers and connecting walls.

Off B6399, 16 miles NE of A7 at Langholm

All year daily except public hols (AMS)

Abbotsford House, Floors Castle, Traquair House

### Manderston

*Near Duns, Berwickshire*

Distinguished Edwardian house in Classical style with interior decoration in Adam manner. Large park and gardens. Marble dairy, interesting group of farm buildings. Lake and woodland.

Duns 3450

2 miles E of Duns off A6105

Mid-May to mid-Sept, Thur, Sun and Bank Hol. Mon 2–5.30

Abbotsford House, Floors Castle, Mellerstain

## Mellerstain

*Gordon, Berwickshire*

Begun c. 1725 by William Adam, and finished between 1770 and 1778 by William's son Robert. Exquisitely decorated, good plasterwork, and well-furnished interiors; library is outstanding. One of most attractive houses in Scotland open to the public. Italian gardens and lake.

☎ Gordon 225

➔ 8 miles NW of Kelso between A6089 and B6397

⏲ May to end Sept daily (except Sat) 1.30–5.30

Abbotsford House, Floors Castle, Manderston

## Traquair House

*Innerleithen, Peeblesshire*

Goes back to 10th C and said to be oldest continuously inhabited house in Scotland. Visitors list is impressive; besides Mary Queen of Scots, 26 Scottish and English monarchs have called. Treasures date from 12th C and include books, embroideries, glass, manuscripts and paintings. Priest's Room with hidden staircase. 18th-C pavilion with previously covered ceiling painting. Famous brewhouse equipped as it was 200 years ago, brewing and selling Traquair ale. Well-known Bear Gates were closed in 1746, the last person passing through them being Bonnie Prince Charlie. They will not be re-opened until a Stuart ascends the throne.

☎ Innerleithen 830323

➔ On B709, just off A72, 8 miles SE of Peebles

⏲ Easter Sat to late Oct daily 1.30–5.30 (July and Aug 10.30–5.30)

Abbotsford House, Bowhill, Floors Castle, Mellerstain

# CENTRAL REGION

## Linlithgow Palace

*Linlithgow, West Lothian*

This quite splendid ruined palace by the Loch was successor to older building burnt down in 1424. Great hall and chapel are late 15th C, and there is richly carved 16th-C fountain in quadrangle. Mary Queen of Scots was born here in 1542 as her father, James V, lay dying at Falkland Palace. In 1746 palace was burnt down, possibly by accident, when garrisoned by General Hawley's troops. In 1914 George V held a court in the Lyon Chamber.

➔ S shore of Loch Linlithgow, off A903

⏲ All year daily, Apr to Sept 9.30–7, Sun 2–7; Oct to Mar 9.30–4, Sun 2–4. Closed public hols

Menstrie Castle, Stirling Castle

⇌ Linlithgow (½ mile)

## Menstrie Castle

*Menstrie, Clackmannanshire*

This 16th-C restored castle was birthplace of Sir William Alexander, James VI's Lieutenant for the Plantation of Nova Scotia. Coats of arms of 107 baronets are displayed. Commemoration rooms only open to public.

➔ On A91, 5 miles NE of Stirling

⏲ May to end Sept, Wed, Sat and Sun 2.30–5

Linlithgow Palace, Stirling Castle

⇌ Stirling (5½ miles)

## Stirling Castle

*Stirling, Stirlingshire*

13th-C and earlier structure, with notable additions from 16th C. Impressive fortress stands 76 m high on great rock. Through it has swirled much of Scotland's history. Wallace recaptured it from English in 1297. Edward I took it back in 1304 but lost it again when Bruce won at nearby Bannockburn in 1314. James II was born here, Mary Queen of Scots and James VI both spent some years in residence. 15th-C great hall, also Renaissance Palace and other noteworthy buildings.

Apr, May and Sept, weekdays 9.30–6.15, Sun 11–6; June to Aug, weekdays 9.30–8, Sun 11–7; Oct to Mar, weekdays 9.30–4, Sun 1–4. Closed public hols

Linlithgow Palace, Menstrie Castle

Stirling ($\frac{3}{4}$ mile)

# DUMFRIES AND GALLOWAY REGION

## Caerlaverock Castle

*Near Dumfries, Dumfriesshire*

£ DoE

Seat of Maxwell family, dating back to 1220. Edward I besieged it in 1300. In 1638 it capitulated to Covenanters after siege of 13 weeks. Triangular with round towers. Heavy machicolation is 15th C. In 17th C interior remodelled as Renaissance mansion. Noteworthy carving.

9 miles S of Dumfries off B725

All year daily (AMS)

Maxwelton House, Rammerscales

Dumfries ($7\frac{1}{2}$ miles)

## Cardoness Castle

*Gatehouse-of-Fleet, Kirkcudbrightshire*

£ DoE

15th-C tower house, 4 storeys high, with vaulted basement. Noteworthy fireplaces. Was home of McCullochs of Galloway.

1 mile SW of Gatehouse-of-Fleet on A75

All year daily (AMS)

Rammerscales

## Carlyle's Birthplace

*Ecclefechan, Dumfriesshire*

£ NTS

Thomas Carlyle was born here in 1795. Little house was built by his father and uncle, both master masons. Of architectural interest. Part of his correspondence with Goethe on view, also other mementoes.

Ecclefechan 666

On A74, $5\frac{1}{2}$ miles SE of Lockerbie

Mid-Apr to end Oct daily (except Sun) 10–6

Carlisle Castle, Rammerscales

Lockerbie (6 miles)

## Drumlanrig Castle

*Near Thornhill, Dumfriesshire*

£

Exotic but impressive castle built of local pink sandstone, resting on site of an old Douglas stronghold. Outstanding treasures such as: a Rembrandt, also works by Holbein, Murillo and Ruysdael; superb silver, including chandelier, 1680, weighing 57 kg; Louis XVI furniture; gifts from Charles II. Memorabilia of Bonnie Prince Charlie. Adventure woodland play area, nature trails.

Thornhill 30248

3 miles N of Thornhill, 1 mile W of A76

Easter weekend (Fri to Mon), then May and June, Mon, Thur and Sat, 12.30–5, Sun 2–6, July and Aug daily (except Fri) 11–5, Sun 2–6

Maxwelton House, Rammerscales

Kirkconnel ($11\frac{1}{2}$ miles)

## Gilnockie Tower

*Canonbie, Dumfriesshire*

£

16th-C border chieftain's tower erected by Johnnie Armstrong of

Gilnockie. Interesting animals in grounds such as the Manx, 4-horned sheep and wild boar.

Off A7, 14 miles N of Carlisle
All year daily 11–5
Drumlanrig Castle, Caerlaverock Castle

## Maclellan's Castle

*Kirkcudbright, Kirkcudbrightshire*

Fine castellated mansion overlooking harbour; dates from 1582. Although ruined, there are interesting architectural details.

Off High Street
All year daily (AMS)
Maxwelton House, Rammerscales

## Maxwelton House

*Near Moniaive, Dumfriesshire*

14th/15th-C house, originally stronghold of Earls of Glencairn. Birthplace of Annie Laurie to whom William Douglas of Fingland wrote his famous poems. Museum of bygones, particularly agricultural and domestic.

Moniaive 384
13 miles NW of Dumfries off A702
May to Sept, Wed and Thur, also 4th Sun each month, 2.30–5
Drumlanrig Castle, Rammerscales

## Rammerscales

*Lockerbie, Dumfriesshire*

Good Georgian manor house dating from 1760 with fine circular staircase and long library. Fine views over Annandale. Walled garden of period. Woodland walks.

Lochmaben 361
5 miles W of A74 at Lockerbie, off B7020
Late June to early Sept, Tues, Wed and Thur, also odd Sun in July and Aug, 2–5
Carlyle's Birthplace, Maxwelton House
Lockerbie (5 miles)

## Threave Castle

*Near Castle Douglas, Kirkcudbrightshire*

4-storeyed tower erected between 1639 and 1690 by Archibald the Grim, Lord of Galloway. Early stronghold of the Black Douglases. When it surrendered to James II in 1455, he used the formidable cannon Mons Meg to blast his way to victory. Threave gardens owned by NT.

$1\frac{1}{2}$ miles W of Castle Douglas, N of A75
All year daily (AMS)
Drumlanrig Castle, Maxwelton House

# FIFE REGION

## Aberdour Castle

*Aberdour, Fifeshire*

14th-C tower is oldest part. Remarkable remains of wall paintings. Circular dovecote nearby.

From Aberdour on A92, 8 miles SW of Kirkcaldy
All year daily (AMS)
Town House and Study (Culross), Culross Palace
Kirkcaldy (7 miles)

## Culross Palace

*Culross, Fifeshire*

The small 'palace' was built between 1597 and 1611 by Sir George Bruce, who fostered the sea-going trade in salt and coal from Culross. Crow-stepped gables, pantiled roofs. Little-changed with years. Decorative painted woodwork and ceilings.

→ 7½ miles w of Dunfermline off B9037
⏱ All year daily except public hols: Apr to Sept 9.30–7, Sun 2–7; Oct to Mar 9.30–4, Sun 2–4
Town House and Study (Culross), Linlithgow Palace
Cowdenbeath (13½ miles)

## Culross: Town House and Study

*Near Dunfermline, Fifeshire*

£ NTS

Noteworthy example of 17th-C Scottish burgh architecture.

☎ Newmills 359
→ 8 miles w of Dunfermline off B9037
⏱ Town House: mid-Apr to mid-Oct, weekdays 9.30–12.30, 2–5.30, Sun 2–5.30. The Study: mid-Oct to early Apr, Sat 9.30–12.30, 2–4, Sun 2–4
Culross Palace, Linlithgow Palace
Cowdenbeath (13½ miles)

## Falkland Palace

*Falkland, Fifeshire*

£ NTS

Charming Royal Palace built between 1501 and 1541 by James IV and James V, replacing earlier castle and palace buildings from 12th C. Favourite with James V who died here, and his daughter Mary Queen of Scots. The roofed South Range contains Chapel Royal, and East Range the King's Bedchamber. The Royal Tennis Court of 1539 is still in use. Attractive gardens.

☎ Falkland 397
→ 5 miles N of Glenrothes, off A912
⏱ Apr to end Oct, weekdays 10–6, Sun 2–6
Hill of Tarvit
Ladybank (6 miles)

## Hill of Tarvit

*Craigrothie, Fifeshire*

£ NTS

Mansion house of 1696, remodelled in 1906 by Sir Robert Lorimer for Mr F. B. Sharp. Contents include: noteworthy Louis XVI, Sheraton and Chippendale furniture; tapestries; Chinese bronzes; porcelain; and paintings by Raeburn and Ramsay.

☎ Cupar 3127
→ 2 miles s of Cupar off A916
⏱ Easter Sat and Sun, then May to end Sept daily (except Fri) 2–6
Falkland Palace, Kellie Castle
Cupar (2½ miles)

## Kellie Castle

*Near St Andrews, Fifeshire*

£ NTS

Excellent example of domestic architecture of 16th/17th Cs, although earliest parts date from *c.* 1360. Restored century ago by Professor James Lorimer. Good plasterwork and panelling painted with 'romantic' landscapes. Room displaying work of Robert Lorimer, the architect. 16 acres of gardens.

☎ Arncroach 271
→ 10 miles s of St Andrews off A921
⏱ Mid-Apr to end Sept daily (except Fri) 2–6
Falkland Palace, Hill of Tarvit
Cupar (12½ miles)

## Ravenscraig Castle

*Near Kirkcaldy, Fifeshire*

£ DoE

Impressive ruin of castle erected by James II in 1460. Later passed to the Sinclair Earls of Orkney. Of interest because it is probably first British castle to be designed for defence by firearms.

→ On rocky promontory between Buckhaven and Kirkcaldy off A935
⏱ All year daily except public hols (AMS)
Falkland Palace, Hill of Tarvit
Kirkcaldy (1 mile)

## St Andrews Castle

*Near St Andrews, Fifeshire*

Founded 1200 and rebuilt in late 14th C. Cardinal Beaton was murdered here in 1546, and first stage of Reformation struggle followed with subsequent siege.

From shore at St Andrews

All year daily except public hols (AMS)

Hill of Tarvit, Kellie Castle

Leuchars (6 miles)

# GRAMPIAN REGION

## Balvenie Castle

*Dufftown, Banffshire*

Romantic ruins of 14th-C moated fortress originally in hands of Comyns. Visited by Edward I in 1304 and Mary Queen of Scots in 1562.

In Dufftown on A941

All year daily except public hols (AMS)

Huntly Castle, Leith Hall

Keith (11 miles)

## Braemar Castle

*Near Braemar, Aberdeenshire*

Turreted stronghold built in 1628 by Earl of Mar, and burned by Black Colonel John Farquharson of Inverey in 1689. Garrisoned by English troops after 1715 Jacobite Rising; after the '45 it was repaired and again garrisoned to protect the military road from Perth across Dee and Speyside to Fort George. Underground pit prison, massive iron 'Yett' and barrel-vaulting.

Braemar 219

Just outside Braemar on A93

May to early Oct daily 10–6

Craigievar Castle

Pitlochry (15 miles)

## Brodie Castle

*Near Nairn, Morayshire*

Ancient seat of Brodies, first endowed with their lands by Malcolm IV in 1160; a Thane of Brodie is recorded in the reign of Alexander III. Burned down in 1645 by Lord Lewis Gordon during the Montrose campaigns, and rebuilt with 18th/19th-C additions. Contents include: important collection of 18th-C Dutch and English paintings; also French Impressionists and English watercolours; French furniture; English, continental and Chinese porcelain.

Brodie 371

6 miles E of Nairn off A96

May to Sept, Mon to Sat 11–6, Sun 2–6

Cawdor Castle

Nairn (6 miles)

## Castle Fraser

*Sauchen, Aberdeenshire*

One of most impressive castles of Mar, begun *c.* 1575 and completed in 1636. The quadrangular building comprises 6 storeys, with square tower to W, and round tower to SW. One of best examples of Flemish style in Scotland. Two

BRAEMAR CASTLE

great families of master masons, Bel and Leiper, helped with work.

Sauchen 463

3 miles S of B993 at Kemnay, on unclassified road to Dunecht

May to end Sept daily 11–6, Sun 2–6

Craigievar Castle, Drum Castle

Inverurie (7½ miles)

(2 miles)

## Corgarff Castle

*Corgarff, Aberdeenshire*

£ DoE

Tower house built in 16th C and converted into garrison post in 1748 by being enclosed with a star-shaped loophole wall.

15 miles NW of Ballater off A939

Apr to Sept daily 9.30–7, Sun 2–7

Craigievar Castle

## Craigievar Castle

*Craigievar, near Lumphanan, Aberdeenshire*

£ NTS

Outstanding baronial tower house, structurally unchanged since completion in 1626 by William Forbe of Aberdeen. Simplicity of lower walls contrasts strikingly with turrets, crow-stepped gables, conical roofs, balustrading and corbelling. Very fine moulded plaster ceilings.

Lumphanan 635

10 miles NW of Banchory off A980

May to end Sept daily (except Fri) 2–7

Corgarff Castle, Crathes Castle, Kildrummy Castle

Inverurie (17 miles)

(1½ miles)

## Crathes Castle

*Crathes, near Banchory, Kincardineshire*

£ NTS

Double square tower of castle dates from 1553. Royal associations pre-date this, when the lands of Leys were granted to Burnett family by Robert the Bruce in 1323. The Horn of Leys, said to have been given by Bruce, is in the great hall. Fine interior includes remarkable ceiling paintings dating from 1599 in the Chamber of the Nine Muses, the Chamber of the Nine Nobles and the Green Lady's Room. Interesting gardens with yew hedges, shrubs and specimen trees.

Crathes 525

Off A93 3½ miles E of Banchory

May to end Sept daily 11–6, Sun 2–6

Drum Castle, Muchalls Castle

Aberdeen (10 miles)

## Delgatie Castle

*Turriff, Aberdeenshire*

£

12th-C tower-house home of the Hays. Painted ceilings, arms and armour. 97-stepped turnpike stair.

Turriff 3479

2 miles E of Turriff off A947 and B9170

To groups all year. Individuals July and Aug, by prior arrangement only

Kildrummy Castle

Huntly (20 miles)

## Drum Castle

*Peterculter, Aberdeenshire*

£ NTS

Great square tower, one of 3 oldest tower houses in Scotland, was work of Richard Cementarius, King's Master Mason, in late 13th C. Charming mansion added in 1619. Furniture, pictures, silver and relics. Pleasant garden with rare trees and shrubs.

Drumoak 204

10 miles W of Aberdeen off A93

May to end Sept daily 11–6, Sun 2–6

Crathes Castle, Muchalls Castle, Provost Skene's House

Aberdeen (10½ miles)

## Druminnor Castle

*Rhynie, Aberdeenshire*

Restored 15th-C building, once stronghold of Clan Forbes, now incorporates museum.

- Rhynie 248
- 10 miles s of Huntly off A97
- By appointment only
- Huntly Castle, Leith Hall
- Huntly (8 miles)

## Duffus Castle

*Duffus, Morayshire*

DoE

Massive ruins of motte-and-bailey castle, surrounded by moat; 14th-C tower crowns motte. Original seat of the de Moravia family, the Murrays, now represented by duchies of Atholl and Sutherland.

- 3 miles NW of Elgin off B9012
- Any reasonable time (AMS)
- Brodie Castle
- Elgin (4 miles)

## Dunnottar Castle

*Near Stonehaven, Kincardineshire*

14th-C fortress on rocky cliff 50 m above sea, once stronghold of Earls Marischal of Scotland. During Commonwealth Wars Scottish regalia were hidden here for safety. Cromwell's troops occupied castle but in 1652 this treasure was smuggled out by wife of the minister at Kinneff, 7 miles away, and hidden under the pulpit.

- Stonehaven 62173
- 1½ miles s of Stonehaven off A92
- All year daily 9–6, Sun 2–5. Closed Sat from Nov to Mar, and public hols
- Drum Castle, Muchalls Castle
- Stonehaven (2½ miles)

## Haddo House

*Methlick, Aberdeenshire*

NTS

Standing on site of earlier building, Haddo House was designed in 1731 by William Adam, pupil of Sir William Bruce and father of Adam brothers. Much of interior is 'Adam Revival' carried out *c.* 1880. Portraits of the Gordons and good furniture. Terraced gardens.

- Tarves 440
- 7½ miles NW of Ellon off B9005
- May to end Sept daily 11–6, Sun 2–6
- Delgatie Castle, Huntly Castle
- Inverurie (10½ miles)

## Huntly Castle

*Castle Street, Huntly, Aberdeenshire*

DoE

Earlier building on site, Strathbogie Castle, was replaced by Huntly Castle *c.* 1600. Elaborate heraldic ornaments on the castle tower. The Marquesses of Huntly lived here – the 'Gay Gordons' after whom the dance was named.

- In Huntly on A97
- All year daily (AMS)
- Delgatie Castle, Leith Hall
- Huntly

## Kildrummy Castle

*Kildrummy, Aberdeenshire*

DoE

Good example of ruins of 13th-C castle with extensive layout. 4 round towers that remain with parts of chapel and hall are more or less original; gatehouse and other parts date from 16th C. Seat of the Earls of Mar, it was an important fortress until 1715.

- 16 miles s of Huntly off A97
- Any reasonable time (AMS)
- Craigievar Castle, Druminnor Castle, Leith Hall

## Leith Hall

*Kennethmont, Aberdeenshire*

NTS

For 300 years home of Leith and Leith-Hay family. Earliest part in north wing dates from 1650. Additions in 18th and 19th Cs. Collections of memorabilia of past lairds; also on display a writing case presented by Prince Charles Edward on eve of Culloden. Extensive and attractive grounds: 2 ponds, a bird observation hide, nature trail and a flock of Soay sheep. 17th-C stables.

Kennethmont 216
7 miles S of Huntly off B9002
May to end Sept daily 11–6, Sun 2–6
Druminnor Castle, Haddo House
Huntly ($7\frac{1}{2}$ miles)

## Muchalls Castle

*Near Stonehaven, Kincardineshire*

£

Small castle overlooking sea built by Burnetts of Leys in 1619. Fine fireplaces and plasterwork ceilings. Secret staircase.

Newtonhill 30217
11 miles S of Aberdeen off A92
May to Sept, Tues and Sun 3–5
Crathes Castle, Drum Castle, Dunnottar Castle
Stonehaven (5 miles)

## Pitcaple Castle

*Near Inverurie, Aberdeenshire*

£

Good example of 15th C 'Z' plan castle that is still lived in. Three monarchs have visited here, and Montrose stayed here on his way to execution in Edinburgh. Family memorabilia.

Pitcaple 204
4 miles NW of Inverurie off A96
May to Sept, 11–6 if convenient
Druminnor Castle, Leith Hall, Tolquhon Castle
Inverurie (4 miles)

## Provost Skene's House

*Guestrow, Aberdeen, Aberdeenshire*

£

Named after Sir George Skene, Provost of Aberdeen 1676–85. Building dates prior to 1545 and is of granite with various external additions such as armorial bearings of Sir George above main doorway. Of interest is Painted Gallery with examples of Reformation religious paintings on wood panels. For years these were obscured by whitewash, but have now, where possible, been restored.

Aberdeen 50086
All year, Mon to Sat 10–5
Crathes Castle, Drum Castle
Aberdeen ($\frac{1}{2}$ mile)

## Tolquhon Castle

*Pitmedden, Aberdeenshire*

£ DoE

Early 15th-C rectangular tower, with quadrangular mansion *c.* 1584. Good carved panel over door, and 2 round towers.

7 miles E of Oldmeldrum off B999
All year daily except public hols (AMS)
Haddo House, Pitcaple Castle
Inverurie (11 miles)

# HIGHLAND REGION

## Castle of Old Wick

*Near Wick, Caithness*

14th-C windowless square tower, on headland above sea, over cleft in rocks. Once known as Castle Oliphant, it was taken in 1569 by Master of Caithness, son of 4th Earl of Caithness who, the following year, was incarcerated in nearby Castle Girnigoe for 6 years.

$1\frac{1}{2}$ miles S of Wick off A9
At all reasonable times,

except when adjoining rifle range is in use (AMS)

Dunrobin Castle

Wick (2 miles)

## Cawdor Castle

*Cawdor, Nairnshire*

14th-C keep, fortified in 15th C, with 17th-C additions. Drawbridge and iron yett, freshwater well within the walls. Shakespeare's Macbeth was Thane of Cawdor. Well laid-out gardens, nature trail.

Cawdor 615

5 miles sw of Nairn off B9090

May to Sept daily 10–5.30

Brodie Castle, Hugh Miller's Cottage

Nairn (5 miles)

## Dunrobin Castle

*Golspie, Sutherland*

Historic home of the Sutherlands situated in park overlooking sea. This magnificent building, not unlike a Loire château, began as a square keep *c.* 1275. In 19th C Sir Charles Barry, architect of Houses of Parliament, carried out extensive alterations. This century further work undertaken by Sir Robert Lorimer, notably fine drawing room. Furniture, paintings and interesting exhibits.

Golspie 377

$12\frac{1}{2}$ miles N of Dornoch (A9)

Phone for details

Castle of Old Wick

Golspie ($\frac{1}{2}$ mile)

## Eilean Donan Castle

*Dornie, Ross & Cromarty*

On an islet, now connected by a causeway, this romantic castle was built *c.* 1220 by Alexander II to guard against Danish raiders. In 1719 garrisoned by Spanish Jacobite troops and bombarded by the *Worcester*, an English warship.

Dornie 202

DUNROBIN CASTLE

8 miles E of Kyle of Lochalsh off A87

Easter to Sept daily 10–12.30, 2–6

Dunrobin Castle

Kyle of Lochalsh (8 miles)

To shore opposite

## Hugh Miller's Cottage

*Cromarty, Ross & Cromarty*

NTS

Thatched cottage, *c.* 1711, birthplace (1802) of stonemason Hugh Miller, later to become eminent geologist, editor and writer. Geological specimens.

Cromarty 245

In Cromarty on A832

May to end Sept, weekdays 10–12, 1–5; also Sun from June to Sept 2–5

Dunrobin Castle

## Urquhart Castle

*Drumnadrochit, Invernessshire*

DoE

Once one of largest castles in Scotland, given by James IV to John Grant of Freuchie, in 1509. Sited on W bank of Loch Ness, from where sightings of the 'monster' have been reported. Castle was blown up in 1692 to prevent a Jacobite takeover.

14 miles SW of Inverness

All year daily (AMS)

Eilean Donan Castle

Inverness (14 miles)

## Blackness Castle

*Near Linlithgow, West Lothian*

£ DoE

15th-C stronghold on River Forth once of considerable importance. One of 4 castles which by Articles of Union were to be left fortified. Prison in Covenanting times; a powder magazine in late 19th C and, more recently, a youth hostel.

→ 4 miles NE of Linlithgow off B909

⏲ All year daily except public hols (AMS)

Hamilton House, Lauriston Castle

Linlithgow (4½ miles)

## Craigmillar Castle

*Edinburgh, Midlothian*

£ DoE

Ruins of huge 14th-C keep enclosed in early 15th C by curtain wall. Within are remains of State apartments from 16th/17th Cs. Mary Queen of Scots often stayed here; in 1566, while she was in residence, the plot to murder Darnley was hatched.

→ 3½ miles SW of city centre close to A68

⏲ All year daily except public hols (AMS)

Edinburgh Castle, Georgian House in Charlotte Square

Edinburgh

## Crichton Castle

*Crichton, Midlothian*

£ DoE

14th-C keep with 15th- to 17th-C additions. Elaborate in style, has arcaded range and faceted stonework. Built by Earl of Bothwell in 16th C.

→ 7 miles SE of Dalkeith off B6367

⏲ All year daily except public hols; closed Fri from Oct to May (AMS)

Craigmillar Castle. Palace of Holyroodhouse

Edinburgh (10 miles)

## Dalmeny House

*Near Queensferry (South), West Lothian*

£

Designed by Wilkins in 1814 in Tudor Revival style. Mentmore French furniture, fine paintings and Napoleonic mementoes.

→ 3 miles E of Queensferry

⏲ Easter Sun to end Sept, Wed and Sun 2.30–5.30

Crichton Castle, Lauriston Castle

Dalmeny

## Dirleton Castle

*Dirleton, East Lothian*

£ DoE

This 13th-C castle has been the scene of much mayhem. Besieged by Edward I in 1311; regained by Scots; captured by Cromwell in 1650. Three drum towers remain. 16th-C dovecote and gardens.

→ 20 miles NE of Edinburgh

⏲ Apr to Sept daily 9.30–7, Sun 2–7; Oct to Mar daily 9.30–4, Sun 2–4. Closed Dec 25–26 and Jan 1–2

Luffness Castle, Tantallon Castle, Winton House

North Berwick (2½ miles)

## Edinburgh Castle

*Castlehill, Edinburgh, Midlothian*

£ OAP

Oldest part is St Margaret's Chapel dating from 11th C. However, there has certainly been fortress here since 7th C. James VI of Scotland and I of England was born here, and it was in rooms used by Mary Queen of Scots that the 'Casket Letters' were found that were used to implicate her in Darnley's murder. Great hall built by James IV with fine timbered roof and Old Palace which houses regalia of Scotland. Famous old piece of artillery 'Mons Meg'.

⏲ May to Oct 9.30–6, Sun 11–6; Nov to Apr 9.30–5, Sun 12.30–4.30. Closed Dec 25–26 and Jan 1–3

EDINBURGH CASTLE

Craigmillar Castle, Georgian House in Charlotte Square

Edinburgh

Summer months

## Georgian House

*7 Charlotte Square, Edinburgh, Midlothian*

£ NTS

A Robert Adam masterpiece of urban architecture. Main floors furnished as they might have been by first owners, illustrating social conditions of period.

Edinburgh 226 5922

Apr to end Oct daily 10–5, Sun 2–5; Nov to mid-Dec, Sat 10–4.30, Sun 2–4.30. Closed public hols

Craigmillar Castle, Edinburgh Castle, Hamilton House

Edinburgh

## Gladstone's Land

*483 Lawnmarket, Edinburgh, Midlothian*

£ NTS

Early 17th-C house with unusual outside staircase and interesting painted ceilings.

Apr to end Oct daily 10–5, Sun 2–5; Nov to mid-Dec, Sat 10–4.30, Sun 2–4.30

Edinburgh Castle, Hamilton House

Edinburgh

## Hamilton House

*Prestonpans, East Lothian*

NTS

Built in 1628 by rich Edinburgh burgess John Hamilton. Bought and restored by NT in 1937.

Prestonpans 811035

$8\frac{1}{2}$ miles E of Edinburgh

Only by prior appointment

Craigmillar Castle, Edinburgh Castle

Prestonpans

## Hopetoun House

*Near Queensferry (South), West Lothian*

£ OAP

Begun in 1696 with designs by Sir William Bruce, then rebuilt and enlarged at beginning of 18th C by William Adam and his sons, John and Robert. Fine collection of paintings by Canaletto, Rembrandt, Rubens and Van Dyck; also fine showing of antiques. Rooftop viewing platform with panoramic vistas over Firth of Forth. Stables' museum. Deer parks, nature trail.

Edinburgh 331 2451/1546

2 miles W of Forth Road Bridge (A90) at Queensferry, on unclassified road

Easter, then end Apr to mid-Sept daily 11–5.30

Craigmillar Castle, House of the Binns

Dalmeny ($5\frac{1}{2}$ miles)

## House of the Binns

*Near Linlithgow, West Lothian*

£ NTS

Parts of house date from 1478, but most from early 17th C. Reflects transition from fortified stronghold to house more suited to gracious living. Fine moulded plasterwork on the ceilings of 4 main rooms; noteworthy paintings. Wide view over Forth.

Philpstoun 255

➜ 4 miles E of Linlithgow off A904

Easter, then May to end Sept daily (except Fri) 2–5.30

Edinburgh Castle, Hopetoun House

Linlithgow (4 miles)

## Lauriston Castle

*Near Edinburgh, Midlothian*

£

Original 16th-C tower, built by Sir Archibald Napier, father of the discoverer of logarithms. Has been added to and converted into pleasant house with good furniture and paintings. John Law (1671–1729), founder of 1st Bank of France, also proposer of ill-fated 'Mississippi Scheme', spent part of his youth here.

Edinburgh 336 2060

➜ N of A90 at Cramond Road S, 4 miles NW of city centre

Apr to end Oct daily (except Fri) 11–1, 2–5; Nov to Mar, Sat and Sun 2–4. Closed public hols

Edinburgh Castle, Hopetoun House, House of the Binns

Edinburgh (4 miles)

## Luffness Castle

*Aberlady, East Lothian*

16th-C castle with keep dating from 13th C; dry moat and traces of old fortifications.

➜ 18 miles NE of Edinburgh off A198

In summer by arrangement

Hamilton House, Manderston, Mellerstain

Drem ($4\frac{1}{2}$ miles)

## Palace of Holyroodhouse

*Edinburgh, Midlothian*

£ OAP DoE

Official residence of HM the Queen when in Scotland. Oldest part is constructed against nave of Holyrood Abbey, of which little survives. Largely rebuilt and remodelled for Charles II by Sir William Bruce. Mary Queen of Scots spent 6 years here and met John Knox. Tapestries and portraits of over 100 Scottish kings.

➜ At foot of Canongate, Edinburgh

Jan to early May, then late July to mid-Dec, Mon to Fri 9.30–5.15, Sat 11–4. Closed during Royal visits

Edinburgh Castle, Georgian House in Charlotte Square

Edinburgh

## Tantallon Castle

*Near North Berwick, East Lothian*

£ DoE

Ruins of 14th-C Douglas stronghold. Survived siege by James V in 1528, but was slighted and destroyed by General Monk in 1651. Clifftop setting with fine views.

➜ 3 miles E of North Berwick off A198

Daily except public hols (AMS)

Luffness Castle

North Berwick (2 miles)

## Winton House

*Pencaitland, East Lothian*

£

Built 1620, good example of Scottish Renaissance style. Exquisite plaster ceilings decorated for visit of King Charles I in 1633. Paintings and furniture. Unique carved twisted stone chimneys. Sir Walter Scott's model for Ravenswood Castle in *The Bride of Lammermoor*. Terraced gardens, fine trees.

Pencaitland 340222

➜ 6 miles SW of Haddington off B6355

For parties only (or those specially interested) by prior arrangement

Hamilton House

Prestonpans (7 miles)

## Bachelors' Club

*Tarbolton, Ayrshire*

17th-C thatched house where in 1780 Robert Burns and his friends founded a literary and debating society. Burns also attended dancing lessons here. Memorabilia of the poet.

Tarbolton 424

7 miles NE of Ayr off B730

Apr to end Sept daily 10–6; other times by appointment

Burns Cottage, Culzean Castle

Ayr ($7\frac{1}{2}$ miles)

## Bothwell Castle

*Bothwell, Lanarkshire*

Impressive giant ruins of one of finest stone castles in Scotland. Dates from 13th C, reconstructed by Douglases in 15th C. Fine setting above Clyde valley.

9 miles SE of Glasgow, $1\frac{1}{2}$ miles from M74 exit 5

All year except public hols (AMS)

Cameron House, Weaver's Cottage

Uddingston (1 mile)

## Burns Cottage

*Alloway, Ayrshire*

Thatched cottage, built by his father, where Robert Burns was born in 1759. Adjoining cottage is museum dedicated to poet. Start of Burns' heritage trail.

2 miles s of Ayr off B7024

Apr to Oct daily 9–7, Sun 2–7 (but Sun from June to Aug 10–7); Nov to Mar daily (except Sun) 10–dusk

Bachelors' Club, Culzean Castle, Souter Johnnie's Cottage

Ayr ($1\frac{1}{2}$ miles)

## Cameron House

*Balloch, Dunbartonshire*

Family home of Smollets of Bonhill, standing within Cameron-Loch Lomond Wildlife Park. House has: literary museum devoted to Tobias Smollett; glass; porcelain; furniture; unusual 'Whisky Galore' room; model aircraft display; Victorian nursery. Pleasant gardens and woodland walk. Wildlife park has bears, bison, children's zoo and adventure playground.

Alexandria 56226

4 miles N of Dumbarton off A82, beside Loch Lomond. House can only be reached from Wildlife Park

Easter to late Sept daily 10.30–6

Stirling Castle, Weaver's Cottage

Balloch ($1\frac{1}{2}$ miles)

($1\frac{1}{2}$ miles)

## Castle Sween

*Argyllshire*

Possibly oldest stone castle on Scottish mainland, erected in mid-

BURNS COTTAGE

12th C. Destroyed in 1647 by Sir Alexander Macdonald.

On E shore of Loch Sween, 15 miles SW of Lochgilphead, off narrow road to Imory

Any reasonable time (AMS)

Cameron House, Stirling Castle

## Craignethan Castle

*Near Lanark, Lanarkshire*

£ DoE

Well-preserved ruin, once chief stronghold of Hamiltons. Recent excavations have revealed possibly earliest example in Britain of a 'caponier'.

6 miles NW of Lanark off A72

All year daily except public hols (AMS)

Bachelors' Club, Burns Cottage, Weaver's Cottage

Carluke (4 miles)

## Culzean Castle

*Kirkoswald, Ayrshire*

£ NTS

One of finest Adam houses in Scotland. Built around ancient tower of the Kennedys, main part dates from 1777. Round drawing room. Superb plaster ceilings and fine staircase. Eisenhower Presentation explaining General's association with Culzean.

Kirkoswald 269

On coast 12 miles SW of Ayr off A719

Apr to end Sept daily 10–6; Oct daily 10–4

Burns Cottage, Souter Johnnie's Cottage

Maybole (4 miles)

## Dumbarton Castle

*Dumbarton, Dunbartonshire*

£ DoE

Built on top of 73-m high rock, it dates from 12th C. Sundial given by Mary Queen of Scots; it was from Dumbarton that she left for France at age of 5.

All year daily except public hols (AMS)

Cameron House

Dumbarton Central

## Inveraray Castle

*Inveraray, Argyllshire*

£ OAP

Headquarters of Clan Campbell since 15th C. Present castle started 1743 when 3rd Duke of Argyll engaged Roger Morris to build it; interior decoration later commissioned by 5th Duke from Robert Mylne. Many fine works of art and antiques.

Inveraray 2203

½ mile N of Inveraray off A83

Apr to end Sept daily 10–1, 2–6, Sun 2–6. Closed Fri in Apr, May, June and Sept

Cameron House

## Newark Castle

*Near Port Glasgow, Renfrewshire*

£ DoE

Turreted mansion of Maxwells, dating mostly from 16th/17th Cs, but with 15th-C tower.

Just E of Port Glasgow, 16 miles W of Glasgow on A8

All year daily except public hols (AMS)

Cameron House, Weaver's Cottage

Port Glasgow (½ mile)

## Pollok House

*Glasgow, Lanarkshire*

£

Built between 1747 and 1752 to designs by William Adam; additions by Sir Rowand Anderson 1890–1908. Houses Stirling–Maxwell collection of Spanish and other paintings and displays of Spanish glass among other decorative arts. In park are rhododendron walk and Royal National Rose Society trial garden.

Glasgow 632 0274

3½ miles from centre off A736

All year daily 10–5, Sun 2–5. Closed Dec 25 and Jan 1

Cameron House, Weaver's Cottage

Pollokshaws West

**Provan Hall**
*Auchinlea Road, Glasgow E4, Lanarkshire*

15th C, probably finest pre-Reformation mansion in Scotland. Given to NT in 1935.

Glasgow 771 6372

Telephone custodian

Pollok House, Weaver's Cottage

Garrowhill (2 miles)

**Souter Johnnie's Cottage**
*Kirkoswald, Ayrshire*

Thatched cottage home of village cobbler (souter) John Davidson at end of 18th C, immortalized by Burns in his 'Tam o'Shanter'. Life-sized stone figures in garden of the souter, Tam, the innkeeper and his wife. Burns' mementoes and cobbler's tools.

Kirkoswald 243

11 miles SW of Ayr, on A77

Apr to end Sept daily (except Fri) 12–5

Burns Cottage, Culzean Castle

Maybole (4½ miles)

**Weaver's Cottage**
*Kilbarchan, Renfrewshire*

Typical cottage of 18th-C weaver, with looms, weaving equipment and domestic utensils.

5 miles W of Paisley off A761

May, Sept and Oct, Tues, Thur, Sat and Sun 2–5; June to end Aug daily 2–5

Pollok House, Provan Hall

Johnstone (2 miles)

## TAYSIDE REGION

**Barrie's Birthplace**
*9 Brechin Road, Kirriemuir, Angus*

J. M. Barrie was born in this 2-storeyed house in 1860. Outside wash-house is said to have been his first theatre. Manuscripts, personal possessions, mementoes of actors and producers associated with his plays are on display.

Kirriemuir 2646

On A928, 18 miles N of Dundee

May to end Sept, Mon to Sat 10–12.30, 2–6, Sun 2–6

Edzell Castle, Glamis Castle

Dundee (18 miles)

**Blair Castle**
*Blair Atholl, Perthshire*

Baronial castle, seat of Duke of Atholl, Chief of Clan Murray. Oldest part is Comyn's Tower built *c.* 1269. Fine collections of portraits, lace, china, furniture, arms and armour, and Jacobite relics. Duke is only British subject allowed to maintain a private army, the Atholl Highlanders.

Blair Atholl 355

7 miles NW of Pitlochry on A9

Easter weekend; Sun and Mon in Apr; May to mid-Oct daily 10–6, Sun 2–6

Braemar Castle

Blair Atholl (½ mile)

**Broughty Castle**
*Broughty Ferry, Angus*

15th-C castle rebuilt as estuary fort in 19th C. On show material concerned with whaling, natural history of the Tay, arms and armour.

4 miles E of Dundee on A930

All year daily (except Fri and Sat) 10–1, 2–5; Sun (June to Sept only) 2–5. Closed public hols

Glamis Castle

Broughty Ferry

## Burleigh Castle

*Milnathort, near Kinross, Kinrossshire*

£ DoE

Good example of tower house *c.* 1500. Seat of Balfours of Burleigh. James VI visited several times.

→ 2 miles N of Kinross off A911

All year daily except public hols (AMS). Key at farm opposite

Falkland Palace, Hill of Tarvit, Scone Palace

Cowdenbeath (10 miles)

## Edzell Castle

*Edzell, Angus*

£ DoE

16th-C castle associated with Mary Queen of Scots. Walled garden laid out by Sir David Lindsay in 1604; heraldic and symbolic sculptures. Courtyard mansion dates from 1580.

→ 7 miles N of Brechin off B996

Apr to Sept daily 9.30–7, Sun 2–7; Oct to Mar daily 9.30–4, Sun 2–4. Closed Dec 25–26 and Jan 1–2

Barrie's Birthplace, Glamis Castle

## Elcho Castle

*Elcho, near Perth, Perthshire*

£ DoE

Preserved fortified mansion, noted for wrought iron grilles to windows and tower-like jambs or wings.

→ On River Tay, 4 miles SE of Perth off unclassified road to Rhynd

All year daily except public hols (AMS)

Glamis Castle, Scone Palace

Perth ($5\frac{1}{2}$ miles)

## Glamis Castle

*Near Kirriemuir, Angus*

£ OAP

Owes present aspect to rebuilding and modifications in 1675–87 when French château style emerged. Portions of high square tower which are $4\frac{1}{2}$ m thick are much older. Fine collections of china, tapestry and furniture. Famous legend of secret chamber. Probable setting for murder of Duncan in *Macbeth*. Grounds laid out by 'Capability' Brown. Childhood home of Queen Elizabeth the Queen Mother.

→ 4 miles S of Kirriemuir off A928

Easter weekend, then May to end Sept daily except Sat 1–5

Barrie's Birthplace, Scone Palace

Dundee (10 miles)

## Huntingtower Castle

*Ruthven, near Perth, Perthshire*

£ DoE

15th-C castellated mansion known as Ruthven Castle until 1600. Scene of Raid of Ruthven in 1528; James VI, when 16, accepted invitation from Earl of Gowrie to his hunting lodge and found himself virtually kidnapped by nobles who wished him to get rid of his royal favourites. James tried to escape, but was barred by Master of Glamis. Ruthven party held power for some months, then Gowrie was beheaded.

→ 3 miles W of Perth off A85

All year daily except public hols (AMS)

Glamis Castle, Scone Palace

Perth (1 mile)

GLAMIS CASTLE

## Loch Leven Castle

*Near Kinross, Kinrossshire*

Erected in 14th C by Archibald the Grim on small island. Strong 4-storeyed tower with courtyard enclosed by curtain wall. Mary Queen of Scots spent 11 months here until her escape in 1568.

→ 2 miles E of Kinross, off B996, reached by ferry from lochside (from May – weather permitting)

May to early Oct daily (AMS)

Falkland Palace, Hill of Tarvit, Scone Palace

Cowdenbeath (11 miles)

## Scone Palace

*Old Scone, Perthshire*

The Stone of Destiny, on which Scottish kings were crowned, was brought here by Kenneth I in 9th C. It remained until 1296 when Edward I had it seized and taken to Westminster Abbey. In 1559 the followers of John Knox sacked and burned the Abbey of Scone. Present palace, largely rebuilt in 1803, incorporates parts of earlier building. Contents include: needlework bed hangings worked by Mary Queen of Scots; French clocks and furniture; ceramics; ivories; Vernis Martin vases. In the grounds a pinetum, with one of the finest collections of rare conifers in the country.

Scone 51416

→ Off A93, 3 miles N of Perth

Mid-Apr to mid-Oct daily 10–6, Sun 2–6

Falkland Palace, Glamis Castle

Perth ($1\frac{1}{2}$ miles)

SCONE PALACE

# WALES

## CLWYD

### Bodrhyddan Hall

*Rhuddlan, near Rhyl*

17th-C manor house. Collections of arms including armour, 2 suits possibly from Wars of the Roses, portraits and furniture. In grounds St Mary's Well with octagonal well-house, dated 1612.

Rhuddlan 590414

4 miles SE of Rhyl off A547

June to Sept, Tues and Thur 2–5.30

Conwy Castle, Rhuddlan Castle

Rhyl (4 miles)

### Chirk Castle

*Chirk, near Wrexham*

Splendid example of Marcher Fortress, built 1310. Exterior unaltered. Neo-Gothic entrance hall, with oak panelling by Pugin, who made some modifications 1835–37. Four-poster bed in which Charles I slept. Portraits and tapestries. Fine 18th-C wrought-iron gates by the Davies brothers of Bersham. Gardens.

Chirk 7701

10 miles S of Wrexham on B4500 off A5

Mid-Apr to end Oct, Sun 2–5; Tues, Wed and Thur 11–5 (2–5 in Apr, May and Oct), also Bank Hol. Mon 11–5

Powis Castle, Erddig

Chirk ($1\frac{1}{2}$ miles)

### Denbigh Castle

*In Denbigh*

Erected between 1282 and 1322 by Henry de Lacy, Earl of Lincoln, and his successor. Massive triangular gatehouse. Refortified and garrisoned for King during Civil War, withstanding 6-months' siege.

All year daily except public hols (DES)

Bodrhyddan Hall, Conwy Castle

Rhyl (12 miles)

### Erddig

*Near Wrexham*

Late 17th-C house with 18th-C additions, containing much of original furniture. Outbuildings include: bakehouse, laundry, sawmill and smithy, all operative. Notable garden has been restored to 18th-C formal design and contains fruit varieties known to have been grown at time. Agricultural museum.

1 mile S of Wrexham off A483

Mid-Apr to end Oct daily (except Mon, but open Bank Hol. Mon) 12–5.30

Bodrhyddan Hall, Chirk Castle, Denbigh Castle

Wrexham ($1\frac{1}{2}$ miles)

Sun only

### Ewloe Castle

*Ewloe, near Flint*

Unusual small castle tucked away in woods between 2 ravines. Two periods of buildings discernible, both of the 13th C.

6 miles SE of Flint off A55

All year daily except public hols (DES)

Flint Castle, Erddig

Hawarden (2 miles)

### Flint Castle

*In Flint*

The ruins of the first of Edward I's Welsh castles, built between 1277 and 1284. Circular keep surrounded by moat. Great tower is mentioned in Shakespeare's *Richard II*. The doomed king heard Mass here on August 22, 1399. In Civil War castle was Royalist until taken by Cromwellians in 1643, then retaken in 1645 and lost once more in 1646.

All year daily except public hols (DES)

Bodrhyddan Hall, Erdigg, Ewloe Castle, Rhuddlan Castle

Flint

### Rhuddlan Castle

*Rhuddlan, near Rhyl*

£ OAP DoE

Concentric castle built to 'diamond' plan by Edward I in 1277; massive curtain walls and gatehouses. Intended to command estuary and crossing of River Clwyd.

3 miles S of Rhyl off A547

All year daily except public hols (DES)

Bodrhyddan Hall, Conwy Castle

Rhyl ($3\frac{1}{2}$ miles)

## DYFED

### Carreg Cennen Castle

*Near Ammanford*

£ DoE

13th C, although there was fortress on site long before present building. Interesting feature is long passage cut into rock and lit by loopholes. In Wars of the Roses, held for a time by Lancastrians. Slighted in 1462 to stop robbers using it as refuge.

5 miles NE of Ammanford, 2 miles E of A483

All year daily except public hols (DES)

Gelly, Llanstephan Castle

Llandeilo ($4\frac{1}{2}$ miles)

### Cilgerran Castle

*Near Cardigan*

£ OAP NT DoE

Dramatically sited on towering crag above gorge of Teifi. Castle's age uncertain, 12th or 13th C. Occupied by Normans as administrative centre of lordship of Emlyn. Reduced to ruins in Civil War. Features in paintings by de Wint and Turner.

3 miles SE of Cardigan, E of A478 at Pen-y-bryn

Mid-Mar to mid-Oct daily 9.30–6.30, Sun 2–6.30; rest of year, daily 9.30–4, Sun 2–4. Closed Dec 24–26 and Jan 1

Gelly, Llanstephan Castle

### Gelly

*Talsarn, near Lampeter*

Early Welsh Gentry House dating *c.* 1680. Possibly elements of design by John Nash. Favourite haunt of Dylan Thomas. Welsh kitchen. Cob walled garden.

8 miles NW of Lampeter on B4337, 2 miles from A482 at Temple Bar

By prior arrangement only. Admission charges on request

Carreg Cennen Castle, Cilgerran Castle

($1\frac{1}{2}$ miles)

### Kidwelly Castle

*Kidwelly, near Carmarthen*

£ OAP DoE

12th-C fortress with semi-circular moat. Earthwork defences raised by Roger, Bishop of Salisbury, during reign of Henry I.

$8\frac{1}{2}$ miles S of Carmarthen off A484

All year daily except public hols (DES)

Llanstephan Castle

Kidwelly ($\frac{1}{2}$ mile)

### Lamphey Palace

*Lamphey, near Pembroke*

£ OAP DoE

Fine unfortified manor house of Bishops of St David's. W wing dates from 13th C, and E from 14th. Additions by Bishop Gower including battlemented parapets, and larger hall.

➔ 2 miles E of Pembroke off A4139

◷ All year daily except public hols (DES)

▦ Llanstephan Castle, Pembroke Castle

⇌ Pembroke (2 miles)

## Llanstephan Castle

*Llanstephan, near Carmarthen*

£ DoE ♜

Romantic castle standing on headland overlooking Towy estuary. 13th-C remains include great keep-gatehouse.

➔ 8 miles SW of Carmarthen

◷ Any reasonable time (DES)

▦ Lamphey Palace, Pembroke Castle

⇌ Carmarthen (8 miles)

## Llawhaden Castle

*Llawhaden, near Haverfordwest*

£ ♟ OAP DoE ♜

Fortified residence of bishops of St David's. Earlier version of timber and earthworks. Curtain and tower came in early 14th C; good gatehouse.

➔ 8½ miles E of Haverfordwest, 1½ miles N of junction of A40 and A4075

◷ All year daily except public hols (DES)

▦ Lamphey Palace, Pembroke Castle

⇌ Narberth (4 miles)

## Manorbier Castle

*Manorbier, near Pembroke*

£ ♟ 🚌

In 12th C stone castle began to replace earlier simple earthworks; powerful de Barri family implemented work. Historian and scholar-priest Giraldus Cambrensis was born here about 1146. He was to call Manorbier 'the most delightful part of Pembroch ... the pleasantest spot in Wales'. In his day, the castle, he tells us, was 'excellently well defended by turrets and bulwarks'. Life-sized wax figures on display.

☎ Manorbier 394

➔ On coast 5 miles SE of Pembroke off B4585

◷ Easter week, then late May to end Sept daily 11–6

▦ Lamphey Palace

⇌ Manorbier

## Pembroke Castle

*In Pembroke*

£ ♟ 🚌 🔒

Earliest work on site dates from *c.* 1090 by Arnulf of Montgomery. Main fortress was begun in 1105; important feature is massive keep nearly 25 m high with walls 5 m thick. Birthplace of Henry VII.

☎ Pembroke 3092

➔ From W end of Main Street

◷ Easter to end Sept, Mon to Fri 10–7, Sat 10–6, Sun 11–7; Oct to Easter, Mon to Sat 10.30–5. Closed Sun and Dec 25

▦ Lamphey Palace, Manorbier Castle

⇌ Pembroke

## Tudor Merchant's House

*Quay Hill, Tenby*

£ ♟ NT 🚌 🔒

15th C, with fine Flemish chimney. Remains of early frescoes on 3 interior walls.

☎ Tenby 2279

◷ Easter to end Sept, Mon to Fri 10–1, 2.30–6, Sun 2–6. Closed Good Fri

▦ Manorbier Castle, Pembroke Castle

⇌ Tenby

## Caerphilly Castle

*In Caerphilly*

£ OAP DoE

Concentrically planned castle begun *c.* 1271 by Gilbert de Clare. One of greatest castles in Wales with comprehensive land and water defences.

All year daily except public hols (DES)

Cardiff Castle, Castell Coch, Coity Castle

Caerphilly

## Cardiff Castle

*In Cardiff*

£ OAP

Rests on Roman fortification which Normans used as framework for wooden building on raised motte; then in late 12th C came a stone keep and later a gatehouse. Robert, Duke of Normandy, was imprisoned here for 28 years after his defeat by younger brother Henry I. Between 1867 and 1875 William Burges, encouraged by 3rd Marquess of Bute, made an almost complete reconstruction of castle, producing another imaginative extravaganza as at Castell Coch. Scenes from the Bible, Greek mythology, *Canterbury Tales* and the Arab world abound, rich in colour and gilding, evocative of King Ludwig II's Schloss Neuschwanstein.

Cardiff 31033 (ex 716)

All year daily: Mar, Apr and Oct 10–5; May to Sept 10–6; Nov to Feb 10–4

Caerphilly Castle, Castell Coch, Coity Castle

Cardiff Central (½ mile)

## Castell Coch

*Tongwynlais, near Cardiff*

£ OAP DoE

Foundations are 13th C, when it was the 'Red Castle' of the Anglo-Norman lords of Glamorgan. Restored and remodelled considerably in 1870s by William Burges for 3rd Marquess of Bute. Designer's imagination had full scope with interior decoration; scenes from Aesop's fables and figures from Greek mythology are disported on walls and ceilings.

5 miles NW of Cardiff, off A470

Mid-Mar to mid-Oct daily 9.30–6.30; mid-Oct to mid-Mar daily 9.30–4, Sun 2–4. Closed Dec 24–26 and Jan 1

Caerphilly Castle, Cardiff Castle, Coity Castle

Taff Wells (1 mile)

## Coity Castle

*Coity, near Bridgend*

£ OAP DoE

Square keep and S and E curtain walls of circular inner ward date from 12th C; other buildings are 14th C, when most of castle was rebuilt. Held by the Turbevilles. 'Marry my daughter and you shall have all my lands without bloodshed', said Morgan, the Welsh ruler of the region, and Payn de Turbeville did just that.

1½ miles NE of Bridgend, 1 mile E of A4061 at Pendre

All year daily except public hols (DES)

Caerphilly Castle, Cardiff Castle, Castell Coch

Bridgend (2 miles)

## Loughor Castle

*Loughor, near Llanelli*

£ DoE

Partly built on Roman fort of Leucarum. Small square tower of 13th or early 14th C, with traces of curtain wall. Intended to command ford through River Loughor.

5 miles SE of Llanelli, off A484

Any reasonable time (DES)

Coity Castle, Newcastle Castle

Gowerton (2½ miles). Not Sun

## Newcastle Castle

*In Bridgend*

Small 12th-C building, overlooking River Ogmore. Massive curtain walls enclosing polygonal courtyard; remarkable elaborately decorated Norman gateway.

½ mile from train station

All year daily (DES)

Castell Coch, Coity Castle

Bridgend

## Ogmore Castle

*Ogmore, near Bridgend*

Built to guard crossing on River Ewenny, well known for its stepping stones. Inner and outer wards each with moat; the inner also with 12th-C keep. With Coity and Newcastle Castle, formed defensive triangle.

2½ miles SW of Bridgend off B4524

All year daily except public hols (DES)

Coity Castle, Newcastle Castle

Bridgend (4 miles)

## Weobley Castle

*Llanrhidian, near Swansea*

Fortified manor house dating from 13th/14th Cs, built by Henry Beaufort, Earl of Warwick, later lived in by de la Bere family. Stands dramatically in commanding position on N Gower coast. Hall and kitchen wing date from 2nd half of 13th C. Variety of towers.

11 miles W of Swansea, 1¾ miles W of junction of B4271 and B4295

All year daily (DES)

Llanstephan Castle, Manorbier Castle, Pembroke Castle

Gowerton (8 miles). Not Sun

# GWENT

## Chepstow Castle

*In Chepstow*

One of earliest recorded masonry castles, begun *c.* 1067 by William FitzOsborn. Set on spur of land overlooking Wye and commanding Roman road leading into South Wales. Fine and extensive ruin with buildings from its beginnings up to Civil War.

Mid-Mar to mid-Oct daily 9.30–6.30; mid-Oct to mid-Mar daily 9.30–4, Sun 2–4. Closed Dec 24–26 and Jan 1

Monmouth Castle, Penhow Castle

Chepstow

## Grosmont Castle

*Near Pontrilas*

Built *c.* 1201 largely by Hubert de Burgh; consists of single ward surrounded by deep moat.

2 miles SE of Pontrilas off B4347

Any reasonable time (DES)

Llanfihangel Court, Skenfrith Castle

Abergavenny (11 miles)

## Llanfihangel Court

*Llanfihangel Crucorney, near Abergavenny*

Early Tudor manor house with reconstructed front dating from 1559. Interior altered in mid-17th C during Restoration.

5 miles N of Abergavenny off A465

1st, 3rd and 5th Sun in June, all Sun in July and Aug, also Easter and Bank Hol. Sun and Mon 2.30–6

Grosmont Castle, Skenfrith Castle

Abergavenny (4½ miles)

## Monmouth Castle

*In Monmouth*

One of chain of 12th-C fortresses built by William FitzOsborn. Added protection provided by fortified Monnow Gate – only surviving example of its kind in Britain. Birthplace of Henry V.

On cliff above the Monnow

Any reasonable time (DES)

Grosmont Castle, Skenfrith Castle

## Newport Castle

*In Newport*

Two large octagonal corner-towers with watergate between them, dating from late 14th C.

On right bank of Usk beside Newport Bridge (A48)

Any reasonable time (DES)

Penhow Castle, Tredegar House

Newport (½ mile)

## Penhow Castle

*Penhow, near Newport*

Oldest inhabited castle in Wales, once home of Seymour family. Dating from 12th C, shows how fortified manor house was developed from early massive keep. Great hall with minstrels' gallery; Charles II rooms; dovecote, with entrance holes opening from side of building.

Penhow 400800

Midway between Chepstow and Newport on A48

Easter to Sept, Wed to Sun and Bank Hol. 10–6

Chepstow Castle, Newport Castle, Tredegar House

Newport (6 miles)

## Raglan Castle

*Raglan, near Monmouth*

Romantic and beautiful remains of one of latest great castles. Built in 15th C, probably on site of small Norman castle. Design of entrance towers and much of interior has a grace that points to increasing desire for gracious living. Massive Yellow Tower of Gwent with its own moat is masterly piece of defensive work. Defended in Civil War by brave old Marquis of Worcester against powerful Cromwellian army; he held out from June 3rd to August 19th 1646. This fine castle was then mutilated.

7 miles SW of Monmouth off A40

All year daily except public hols (DES)

Monmouth Castle, Skenfrith Castle

Abergavenny (10 miles)

## Skenfrith Castle

*Skenfrith, near Monmouth*

Norman castle built as defence against Welsh; keep stands on remains of motte; 13th-C curtain wall with towers.

6 miles NW of Monmouth off B4521

At any reasonable time

Monmouth Castle, Raglan Castle

Abergavenny (12 miles)

Fri only

## Tredegar House

*Near Newport*

One of outstanding 17th-C brick houses in Wales; part of earlier building also survives. Formerly home of Lords of Tredegar; family portraits. Extensive grounds, fishing and boating lake, aquarium, children's farm. Coarse angling by permit in season.

Newport 62568

2 miles SW of Newport near junction of M4 (exit 28) and A48

Apr to end Sept daily (except Mon and Tues, but open Bank Hol. Mon) 2–6

Castell Coch, Newport Castle

Newport (3 miles)

### White Castle

*Near Abergavenny*

In 1201 King John granted White Castle, Grosmont and Skenfrith to Hubert de Burgh, the 3 castles forming defensive triangle. Traces of white plaster indicate how this structure got its name. Much still standing. Moated.

5 miles E of Abergavenny off B4233

All year daily (DES)

Grosmont Castle, Skenfrith Castle

Abergavenny (5 miles)

## GWYNEDD

### Aberconwy House

*Castle Street, Conwy*

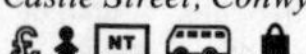

Medieval house dating from 14th C, 3-storeyed with asymmetrical front. Displays illustrating life of borough of Conwy from Roman times to present.

Conwy 2246

Mid-Apr to end Sept daily (except Wed in Apr and May) 10–5.30, Oct, Sat and Sun 10–5.30. Parties all year by arrangement

Caernarfon Castle, Cochwillan Old Hall, Conwy Castle

Llandudno Junction ($\frac{1}{2}$ mile)

### Beaumaris Castle

*Beaumaris, near Menai Bridge*

Started at end of 13th C, was last fortress set up in North Wales by Edward I. Possibly finest of concentrically planned strongholds in Britain. Moated, Beaumaris is entered by gate next to sea, where modern wooden bridge replaces original drawbridge.

On Anglesey, 4 miles NE of Menai Bridge, off A545

All year daily except public hols (DES)

Caernarfon Castle, Plas Newydd

Llanfairpwll ($5\frac{1}{2}$ miles)

### Bryn Bras Castle

*Llanrug, near Caernarfon*

Earlier structure on site dates from before 1750. Present building built in 1830s in Romanesque style. Large gardens with waterfalls, pools, woodland walks and wonderful views of Anglesey and Snowdonia.

Llanberis 210

$4\frac{1}{2}$ miles E of Caernarfon off A4086

Spring Bank Hol. to end Sept daily (except Sat) 1–5 (mid-July to end Aug 10.30–5)

Caernarfon Castle, Dolwyddelan Castle

Bangor ($9\frac{1}{2}$ miles)

### Caernarfon Castle

*In Caernarfon*

Most splendid of Edward I's castles in North Wales, begun in 1284 on site of earlier Norman castle built there *c.* 1090. Castle is defended by massive walls, 7 huge towers and 2 great gatehouses. Birthplace of Edward II, first Prince of Wales. Scene, in 1969, of investiture of present Prince of Wales.

All year daily: mid-Mar to mid-Oct 9.30–6.30, rest of year 9.30–4, Sun 2–4. Closed Dec 24–26 and Jan 1

Beaumaris Castle, Plas Newydd

Bangor (9 miles)

### Cochwillan Old Hall

*Tal-y-bont, near Bangor*

Noteworthy example of medieval architecture. Restored in 1971.

Bangor 4608

CAERNARFON CASTLE

→ 3 miles SE of Bangor off A55
By appointment only
Penrhyn Castle, Plas Newydd
Bangor (3½ miles)

## Conwy Castle

*In Conwy*

£ OAP DoE

Built by Edward I between 1283 and 1289 to command ferry at Conwy and main road to Snowdonia. Originally 27 towers with extensive and formidable town walls. King's Tower was probably more ornate than others and had extra storey.

All year daily: mid-Mar to mid-Oct 9.30–6.30; rest of year 9.30–4, Sun 2–4. Closed Dec 24–26 and Jan 1
Aberconwy House, Caernarfon Castle
Llandudno Junction (1 mile)

## Criccieth Castle

*Criccieth, near Porthmadog*

£ OAP DoE

Native Welsh castle dating mainly from first half of 13th C, altered and strengthened by Edward I. Sited on top of rocky peninsula commanding Tremadog Bay.

→ 6 miles S of Porthmadog, off A497
All year daily (DES)
Harlech Castle, Portmeirion
Criccieth. Not Sun

## Dolwyddelan Castle

*Near Betws-y-Coed*

£ OAP DoE

12th-C Welsh castle perched high on ridge, looking over magnificence of Moel Siabod and meadow of Gwyddelan. Well-preserved rectangular keep. Traditionally the birthplace of Llywelyn the Great.

→ 6 miles SW of Betws-y-Coed, up rough track off A470
All year daily (DES)
Gwydir Castle, Portmeirion
Dolwyddelan

## Gwydir Castle

*Llanrwst, near Conwy*

£

Fine ivy-covered Tudor mansion, historic royal residence, built round 14th-C hall of Maredudd. Notable Tudor furniture. Fireplace hiding priest's hole. Bedroom where Charles II slept. Tropical birds and peacocks in grounds.

Llanrwst 640261
→ 12 miles S of Conwy, ½ mile from Llanrwst on A470
Easter to mid-Oct daily (except Sat) 10–5
Caernarfon Castle, Conwy Castle
Llanrwst (¾ mile)

## Harlech Castle

*In Harlech*

£ OAP DoE

Built by Edward I between 1283 and 1290, notable example of concentric plan fully developed at Beaumaris. Great master mason James of St George worked here. Site is a precipitous rock from where castle looks over Tremadog Bay to Ireland.

Mid-Mar to mid-Oct daily 9.30–6.30; mid-Oct to mid-Mar daily 9.30–4, Sun 2–4. Closed Dec 24–26 and Jan 1
Portmeirion, Ty Mawr
Harlech (¾ mile)

## Penrhyn Castle

*Near Bangor*

19th-C neo-Norman castle. Industrial railway museum, collection of dolls, natural history display. Victorian garden.

Bangor 53084

1 mile E of Bangor, N of A5 at Llandegai

Apr to end Oct daily 2–5 (late May to end Sept and all Bank Hol. weekends 11–5)

Caernarfon Castle, Plas Newydd

Bangor (2 miles)

## Plas Mawr

*High Street, Conwy*

Notable town house by Robert Wynne built late 16th C. Royal Cambrian Academy of Art.

Daily, summer 10–5.30, winter 10–4. Closed Dec to mid-Jan

Aberconwy House, Cochwillan Old Hall, Penrhyn Castle

Llandudno Junction ($\frac{3}{4}$ mile)

Summer only

## Plas Newydd

*Llanfairpwll, Anglesey*

18th-C Georgian-Gothic style mansion by James Wyatt assisted by Joseph Potter. Rex Whistler room decorated by painter's largest mural. Military museum with relics from Waterloo. Pleasant grounds sloping down to Menai Straits.

Bangor 714795

In Anglesey, 2 miles SW of Menai Bridge off A4080

Mid-Apr to end Oct daily (except Sat) 12–5

Beaumaris Castle, Caernarfon Castle, Conwy Castle

Llanfairpwll (1 mile)

Not Sun

## Plas-yn-Rhiw

*Rhiw, near Pwllheli*

Small manor house, part medieval with Tudor and Georgian additions. Ornamental gardens; woodlands down to W shore of Porth Neigwl (Hell's Mouth Bay).

Rhiw 219

12 miles SW of Pwllhelli on unclassified coast road to Aberdaron

Apr to end June, Wed and Thur 3–4.30, strictly by appointment only

Portmeirion

Pwllheli (10 miles)

## Portmeirion

*Penrhyndeudraeth, near Porthmadog*

Village designed by late Sir Clough Williams-Ellis with pastel-washed cottages and other buildings that incorporate various architectural styles. 175 acres of sub-tropical woodlands with masses of flowering shrubs, the whole set on private peninsula.

Penrhyndeudraeth 770 228

3 miles SE of Portmadog, off A487 at Minffordd

Easter to end Oct daily 9.30–6

Harlech Castle, Ty Mawr

Minffordd ($1\frac{1}{2}$ miles)

## Ty Mawr

*Wybrnant, near Penmachno*

Birthplace of Bishop William Morgan (*c.* 1541–1604), first translator of Bible into Welsh. His work is considered a masterpiece and has become foundation of modern Welsh literature.

Penmachno 213

$3\frac{1}{2}$ miles SW of Betws-y-Coed, 2 miles W of B4406 at Penmachno

Mid-Apr to end Oct daily (except Sat) 12–5

Dolwyddelan Castle, Gwydir Castle, Portmeirion

Betws-y-Coed ($3\frac{1}{2}$ miles)

# POWYS

## Powis Castle

*Near Welshpool*

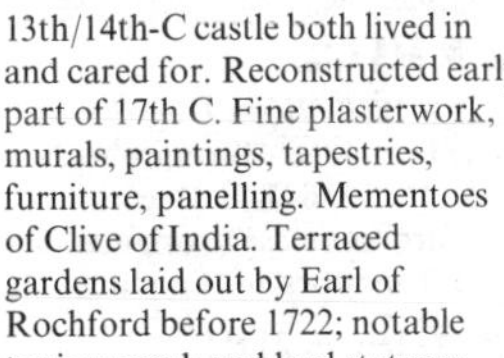

13th/14th-C castle both lived in and cared for. Reconstructed early part of 17th C. Fine plasterwork, murals, paintings, tapestries, furniture, panelling. Mementoes of Clive of India. Terraced gardens laid out by Earl of Rochford before 1722; notable topiary work and lead statuary.

Welshpool 2554

1 mile from Welshpool off A483

Mid-Apr to late Sept, Wed to Sun 2–6; Bank Hol. Mon 11.30–6. Closed Good Fri

Attingham Park, Trelydan Hall. Wilderhope Manor

Welshpool (1 mile)

POWIS CASTLE

## Trelydan Hall

*Near Welshpool*

Fine black-and-white Tudor house sited on foundations of secluded medieval Catholic hospice, in turn reputedly built over a Roman Villa. Once home of John Gwyn, armourer to Charles I and writer of *The Military Memoirs of the Civil War.* Rare collection of Victorian wedding dresses and antique lace.

Welshpool 2773

1 mile N of Welshpool off A490

Easter to Dec 24 daily 11–5

Powis Castle, Wilderhope Manor

Welshpool (1 mile)

(1 mile)

## Tretower Court and Castle

*Tretower, near Abergavenny*

Notable medieval house with nearby ruined Norman and 13th-C castle with interesting cylindrical keep.

8 miles NW of Abergavenny near junction of A40 and A479

Mid-Mar to mid-Oct daily 9.30–6.30, Sun 2–6.30; rest of year 9.30–4, Sun 2–4. Closed Dec 24–26 and Jan 1

Grosmont Castle, Llanfihangel Court

Abergavenny (8 miles)

# THE OFFSHORE ISLANDS

## CHANNEL ISLANDS: GUERNSEY

### Castle Cornet

*In St Peter Port*

Old castle with features and additions dating from 13th C. Garrisoned during Civil War by Sir Peter Osborne, who held out until Dec 1651. Spencer collection of badges and uniforms; armoury.

Guernsey 21657

Apr to Oct daily 10.30–6

Hauteville House

### Hauteville House

*In St Peter Port*

Built *c.* 1800. Victor Hugo lived there from 1856–70, returning in 1872, 1875 and 1878. Decoration and furniture close to original state. Tapestries and paintings.

Guernsey 21911

All year daily (except Thur afternoons) 10–12, 2–4.30

Castle Cornet

## CHANNEL ISLANDS: JERSEY

### Elizabeth Castle

*Near St Aubin's*

Built on L'Islet rock, which is about 1 mile out in St Aubin's Bay. Raleigh named it Fort Isabella Bellissima, and it has had lively history back to time of Elizabeth I. German bunkers and military relics.

Jersey Central 23971

From St Aubin's by boat

Mar to Oct daily 9.30–6.30

Mont Orgueil Castle

### Mont Orgueil Castle

*Near Gorey*

Medieval concentric castle from 12th/13th Cs. Poised on headland, site of Iron age settlement.

Jersey Central 53292

Near Gorey off A3

Mar to Oct daily 9.30–6

Elizabeth Castle

## ISLE OF ARRAN

### Brodick Castle

*In Brodick*

14th-C ancestral seat of Dukes of Hamilton, sited on fortress of Viking days. Extensions in 1652 and 1844. Collections of fine silver, porcelain, paintings and trophies. Two gardens, formal (1710) and woodland (1923), with one of finest rhododendron displays in Britain.

Brodick 2202

1½ miles from Brodick pier

Apr, Mon, Wed and Sat 1–5; May to Sept, Mon to Sat 1–5, Sun 2–5

Lochranza Castle

Ardrossan, for passenger and car ferry to Brodick (crossing 55 min). Ferry information tel. Gourock 33755

To Ardrossan

### Lochranza Castle

*Lochranza, near Brodick*

Romantic ruin with 2 square towers, built 13th/14th Cs, additions in 16th. Tradition says

Robert the Bruce landed here in 1307 on return from Rathlin in Ireland to start his Scottish Independence campaign.

On N coast of Arran via Brodick pier and A841

All year daily except public hols (AMS). Apply to Custodian

Brodick Castle

As for Brodick Castle

As for Brodick Castle

# ISLE OF BUTE

## Rothesay Castle

*In Rothesay*

Among most important medieval castles in Scotland. Stormed by the Normans in 1240; traces of the breach they made can still be seen. 4 round towers added in late 13th C. Unique circular courtyard.

Just W of Rothesay off A844

All year daily (AMS)

Kames Castle*

Wemyss Bay, for ferry to Rothesay (crossing 30 min)

# ISLE OF MAN

## Castle Rushen

*Near Castletown*

Dates from 13th C, with signs of earlier building. Long the royal residence of Lords of Mann, the Earls of Derby, it was last Royalist stronghold to surrender to Cromwell. Famous one-handed clock said to have been presented by Elizabeth I in 1597.

CASTLE RUSHEN

Castletown 3326

Just E of Castletown

All year daily: May to Sept 10–7; Oct to Apr 10–5, Sat 10–12 (closed public hols and Sun in winter)

Peel Castle

## Peel Castle

*St Patrick's Isle, near Peel*

Massive grey building dating back nearly 1,000 years, ancient home of the Kings of Mann. Gatehouse features in Scott's *Peveril of the Peak*. Legends are many: Mauthe Dhoo the large black dog; a 27-m long Giant's grave; the Vikings sounding their horns on May Day Eve to frighten away evil spirits. Red sandstone walls of castle group encircle the 7 acres of St Patrick's Isle.

Douglas 26262

On coast W of Peel

Easter weekend, then May to end Sept daily 10–6, Sun 2–5.30

Castle Rushen

# ISLE OF MULL

## Duart Castle

*Near Craignure*

Built in 13th C, the keep dominates the Sound of Mull. Royal Charter of 1390 confirmed lands, including Duart, to the Macleans. During 1745 Rising Sir Hector Maclean was imprisoned in the Tower of London, his lands forfeited; they were not reclaimed until 1911 by Sir Fitzroy Maclean.

From Craignure, off A849, via ferry from Oban

May to Sept daily 10.30–6

Torosay Castle

Oban for ferry to Craignure

## Torosay Castle

*Near Craignure*

OAP

Victorian castle in Scottish Baronial style. 11 acres of Italian terraced gardens by Lorimer. Statue walk, water garden, miniature railway from castle to Craignure.

Craignure 421

1½ miles SE of Craignure off A849

Mid-May to early Oct daily 11–5. Gardens all year

Duart Castle

Oban for ferry to Craignure (crossing 45 min)

# ISLE OF SKYE

## Dunvegan Castle

*Near Dunvegan*

OAP

Seat of chiefs of Clan Mcleod of Macleod since at least 1200. Treasures on view: drinking horn of Rory Mor, the 16th chief; priceless Fairy Flag; portraits by Raeburn and Ramsay; bagpipes of the Chief's Hereditary Pipers, the MacCrimmons. Seals can often be seen on rocks near castle.

Dunvegan 206

40 miles NW from ferry at Kyleakin via A850 and A863

Early Apr to mid-May and 3 weeks in Oct daily 2–5; mid-May to early Oct daily 10.30–5. Closed Sun

DUNVEGAN CASTLE

# ISLE OF WIGHT

## Arreton Manor

*Arreton, near Newport*

Manor house dating from 17th C. Good panelling. Folk bygones, toys, dolls and their houses.

Arreton 255

4 miles SE of Newport, off A3056

1 week before Easter to end Oct daily 10–6, Sun 2–6

Carisbrooke Castle, Old Town Hall (Newtown)

Brading (6 miles)

## Carisbrooke Castle

*Near Newport*

Fine medieval castle, with 12th-C and later buildings. Charles I was imprisoned here. Donkey operated wheel for drawing water from very deep well. Many notable rarities in museum: chamber organ by Hoffheimer, 1602; mantraps; lace nightcap believed to have been worn by Charles I the night before his execution.

- 1½ miles SW of Newport off B3401
- Mar and Oct daily 9.30–5.30, Sun 2–5.30; Apr to Sept daily 9.30–7. Nov to Feb daily 9.30–4. Closed Maundy Thur, Good Fri, Dec 24–26 and Jan 1
- Old Town Hall (Newtown), Osborne House, Yarmouth Castle
- Brading (8½ miles)
- Summer months

CARISBROOKE CASTLE

## Old Town Hall

*Newtown, near Newport*

18th-C stone and brick building, later used as meeting house and school. Copies of old documents; copy of mace once used.

- 6 miles W of Newport, 1 mile N of A3054 at Shalfleet
- Easter to end May, Wed, Sun and Bank Hol. Mon; June, July and Sept, Wed, Thur, Sat and Sun; Aug daily 2.30–5.30
- Carisbrooke Castle, Arreton Manor, Osborne House
- (1 mile)

## Osborne House

*Near East Cowes*

19th-C mansion, once Queen Victoria's favourite home. Designed in Palladian style by Prince Albert and Thomas Cubitt. State apartments are open to public and contain feast of Victorian splendour, trophies, paintings, furniture and memorabilia. In the grounds: Swiss Cottage; play earthworks of Royal children; their gardening tools; many fascinating curios.

- 1 mile E of East Cowes off A3021
- Easter Mon to June, Mon to Sat 11–5; July and Aug, Mon to Sat 10–5; Sept and early Oct, Mon to Sat 11–5
- Old Town Hall (Newtown), Yarmouth Castle
- Ryde Esplanade (7 miles)

## Yarmouth Castle

*In Yarmouth*

Built for Henry VIII as part of his defences against King of France and the Holy Roman Emperor. Modified in Elizabethan and Jacobean periods. Surrendered to Cromwell by Captain Burley. Master gunner's house, long room and platform are worth studying.

- All year daily except public hols (DES)
- Carisbrooke Castle, Old Town Hall (Newtown), Osborne House
- Lymington Pier for ferry to Yarmouth (crossing 30 min)

## ISLES OF SCILLY

### Cromwell's Castle

*On Tresco*

Fortification with solid round tower of 1651, modified after Civil War and again a century later.

→ From St Mary's by boat

Any reasonable time (DES)

King Charles's Castle

### King Charles's Castle

*On Tresco*

Erected by Henry VIII as part of his coastal defence scheme. Altered during Civil War.

→ From St Mary's by boat

Any reasonable time (DES)

Cromwell's Castle

## ORKNEY ISLANDS: MAINLAND

### Bishop's Palace

*In Kirkwall*

Dates from 13th C. 16th-C round tower put up by Bishop Reid.

All year daily except public hols (AMS). Apply to Custodian of Earl Patrick's Palace

Earl Patrick's Palace, Noltland Castle

### Earl Patrick's Palace

*Near Kirkwall*

Built *c.* 1607, has been praised as 'most mature and accomplished piece of Renaissance architecture left in Scotland'. Note oriel windows.

Apr to Sept daily (AMS)

Bishop's Palace, Noltland Castle

## ORKNEY ISLANDS: WESTRAY

### Noltland Castle

*Near Pierowall*

Impressive ruins of building put up in 1420 by Thomas de Tulloch. Later suffered siege and damage; additions in 16th C. Hall, kitchen and winding staircase of note.

→ On small isle of Westray, to NW of group. By boat

All year daily except public hols (AMS)

Bishop's Palace, Earl Patrick's Palace

## SHETLAND ISLANDS: MAINLAND

### Fort Charlotte

*Near Lerwick*

Roughly pentagonal shaped fort with high walls and gun ports. Built by John Mylne about 1655, restored in 1781.

→ From town

All year daily (AMS)

Scalloway Castle

### Scalloway Castle

*Near Lerwick*

Built in medieval style by Earl Patrick Stewart in 1600. Fell into disuse after execution of Earl who was a brutal character.

→ 6 miles W of Lerwick

All year daily (AMS)

Fort Charlotte

# PRINCIPAL ARCHITECTS, DESIGNERS, LANDSCAPE GARDENERS, CRAFTSMEN AND PAINTERS

*Places prominently connected with each person are given in parentheses.*

## Architects and Designers

**Adam, James (1730–94)**
Younger brother of Robert with whom he worked on many projects, notably the design of furniture. James succeeded Robert as architect to George III.

**Adam, John (1721–92)**
Elder brother of Robert.

**Adam, Robert (1728–92)**
One of the most inspired of architects, he believed that a designer should be responsible not only for the fabric of a building but also for details of the interior. His involvement took in furniture and fireplaces and he applied decoration down to the smallest items such as door-handles. From this dedication came the harmony and unity of his works (Kenwood House; Syon House; Osterley Park House; Kedleston Hall; Infirmary at Glasgow; Adelphi Terrace). Published works: *The Ruins at Spalatro* and *Works in Architecture.*

**Adam, William (1689–1748)**
Scottish architect and father of the four brothers, James, John, Robert and William the Younger (Hopetoun House; Castle Kenmure; Floors Castle; three hospitals in Edinburgh).

**Barry, Sir Charles (1795–1860)**
London born and where many of his finest works were built. He achieved a harmonious union of classical proportion with medieval detail, the latter often in the hands of A.W.N. Pugin. He also mastered the art of landscape gardening (Houses of Parliament; Reform Club with its ingenious use of mirrors to extend the feeling of space; Privy Council Office; lay out of Trafalgar Square; Trentham Hall; Royal Institute at Manchester).

**Bentley, John Francis (1839–1902)**
Follower of the Neo-Gothic principally concerned with ecclesiastical work. Appointed architect in 1894 for the intended Westminster Cathedral.

**Bindon, Francis (1700–65)**
From Limerick, he was also a talented painter (mansions in Wicklow for the Earl of Milltown and in Kilkenny for Lord Bessborough and Sir William Fownes).

**Blomfield, Sir Reginald Theodore (1856–1942)**
An adapter of traditional styles and manners (Lady Margaret Hall, Oxford; Usher Gallery, Lincoln; the memorial at the Menin Gate, Yprès).

**Blore, Edward (1787–1879)**
Leading exponent of the Gothic Revival. His best known work in his time was the main East front of Buckingham Palace, but this was later hidden by the work of Sir A. Webb (Abbotsford for Sir Walter Scott; Palace of Aloupka, Crimea for Prince Woronzow; Cranford Hall; notable restorations at Lambeth Palace; Merton College Chapel, Oxford; Windsor Castle). Published works include: *The Monumental Remains of Noble and Eminent Persons.*

**Bodley, George Frederick (1827–1907)**
Primarily an ecclesiastical architect, strong tendency to Gothic Revival, pupil offSir Giles Gilbert Scott (St Martin's-on-the-Cliff, Scarborough; St Augustine, Pendlebury, Lancashire; cathedral in Washington D.C.).

**Brettingham, Matthew (1699–1769)**
Pupil of William Kent, exponent of the Palladian style (Holkham Hall to the designs of Kent; Benacre Hall; wing of Kedleston Hall).

**Bruce, Sir William (*c.* 1630–1710)**
Architect to Charles II in Scotland (restored Holyrood House).

**Burges, William (1827–81)**
Neo-Gothic, fantasy and ultra-romantic in style of King Ludwig of Bavaria with Neuschwanstein (Castell Coch; Cardiff Castle; Brisbane Cathedral; Cork Cathedral; Art School at Bombay).

**Burn, William (1789–1870)**
Scotsman working in the Classical manner (Buccleuch House, Whitehall; John Watson Hospital and Melville Monument in Edinburgh; Bowhill).

**Campbell, Colen (died 1729)**
Scotsman working in the Palladian style (Rolls House, Chancery Lane; Houghton Hall; part of Greenwich Hospital; Mereworth Castle, based on the Villa Rotunda by Palladio). Published work: *Vitruvius Britannicus* (3 vols) and a translation of Palladio's *Quattro Libri.*

**Carr, John, of York (1723–1807)**
(Harewood House; Kirby Hall; Tabley House; Lytham Hall; Burton Constable House; Court House at York; County Lunatic Asylum).

**Castle, (also Cassel, Cassels) Richard (*c.* 1690–1751)**
German who was invited to Ireland by Sir Gustavius Hume (Bessborough; Carton House; Leinster House; Powerscourt).

**Chambers, Sir William (1723–96)**
Born and grew up in Sweden, working at first for that country's East India Company. His work is a combination of the Palladian and Neo-Classical styles. (Somerset House; Pagoda at Kew; villa at Roehampton for the Earl of Bessborough; Casino at Dublin for Lord Charlemont). Published *The Decorative Part of Civil Architecture*, also works on Chinese architecture and oriental gardening.

**Cockerell, Charles Robert (1788–1863)**
In the Classical manner encouraged by a friendship with Lord Byron (Sun Fire Office, Threadneedle Street, London; Philosophic Institution, Bristol; Ashmolean and Taylorian Institute, Oxford).

**Cubitt, Lewis (1799– death not known)**
Working with his brothers Joseph and Thomas designed a number of streets and squares in London including: Endsleigh Street; Chesham Place; Gordon Square; Lowndes Square and Belgrave Square (King's Cross Station).

**Dance, George, Senior (died 1768)**
Clerk of the London City Works (Mansion House; St Botolph's, Aldgate; St Luke's, Old Street).

**Dance, George, Junior (1741–1825)**
After study in Italy he followed his father as Clerk of the City Works (Newgate Prison; College of Surgeons; Lincoln's Inn Fields).

**Flitcroft, Henry (1697–1769)**
Started his career as a carpenter, then became a draughtsman under the patronage of Lord Burlington (St Giles-in-the-Fields; Woburn Abbey alterations and forming of the State rooms).

**Galilei, Alessandro (1691–1737)**
Encouraged the Italian influence on his visits to this country (Façade of S. Giovanni in Laterano, Rome and the open Loggia).

**Gandon, James (1743–1823)**
Born in London he went to Ireland (Custom House; Four Courts; designs for Carlisle Bridge, Court House and Gaol at Waterford).

**Gibbs, James (1682–1754)**
A Scot who travelled to and studied in Rome and returned to exercise some influence on building in England. He was a member of the board superintending the erection of 50 churches in London. Wren and Hawksmoor were an inspiration (Radcliffe Library, Oxford; St Martin's-in-the-Fields; Bartholomew's Hospital; Smithfield; Senate House, Cambridge). Published several treatises on architecture.

**Hawksmoor, Nicholas (1661–1736)**
A pupil of Sir Christopher Wren and later worked in association with Sir John Vanbrugh (Clarendon Building, Oxford; All Saints College, Oxford; worked with Vanbrugh at Castle Howard and Blenheim).

**Holland, Henry (1754–1806)**
Worked in collaboration with 'Capability' Brown and married his daughter. Parts of Chelsea and Sloane Street are evidence of his work as an early speculative builder (Claremont; Carlton House; parts of Woburn Abbey; Trentham; Althorp).

**Ivory, Thomas (1709–79)**
Leading member of a Norwich family of architects

(Freemason's Hall, Norwich; alterations to the interior of Blickling Hall).

**Johnson, John (1754–1814)**
(County Hall, Chelmsford; alterations to Bradwell Lodge)

**Jones, Inigo (1573–1652)**
Studied in Italy, notably the work of Palladio. Apart from architecture he was much employed on court masques and pageants and can be considered the founder of scenic design in the British theatre (Queen's House, Greenwich; Banqueting House, Whitehall; Surgeon's Hall; St Paul, Covent Garden; Stoke Park; Wilton House with John Webb).

**Kent, William (*c.* 1685–1748)**
Early career as a painter was under the patronage of Lord Burlington; considerable talent not only for architecture but also interior design and gardens. (Holkham Hall; alterations to Kensington Palace; Rainham House; Rousham House; Badminton). Published Inigo Jones's *Designs.*

**Leoni, Giacomo (*c.* 1686–1746)**
Born in Venice he worked in Britain and Germany (Clandon Park;alterations and additions to Lyme Park; Bramham Park; Moor Park). Published Palladio's work on architecture with his engravings, the first English edition.

**Lutyens, Sir Edwin Landseer (1869–1944)**
A prodigy, he received his first commission at 19. Exponent of large and impressive projects as well as an accomplished restorer (Government Buildings, New Delhi; British Embassy, Washington; prepared plans which were not used for Liverpool Catholic Cathedral; Cenotaph; alterations to Lindisfarne Castle; Great Dixter).

**Lyminge, Robert (active early part of 17th C)**
Leading exponent of red-brick (Blickling Hall 1616–28; Hatfield House, 1607–11).

**Miller, Sanderson (1717–80)**
Amateur with an interest and flair for the Gothic (Hagley Hall; Arbury with Couchman of Warwick and Henry Keene; alterations to Lacock Abbey).

**Nash, John (1752–1835)**
Leading exponent of the Classical style. For a time in partnership with Repton the landscape gardener. He also had a flair for the romantic Gothic (Brighton Pavilion; Buckingham Palace; Haymarket Theatre; Regent Street).

**Paine, James (1725–89)**
Leading figure in the Palladian manner (worked on Nostell Priory and Kedleston, both later worked on by Robert Adam; alterations and additions at Chatsworth, Bramham Park, Wardour Castle, Worksop Manor House).

**Paxton, Sir Joseph (1803–65)**
Leading expert in the handling of iron framing with glass. He started as the Duke of Devonshire's gardener (Crystal Palace; Conservatory for the Victoria Regia at Chatsworth).

**Pugin, Auguste-Charles (1762–1832)**
Refugee from the French Revolution, for a period worked in the draughting office of John Nash. Serious student of the Gothic. Published *Specimens of Gothic Architecture*, *Examples of Gothic Architecture* and *Antiquities of Normandy*.

**Pugin, Augustus Welby Northmore (1812–52)**
More than anyone else he was responsible for bringing about the Gothic Revival in Britain. Son of Auguste-Charles. Interests included: interior decoration, furniture and stained glass (worked on the Houses of Parliament with Sir Charles Barry; Cathedral of St George, Southwark; cathedrals at Enniscorthy and Killarney; alterations at Albury Park and Chirk Castle). Published *Contrasts*, *True Principles* and *Designs for Metal and Timber*.

**Salvin, Anthony (1799–1881)**
Accomplished restorer and an interior decorator with imagination (worked on Windsor Castle; Capesthorne Hall; Rockingham Castle; Alnwick Castle; Thoresby Hall; Dunster Castle; Longford Castle; Beauchamp Tower; Traitor's Gate at the Tower of London).

**Scott, Sir George Gilbert (1811–78)**
A Gothic enthusiast and a great renovator particularly of churches, not always happily (Albert Memorial; St Pancras Station; Foreign Office; worked on and restored many cathedrals). Published *Gleanings from Westminster Abbey*, *Remarks on Secular and Domestic Architecture* and *Lectures on the Rise and Development of Medieval Architecture*.

**Smirke, Sir Robert (1781–1867)**
Holder of a number of official posts, primarily he worked in the Neo-Classical manner (worked on, added to, or altered: Eastnor Castle; Luton Hoo; British Museum; Inner Temple; King's College; Royal Mint; York Minster; Wellington Testimonial, Dublin; Lowther Castle; Drayton Manor).

**Soane, Sir John (1753–1837)**
Apart from his professional work he was an educated collector of the fine and rare (Bank of England; Board of Trade; worked on St James Palace; Houses of Parliament; Dulwich Gallery).

**Stuart, James (1713–88)**
Sent by the Society of Dilettanti with Nicholas Revett in 1751 to make measured drawings of the buildings still standing on the Acropolis; hence his nickname 'Athenian'. Influential in encouraging the Classical Revival. Published *Classical Antiquities of Athens*.

**Talman, William (1650–1719)**
Designer of many country houses, although sadly many now demolished (worked on Chatsworth; Thoresby Hall).

**Taylor, Sir Robert (1714–88)**
From humble beginnings as a monumental mason he rose to be one of the most popular architects of his period (Gorhambury; Duke of Grafton's house in Piccadilly; Ely House, Dover Street).

**Vanbrugh, Sir John (1664–1726)**
His inspiration has given rise to some of the finest stonework and façades. Arrested in France as a spy he spent some time in the Bastille; whilst there he wrote *The Provoked Wife* (worked on or designed: Blenheim; Castle Howard; Eastbury; King's Weston; Clarendon Printing Office; part of Greenwich Hospital; Lumley Castle; Audley End; Kimbolton Castle; Kensington Palace; Seaton Delaval).

**Wood, John the Elder (1704–54)**
Known as 'John Wood of Bath' he worked in the Palladian manner (Crescent, Circus and Queen Square amongst other places in Bath; also Exchange, Bristol; Prior Park; Buckland Park; Bramham Park; Capesthorne Hall).

**Wren, Sir Christopher (1632–1723)**
He studied mathematics and astronomy, becoming a professor in the latter discipline. After the Fire of London he worked out a comprehensive plan for a general rebuilding but this was not adopted (designed or worked on some 50 churches and the great St Paul's, started in 1675 and finished by Wren in 1710; College of Physicians; Lecture Theatre at Oxford; Chelsea College; Marlborough House; part of Hampton Court Palace; the Monument; Winslow Hall; Kensington Palace).

**Wyatt, James (1747–1813)**
Travelled extensively in Italy for 6 years and on his return his production of ideas for houses was prolific (designed or worked on Dodington House; Heaton Hall; Belvoir Castle; Belton House; Goodwood House; Wilton House; Plas Newydd; Castle Coole; Pantheon Assembly Rooms; Fonthill Abbey – an extravaganza in the Gothic manner, with an immense central tower 69 m high which collapsed about 30 years after it was built).

**Wyatville, Sir Jeffry (1766–1840)**
Nephew of James Wyatt (State apartments at Windsor Castle; worked on Lyme Park; Chatsworth; Wollaton Hall; Longleat; Browsholme Hall).

## Landscape Gardeners

**Bridgeman, Charles (died 1738)**
A claimant to be the innovator of the 'Ha-ha', a form of sunken barrier to allow uninterrupted vistas (Blenheim, though sadly his work was erased by the landscaping of 'Capability' Brown. Good examples of 'Ha-has' can be seen at Rousham; Syon House; Levens Hall).

**Brown, Lancelot 'Capability' (1716–83)**
Starting life as a kitchen gardener he progressed to being the greatest of landscape builders, heading a rejection of the formal garden manner of the French. His nickname arose from his habit of encouraging clients with the words that their properties had 'great capabilities'. Seeing some of his schemes now that they have grown to maturity, it is amazing that he could have moved so much around with the equipment available to him. What he could have done with bulldozers, graders, excavators and the rest! (Luton Hoo; Chatsworth;

Dodington House; Moor Park; Syon House; Burghley House; Alnwick Castle; Blenheim; Clandon Park; Warwick Castle; Longleat; Wilton House; Harewood House).

**Caus, Isaac de (active mid-17th C)**
He was responsible for the original Renaissance garden at Wilton; practically no vestiges of this remain as change followed change.

**Cooke, Edward (active mid-19th C)**
Artist gardener who with James Bateman the owner of Biddulph Grange, Staffordshire, created a 'China' garden, that was entered by traversing a tunnel that came out on to a pavilion with a view of an oriental landscape.

**Flitcroft, Henry (1697–1769)**
See also under architects. At Stourhead he laid out the gardens for Henry Hoare. His free romantic treatment was one of the first to break with the highly formal manner of the French as epitomized by Le Nôtre.

**Gilpin, William Sawrey (1762–1845)**
His *Practical Hints for Landscape Gardening* was a factor in the growth of smaller, romantic and intimate gardens.

**Jekyll, Gertrude (1843–1932)**
After a meeting with William Robinson she was inspired to turn to the art of garden-making. For lengthy periods she worked with Sir Edwin Lutyens, giving the settings to his buildings (Great Dixter; Hestercombe; her influence can be noted at the famous Wisley Gardens, Surrey). Published: *Wood and Garden*, *Home and Garden*, *Gardens for Small Country Houses* and *Garden Ornaments*.

**Loudon, John Claudius (1783–1843)**
A prime mover and influence towards the British informal and at times secluded garden of the 19th C. He advocated collecting numerous specimen plants, and at one time was reputed to have had around 2,000 different plants in his small London garden. Possibly he was the introducer of the herbaceous border. Published lists of plants with suggestions for their placing in borders.

**Mason, William (active last half of 18th C)**
A romanticist, a garden-poet (Flora's Garden at Nuneham).

**Repton, Humphry (1752–1818)**
Born in Bury St Edmunds, he went to study in Holland. On his return he settled at Romford. His work at first tended towards that of 'Capability' Brown; later he developed a 'marriage' style between this and the formalities of Le Nôtre. (Harewood; Uppark, Sheringham Hall; West Wycombe; Attingham). Published *Observations on the Theory and Practice of Landscape Gardening*, and also left behind a couple of hundred of his so-called 'Red Books' in which were many 'before' and 'after' sketches for varying landscape treatments.

**Robinson, William (active last half of 19th C)**
Writer and theorist on plants and gardens. His influence had much to do with fashion of rock gardens. Published: *Alpine*

*Flowers for English Gardens*, *The Wild Garden* and *The English Garden*.

**Wise, Henry (active early part of 18th C)**
Gardener to Queen Anne. Follower of Le Nôtre. As with others, his work at Blenheim was erased by 'Capability' Brown. Between 1900 and 1910 the 9th Duke of Marlborough employed the Frenchman Achille Duchêne to reconstruct much of the formal work of Wise.

## Craftsmen and Painters

**Artari, Guiseppe (1697–1769)**
Skilled plasterer born in Switzerland, he came to England to be employed by James Gibbs from 1721 (St Martin-in-the-Fields; Ditchley Park; Moor Park; Orleans House, Twickenham).

**Bakewell, Robert (1685–1752)**
Talented smith from Derbyshire (Arbour at Melbourne Hall).

**Barry, James (1741–1806)**
Son of a ship-master from Cork he studied with Mr West in Dublin. Encouraged by Mr Burke, he travelled to Italy, thence to London, was elected to the Royal Academy and later became Painting Professor (Murals at the Royal Society of Arts building, Adelphi; much work carried out gratuitously).

**Gibbons, Grinling (1648–1721)**
Wood carver supreme, probably born of Dutch parents in Rotterdam. When he came to London he was discovered by John Evelyn who greatly admired his virtuosity and skill. He also modelled, for bronze casting, noteworthy statues of Charles II and James II. Sir Christopher Wren often called on him for his talent and quality. Master wood carver to George I (St Paul's; Belton House; Burghley House; Petworth House).

**Laguerre, Louis (1663–1721)**
Called 'Old Laguerre' he was born in Paris; his father became the master of the Menagerie at Versailles. He came to England in 1683 and at first worked as an assistant to Antonio Verrio (Blenheim; Chatsworth; Petworth House; Burghley House; Hampton Court, restoring Mantegna's cartoons of 'The Triumphs of Julius Caesar'; St Bartholomew's Hospital).

**Lanscroon, Gerard (1677–1737)**
Native of Flanders, he came over to England to assist Laguerre and Verrio. His son carried on his work (Windsor Castle; Hampton Court; Powis Castle).

**Morris, William (1834–96)**
Poet and artistic decorator with architectural training. He was inspired by the medieval, and by the writings of John Ruskin. In 1863 with Marshall and Faulkner he set up a business concerned with the decorative arts, mainly interiors and especially stained glass. This prospered and in 1865 was moved to Queen Street with showrooms in Oxford Street. In 1881 a final move was made to the famous workshops at Merton Abbey.

**Pellegrini, Giovanni Antonio (1674–1741)**
Worked in Venice and later in Paris. The Duke of Manchester invited him to England where he lived for several years working in a number of mansions. His work was strong in line and composition but lacked colour and chiaroscuro. It has been much restored and today is not always easy to identify.

**Rebecca, Biagio (1735–1808)**
Painter and ornamental decorator of Italian descent who lived in England. Attended the Royal Academy Schools and was elected an Associate in 1771 (Windsor Castle; Heaton Hall; Heveningham Hall; Audley End; Harewood House).

**Rose, Joseph, Junior (1745–99)**
Member of a family of plasterers, and the most talented. During this period much exquisite decorative plasterwork was produced both in Britain and Ireland (Castle Coole; Nostell Priory; Sledmere House).

**Thornhill, Sir James (1676–1734)**
After studying with Thomas Highmore he travelled through Holland, Belgium and France. On his return he rose to fame, the only British painter who worked in the Grand Baroque manner. Although in demand he found that he was ill paid, receiving only forty shillings a square yard for his work in St Paul's and at Greenwich (Painted Hall, Greenwich Hospital, where his 'Triumph of Peace and Liberty', a huge oval of 32 m × $15\frac{1}{2}$ m, is the largest painting in Britain; Moor Park; Hanbury Hall; Hampton Court).

**Tijou, Jean (last half of the 17th C–1712)**
Master ironsmith (St Paul's; Hampton Court; Burghley House; Chatsworth).

**Verrio, Antonio (1639–1707)**
Born in Italy he moved to France and settled in Toulouse. Charles II asked him to come to England to revive the Mortlake tapestry works which had been ruined by the Civil War. He had considerable success as a mural painter receiving no less than £7,000 for work at Windsor (Hampton Court; Chatsworth, Burghley House).

**Watson, Samuel (1663–1715)**
Born in Derbyshire he became a talented wood carver, much in demand (Chatsworth).

**Whistler, Rex (1905–44)**
After winning prizes at the Royal Drawing Society's exhibitions he attended both the Royal Academy School and the Slade School. He developed a highly personal style of decorative scenes for mural work (Mottisfont Abbey; Plas Newydd).

**Zucchi, Antonio (1726–95)**
Born in Venice and studied architectural drawing and perspective with his uncle, Carlo Zucchi, and historical painting under Fontebasso. He met the Adam brothers and travelled with them through Italy, finally being persuaded by them to come to England (Osterley Park House; Luton Hoo; Caen Wood).

# GLOSSARY

*Architectural and other terms likely to be encountered when visiting a stately home or castle.*

**Abutment** Solid masonry erected to resist the lateral pressure of an arch or vault.
**Apron** Raised panel below a window-sill sometimes decorated and shaped.
**Apse** Semicircular (sometimes polygonal) recess, either arched or domed-roofed.
**Apsidal** Having the form of an apse.
**Arabesque** Involved and imaginative surface decoration often using combinations of flowing lines interwoven with flowers, fruit, spirals and sinuous sweeping lines.
**Arcade** Range of arches carried on columns or piers, either free-standing or attached to a wall.
**Architrave** Beam or lowest division of the entablature; also the moulded frame round a door or window.
**Archivolt** Moulding on the face of an arch which follows its contour.
**Ashlar** Masonry of smooth squared stones laid in horizontal courses with vertical joints.
**Attic** Upper storey of a building above the main cornice, a term first applied in the Renaissance period; also room in a roof.
**Bailey** Open space or court of a fortified stone-built castle.
**Baldachino** Canopy, often supported by columns, over a throne, altar or doorway.
**Baluster** Short pillar supporting a coping or handrail; a series of balusters form a *balustrade*.
**Barbican** Outwork of a medieval castle intended to protect the drawbridge or entrance.
**Bargeboards** Boards fixed to the gable-edge of a pitched roof.
**Baroque** The architecture of the 17th and part of the 18th Cs. It was characterized by exuberant, rich and bold decorations and forms.
**Bartizan** Small turret projecting from a tower or parapet.
**Batter** Inclined face of a wall.
**Battlement** Parapet with indentations or embrasures; the raised portions in between each embrasure are known as *merlons*.
**Bawn** Fortification enclosing a house or dwelling.
**Boss** Knob or projection at the intersection of ribs in vaulting, often decorated with carving.
**Bucrane** (or **Bucranium**) Classical ornament in the shape of an ox skull, generally with garlands.
**Buttress** Mass of masonry built against a wall to give added strength. A *flying buttress* is an arch that starts from a detached pier, to transmit the thrust of a vault or roof.
**Cames** Strips of lead with grooves to take the pieces of glass in stained glass or casement windows.
**Capital** Head or crowning feature of a column or pilaster.
**Caponier** Covered passageway over a defensive ditch.
**Caroline** Of or pertaining to the reigns of Charles I and Charles II.
**Caryatids** Sculptured female figures used as columns to support an entablature or included with decorative features.

**Castellation** Towers and/or battlements originally fortifying a building; later employed as form of architectural decoration.
**Chequer-work** Decoration applied to walls and pavements with alternate squares of contrasting materials.
**Cladding** Non-structural materials applied to a building for aesthetic or protective reasons.
**Classical** The architectural styles originating in ancient Greece and Rome, and revived during the Renaissance.
**Clerestory** (also **Clearstory**) Upper stage in a building pierced with windows above adjacent roofs.
**Coffers** Ceiling decoration with sunken ornamental panels.
**Collar-purlin** Horizontal beam of timber connecting or bracing two opposite rafters.
**Colonnade** Line of columns spaced out at regular intervals.
**Coping** Top course of masonry in a wall, usually sloping.
**Corbel** Block of projecting stone, often decorated, that supports the beams of a roof, vault or oriel window.
**Cornice** Moulded projection along top of building, doorway, window, etc. Also ornamental plaster moulding round wall just below ceiling.
**Crown post** One standing upright on the tie-beam of a timber roof. It gives support to a central collar-purlin and nearby rafters by means of braces and struts.
**Crucks** Pairs of curved timbers to act as the principal framing for a house.
**Cupola** Small dome crowning a roof or turret.
**Curtain wall** Non-load-carrying wall surrounding a courtyard, usually containing towers spaced out at regular intervals.
**Donjon** See *Keep*.
**Dormer** Window in a sloping roof.
**Entablature** Part of structure surmounting columns and resting upon the capitals.
**Entasis** Slight swelling given to a column to counteract the optical illusion by which the column appears to curve inwards.
**Façade** Elevation or face of a building.
**Faience** Glazed earthenware, often ornamented, used for decoration. First made at Faenza, Italy, *c*. 1300.
**Fan vaulting** Associated with the Perpendicular period. All the supporting ribs of the vault have the same curve, and radiate as with a fan-shape.
**Fenestration** Placing of windows in a building.
**Festoon** Carved ornament forming a garland of flowers, leaves, stems and fruit tied with ribbons.
**Finial** Ornament topping a bench-end, pinnacle or gable.
**Framed building** One in which the structure is carried on a framework as opposed to load-bearing walls.
**French window** Long window that reaches to the ground or floor and opens in two halves.
**Fresco** Painting carried out directly on to the moist plaster as it is laid; either on walls or ceilings.
**Frieze** That part of entablature (*q.v.*) between architrave and cornice.
**Gable** Triangular portion of a wall at the end of a pitched roof.
**Garderobe** Wardrobe, also medieval name for a lavatory.
**Gargoyle** Spout that projects to throw water off a roof, often carved into grotesque heads.
**Georgian** British architecture from approximately 1702 to 1830.

**Gothic** Term given to the pointed style of medieval architecture dominant in Europe from the 13th to the 15th C.
**Gothic Revival** Fashion that began at the end of the 18th C and flourished during the 19th C. Based on medieval Gothic.
**Grotesque** Painted or stuccoed highly imaginative decoration close to arabesque. Used on medallions, sphinxes, foliage, masks, etc.
**Grotto** Man-made cave, often with fountains, pools, and shellwork decoration. Popular fashion in the 18th C.
**Ha-ha** Sunken fence or ditch protecting formal gardens or grounds from straying cattle without spoiling the view.
**Half-timbered** Building with timber posts, rails and struts, in-filled with brickwork and sometimes plastered.
**Hammer-beam roof** Introduction during the late Gothic period; a roof without a direct tie.
**Intarsia** Decorative inlay of different coloured woods, popular in the 15th and 16th Cs for the decoration of studies, private rooms.
**Jacobean period** English Renaissance architecture *c.* 1603–25.
**Jambs** Sides of doors and windows.
**Keep** (also **Donjon**) Inner great tower of a castle, with sufficient accommodation for its inhabitants and dependents during times of siege.
**Keystone** Central stone of an arch, sometimes with carved decoration.
**King post** Vertical timber between the tie-beam and the ridge.
**Lantern** Small circular or polygonal turret surmounting a roof or dome.
**Linenfold** Carving that imitated folded linen, popular in the late 15th and 16th Cs.
**Loggia** Gallery behind an arcade or colonnade, open on one or more sides.
**Machicolation** Gallery or parapet that projects on brackets on the outside of castle walls or towers. There were holes at intervals through which stones and molten lead or pitch could be dropped on attackers.
**Mansard roof** Roof with steep lower slope and flatter one at the top. Named after François Mansart (1598–1666).
**Mausoleum** Elaborate and stately tomb.
**Meander** Running ornament with fret or key motif.
**Misericord** Hinged seat to support a standing person; underside often carved with grotesque designs.
**Motte** Steep conical mound; prominent feature of 11th- and 12th-C castles.
**Motte-and-bailey** Motte surmounted with a wooden tower within a bailey, plus ditch and palisade.
**Mullions** Vertical members dividing windows.
**Neo-Classical** Belonging to or designating a revival of Classical style, design, taste, particularly with regard to architecture and interior decoration.
**Neo-Gothic** Buildings and interior decoration in style and design evolved from close study of medieval Gothic work.
**Newel** Central shaft around which the steps of a circular staircase wind; also the post into which a handrail is framed.
**Niche** Recess in a wall, generally semi-circular in plan, in which a statue or ornament might stand.
**Norman** Design, style and taste of 11th and 12th Cs; also termed *English Romanesque*.
**Obelisk** Tall square pillar that tapers upwards and ends in a pyramid.
**Ogee** Moulding made up of

a concave and convex curve; also an arch with this shape.
**Opus Alexandrinum** Mosaics inlaid in a marble or stone paving.
**Opus listatum** Walling with courses of brick and stone alternating.
**Opus sectile** Decorative wall covering or paving using marble slabs cut in geometrical shapes.
**Orangery** Garden building with large south-facing windows for growing oranges.
**Oratory** Small private chapel.
**Oriel window** Window projecting from face of wall on bracket or corbel (*q.v.*).
**Palladian** Style originating from the work and publications of Andrea Palladio (1508–80). Early exponent was Inigo Jones (1573–1652).
**Palladian window** Arch or twin columns, flanked by flat-headed openings.
**Parapet** That portion of a wall above the roof-gutter; sometimes battlemented.
**Pargetting** Outside decorative plasterwork, with patterned and tool-made textures. Fashion from Tudor period, particularly in East Anglia.
**Parquet** Thin wood block flooring, usually about $\frac{1}{4}$ in thick, laid in formal geometric patterns.
**Parterre** Space, usually close to house, laid out with formal flower beds.
**Pediment** Structure, usually triangular but sometimes rounded, over a portico, door, window etc.
**Pele tower** Small tower or fortified house designed to repel a sudden attack.
**Pilaster** Rectangular column or pier projecting slightly from a wall.
**Portcullis** Gate of iron or iron-reinforced wood that could be lowered or raised, sliding in vertical grooves.
**Porte-cochère** Porch large enough to accommodate a wheeled vehicle.
**Portico** Roofed space, open or partly enclosed, forming the entrance to a house, church or temple. Often the principal feature of the building's main façade.
**Postern** Small gate, often hidden at the back of a castle, house or monastery.
**Purlin** Timber beam lying across the principal rafters to support the subsidiary ones.
**Quoins** Dressed stones laid at the corners of buildings so that faces appear large and small alternately.
**Rampart** Defensive earthwork round a castle, sometimes with a stone parapet.
**Regency** The period (1811–20) during which the Prince of Wales acted as Regent when his father George III had bouts of insanity.
**Rococo** In architecture term refers to the latter period of Baroque when decoration became fussily flamboyant and almost overpowered the form of the buildings.
**Rustication** Masonry with large blocks with roughened surface separated by deep recessed joints.
**Sarcophagus** Richly carved coffin.
**Sgraffito** Technique for decoration by which an upper coat or stucco is partially cut away to expose an undercoat.
**Slighting** Indefinite term which in this context implies damaging a castle sufficiently to render it no longer viable as a defendable fortress. A favourite activity of Oliver Cromwell and his New Model Army.
**Solar** Medieval name for an upper room usually reserved for the privacy of the owner (from the Latin *solarium*).
**Strapwork** Relief decoration representing intertwined leather straps.
**Stucco** Fine quality plasterwork capable of taking

low relief decoration. Popular in Britain during the late 18th and early 19th Cs.
**Terracotta** Reddish clay that has been fired but not glazed. Much used for ornamental features.
**Terrazo** Floor of marble chips set in cement and then ground and polished.
**Tie-beam** Piece of timber connecting lower ends of rafters to prevent movement.
**Tracery** Decorative stonework filling the upper part of a Gothic window. It can be 'bar' or 'plate', the latter giving the impression that it has been cut out of stone.
**Tudor** British Gothic 1485 to 1558.
**Voussoirs** Blunt-ended wedge-shaped blocks that form an arch and are held at the top by the keystone.
**Wattle and daub** Infilling sometimes used with timber framing, framework of branches or laths roughly plastered with clay.
**Yett** Protective gateway grille; somewhat similar to a portcullis.

# INDEX OF ARCHITECTS, DESIGNERS AND CRAFTSMEN

# INDEX OF PROPERTIES